The World of Malgudi

Dynamics of Creativity and Social Ethos in R. K. Narayan's Novels

The World of Malgudi

Dynamics of Creativity and Social Ethos in R. K. Narayan's Novels

Manju Roy

SERIALS PUBLICATIONS
NEW DELHI (INDIA)

First Published – 2010

ISBN: 978-81-8387-343-7

Published by

SERIALS PUBLICATIONS
4830/24, 1st Floor, Ansari Road
Darya Ganj, New Delhi-110002 (India)
Phone : 23245225. Fax : 91-11-23272135
E-mail: serials@satyam.net.in

Dedicated to

My Parents

CONTENTS

FOREWORD

Narayan is fascinating to read, but difficult to write about. Anyone who approaches him with pre-conceived ideas about the nature and function of novel is in for disappointment. An attempt to write about Narayan is to catch the shimmering rays of the sun. He escapes all generalizations. He creates humour, irony, gentle satire, and pathos out of ordinary life. His humour is all-pervasive; a quotation or two cannot do justice to him.

Instead of easy generalisations about Narayan's works as a whole, Manju Roy has wisely discussed the novels chronologically. She competently analyses characters, episodes and cultural values in which Narayan's fiction is rooted. She, however, constantly compares characters and episodes in various novels. Her judgement of the novels that are considered weak (like *The Dark Room* and *Waiting for the Mahatma)* is balanced. Her praise is rightly reserved for the 'middle novels' for their well-knit plot, characterization and maturity of vision.

Manju Roy's vivid presentation of the people who inhabit Malgudi is a strong feature of her book. She brings out the wide range of Malgudi characters, remarkable in ordinariness with short-lived extraordinariness, typically Indian yet universal, generally a mixture of good and evil. Particularly good is she in showing how they feel the winds of change, yet remain essentially rooted in traditional values. They cannot be categorized, as the common humanity cannot be, into flat and round characters.

Another strong feature of the book is the author's command of the latest secondary sources. Using observations of the critics and reviewers with discrimination, Manju Roy moves forward to present her own insights. She points out the near circularity of the movement of almost each of the stories, the protagonist ending from where he began. Many of her insights are refreshingly new. For example, she explains the mystery of how Margayya is able to give high rate of interest on the deposits he receives. Her view seems reasonable that he wishes "to spread the impression that he did not earn money by publishing an erotic book."

Manju Roy's book is a valuable addition to Narayan scholarship.

Harsharan S. Ahluwalia,
Ph.D. (Wisconsin)
Professor of English (Retd.)
Guru Nanak Dev University, Amritsar

PREFACE

Yet another book on R .K.Narayan! The justification for this book lies in the celebration of Narayan's birth centeneary only about two and a half years ago. As is usual with this kind of celebration, this has started a fresh stimulus for reading and reassessing him. In Mysore, on this occasion, a birth centeneary conference on Narayan was organised from 10 to 12 October 2006 by the Indian Association for Commonwealth Literature and Language Studies (IACLALS). Twenty-seven scholars from India and eight other countries presented thought provoking papers to increase interest in Narayan's work in this conference.

R.K. Narayan's greatness lies in presenting ordinary men and women and translating their experiences into English easily and majestically. Besides, his spatio-temporal awareness makes his work more real and superbly artistic. Narayan is the master of Malgudi which is the microcosm of traditional Indian society. Naturally, what is true for Malgudi appears to be true for the whole of India. In fact, the place becomes the backdrop for the tradition, customs, and beliefs of its inhabitants. Thus, the people and palce become inseperable. Arguably, a detailed study of Narayan's characters seems to be the best way of understanding Narayan's art. In fact, after Malgudi, charcters are the most important element in his novels. His characters vibrate with a great deal of life and energy and have a vision of their own. The book analyses their oddities and eccentricities and their inter-personal relationship. Narayan also accepts the significance of these relationships as they make one's existence worthwhile. In adition, this book also tries to answer the following questions: To what extent do socio-economic changes affect characters? Do all of them belong to the same socioeconomic class? Is there any significantly valid pattern among Narayan's charcters?

I should like to put on record my gratitude to the following persons for helping me in numerous ways: Dr. D. Thakur (Professor & the Head of the English Department, Sana'a University, Sana'a, Yeman), Dr. H. S. Ahluwalia (Professor of English [Retd.], Guru Nanak Dev University, Amritsar), Dr. Mohan Jha (Professor of English [Retd.], Bihar University, Muzaffarpur) Dr. Vijay Singh Thakur, (Assistant Professor of English, Dhofar University, Salalah, Oman), Mr. Mohammed Athar Khan (Testing Co-ordinator, Language Centre, Sultan Qaboos University, Muscat), Dr. P. N. Jha (Reader in English, C.M. College, Darbhanga), Mr. S. K. Jha (Manager, Serials Publication) and Mr. Mukesh Uniyal (Composer). I am also indebted to my parents, my husband, Dr. Amrendra K. Sharma, and my daughters–Amrita and Ankita–for giving me encouragement and moral support.

Manju Roy
C.M. College, Darbhnaga

1

INTRODUCTION

> What we call the beginning is often the end.
> And to make an end is to make a beginning.
>
> —T. S. Elot

NARAYAN'S LIFE AND ACHIEVEMENTS

R. K. Narayan, along with Mulk Raj Anand and Raja Rao, is regarded as one of the best Indian writers of English fiction. His exquisite use of the language, his ability to fuse character and action, his steady perception of life, his authentic portrayal of Indians, his relentless search for a moral centre, and his utilization of Indian myths and legends, are all features of his art that have helped in making him a recognised and established man of letters. Critics of Indo-English literature place him on a very high pedestal. Almost all agree that Narayan's stature as one of the finest Indo-English novelists is assured. Very rarely does one hear a detracting voice.

Like Anand, R. K. Narayan is also a prolific writer. He has written a number of novels and short stories, besides essays and memoirs, and what is interesting is that he wrote and published until his last days. His first novel, *Swami and Friends,* came out in 1935. It has been followed, almost in a quick succession, by such other novels and short-story collections as *The Bachelor of Arts* (1937), *The Dark Room* (1938), *Malgudi Days* (1941), *Dodu and Other Stories* (1943), *Cyclone and Other Stories* (1944), *The English Teacher* (1945), *An Astrologer's Day and Other Stories* (1947), *Mr. Sampath* (1949), *The Financial Expert (1952), Waiting for the Mahatma* (1955), *Lawley Road* (1956), *The Guide* (1958), *Next Sunday* (1960), *My*

Dateless Diary (1960), *The Man-Eater of Malgudi* (1962), *Gods, Demons and Others* (1965), *The Vendor of Sweets* (1967), *A Horse and Two Goats* (1970), *The Ramayana* (1972), *My Days* (1974), *The Painter of Signs* (1976), *A Tiger for Malgudi* (1983), *Under The Banyan Tree and Other Stories* (1985), *The Talkative Man* (1986), *A Writer's Nightmare: Selected Essays 1958-1988* (1988), *A Story-teller's World* (1989), *The World of Nagaraj* (1990), *Malgudi Landscapes: The Best of R. K. Narayan* (1992), *Grandmother's Tale* (1993) and *Salt and Sawdust: Stories and Table Talk* (1993).

R. K. Narayan (Rashipuram Krishnaswamy Narayan) was born in 1906 in Madras in a South Indian family. He spent his early days with his grandmother and maternal uncle in Madras. When he was a high-school student, his father brought him to Mysore from Madras because at that time his father was the headmaster of a collegiate school at Mysore. Narayan did not believe in the conventional system of education. In his book, *My Days,* he says:

> I instinctively rejected both education and examinations, with their unwarranted seriousness and esoteric suggestions. Since revolt was impractical, I went through it all without conviction, enthusiasm or any sort of distinction.[1]

He once failed in his university entrance examination in English, the subject in which he was most confident. After failing in the university entrance examination, he got one full year at his disposal because he could appear at the next examination only after a year, without attending classes. He spent this time in studying English Literature keenly. He read Keats, Shelley, Byron, Browning, and Tagore, and all this reading did indeed deepen his sensibility. In 1926, he passed the university entrance examination and got himself admitted to B. A. at Maharaja College, Mysore. In 1930, he did his graduation. First, he thought of studying for an M. A. degree in literature and thus becoming a college lecturer, but one of his friends persuaded him against taking admission to M. A., convincing him that this would be a sure way of losing interest in literature. Thus, after dropping the idea of doing M. A., he began to search for a job according to his father's wishes. His search for a job did not bear any fruit, and he spent his time mainly in typewriting. It was at this time that his father retired from service.

When R. K. Narayan did not find anything to do in Mysore, he came to Bangalore to stay with his grandmother. There he spent his time in dreaming and planning about his future. One fine day, selected by his grandmother for its auspiciousness, he bought an exercise book and wrote the first line of a novel. He sat in his room wondering what to write. As his meditation deepened, Malgudi with its little railway station swam into his view, ready-made, with a character called Swaminathan. It was a satisfactory beginning for him, and then, he regularly wrote a few pages.

At about this very time his father's efforts to get him a job materialised, and Narayan got an appointment as a teacher at a government school in Chennapatnam. This very school had witnessed his father as a teacher and R. K. Narayan as a student. He taught in that school for a very short period and came back to Mysore, determined never to return. His decision caused anxiety to his parents, and it was only after a good deal of persuasion from his parents that he agreed to return once again to Chennapatnam and resume his job. Again, he found his job at the school very irksome and returned to Mysore after a brief stay there.

Now he felt contented and began to work on his first novel with a new zeal. Besides, he wrote many short stories and essays. At this time, his maternal uncle came to his place and took him to Bangalore to find a better prospect for his writings. There he ran from one editor to another for the publication of his stories, but of no avail. After some time a small piece written by him was accepted by *Punch* and that was his first prestige publication. The piece was titled "How (Not) to Write an Indian Novel," and it lampooned Western writers who visited India to gather material for their creative writings. By this time, he had succeeded in marrying a headmaster's daughter after many hurdles because their horoscopes did not tally and the girl's father was not ready to take a risk. In spite of all odds, R. K. Narayan and Rajam got married. Soon after his marriage, his father suffered a paralytic stroke causing him to remain bed-ridden for a long time. That is why, with a view to increasing his income, he became a reporter in Mysore for a Madras-based newspaper named *The Justice*. While he was working for *The Justice,* the manuscript was changing hands from one publisher to another, and later it was returned to him with a rejection slip. As he was getting discouraged, his old friend, Purna, who was at Oxford, came to his rescue and managed to get his novel published by Hamish Hamilton on the recommendation of Graham Greene. It is since then that the friendship between R. K. Narayan and Graham Greene continued unabated. Subsequently, Narayan left his job as a newspaper reporter.

His first novel, *Swami and Friends,* was published in 1935, but it did not sell well, so much so that Hamish Hamilton refused to publish his next novel, *The Bachelor of Arts,* with the words: 'S*wami and Friends* was a sad failure. I do not think Chandran (*The Bachelor of Arts)* is going to do any better. I hope someone will prove me wrong some day.'[2] *The Bachelor of Arts* was published in 1937 by Nelson again on Graham Greene's recommendation. In 1937, his father died, and to earn more he began to write one humorous article every week for a Magazine at ten rupees a week. In the meantime, he had also begun his third novel, *The Dark Room. The Dark Room* was once again read and approved by Graham Greene, and consequently, was published by Macmillan in 1938. In *My Days* R. K. Narayan says: 'I had the unique experience of having a new publisher for each book.'[3] Then the Second World War began, and Narayan kept himself pre-occupied with editing the short lived *Indian Thought.* In June 1939, his wife died of typhoid leaving behind a three-year old daughter, Hema. R. K. Narayan has described this part of his experience of her sickness and death in *The English Teacher. The English Teacher* is autobiographical in content, and only a very small part of it is fictional.

Since then he wrote continuously, and it is no surprise that he could write fifteen novels, a large number of short stories, besides essays and memoirs. Narayan is a comic novelist. His attitude to comedy grows out of a holistic view of man's condition in the universe. As such, the criticism of society and observation of the social predicament implicit in his works are only incidental. For Narayan, society is not man-made by choices, but exists as part of a universal mixture of the serious and the comic, and it is this combination that distinguishes his works from the writings of others. This simple and unpretentious writer has delighted countless readers with his charming novels relating to Malgudi for over seventy-five years.

Mostly R. K. Narayan is not a writer of problem novels. He is content with depicting the contours of Malgudi and portraying the sorrows, joys and ironies in the lives of the various types of peoples, who live and die in Malgudi, or of those who pass through Malgudi. His main aim is to acquaint his readers thoroughly with these 'ins and outs' of the human drama that is always taking place in the lives of the Malgudi people. Politics, war, sex, crime, topical problems and such other themes that a novelist generally exploits to keep pace with the moving times fail to tempt him. His only novel with a political background, *Waiting for the Mahatma,* is also primarily a love-story. War, the negation of life, has no place in his positive acceptance of life. Sex is only incidental. If it acquires thematic significance, as in *The Painter of Signs,* the way it is tackled is essentially ironical and mocking. Of all his characters, Vasu, the 'Man-eater' alone, has a criminal passion which turns him into a diabolic and abominable figure, ending in self-destruction. Narayan's art has a quality of imperturbable placidity. It has no use for ephemeral topical subjects. *The Painter of Signs* may be regarded as an exception. Narayan uses the current family-planning programme as the backdrop to much of the action in it, but the topicality of the background is not allowed to grow into the centrality of the theme.

Narayan's portrayal of life is, thus, severely restrained by a rigorous discipline of art. It precludes all that falls outside his periphery of observation and knowledge. The urban middle-class setting in South India is his milieu as a painter of life. The substance of his work, in fifteen novels and numerous short stories, has thus an essential homogeneity.

His humour has a universal quality, and it places him 'in the mainstream of the great comic traditions.'[4] He carries on the great tradition of comedy in his own distinctive manner. He shares his comic vision with the world's great humorists from Chaucer to those of the modern times. Narayan's humour is genial. Of Narayan's humour, Graham Greene says in his Introduction to *The Bachelor of Arts:* '... a humour strange to our fiction, close to Chekov than to any English writer with the same underlying sense of beauty and sadness.'[5] Harvey Breit is also aware of the likeness between the two great humourists, Narayan and Chekov, in the following lines: 'Narayan is to India what Chekov was to Russia; he has the same dispassionate mind and compassionate heart.'[6] Unlike Graham Greene and Harvey Breit, Anthony West underscores Narayan's kinship with the great Russian humorists when he describes him as 'a writer of Gogol's stature.'[7] Narayan's humour is essentially free from the satiric spirit of condemnation and censure. It aims at portraiture rather than exposure of human nature. As a comic writer, he is closer in spirit to Chaucer, Shakespeare and Dickens than to Swift, Voltaire and Thackeray.

Narayan has the keen eye, the tolerant mind and the compassionate heart which constitute the basic equipment of a true humorist. 'Narayan's comic vision is one of his great gifts,'[8] says Rosanne Archer. It enables him to perceive the comic and the incongruous in the ordinary. Narayan's observation on two of his lovable child-characters in *Swami and Friends,* Swami and Samuel, may be taken as expressive of his own comic vision:

> The bond between them was laughter. They were able to see together the same absurdities and incongruities in things. The most trivial and unnoticeable things to others would tickle them to death.[9]

Narayan has preserved this freshness of vision throughout his long creative career.

The basic comic situation in Narayan's novels is one of the deviations from the normal. *The Bachelor of Arts* struck the first significant note of ironic comedy in the character of Chandran, and with each successive novel, it grew into Narayan's signature. With *Mr. Sampath,* Narayan's comic genius became manifest. With *The Financial Expert,* it blossomed into maturity. Then came *The Guide,* 'a remarkable example of the especially difficult genre to which most of Narayan's work belongs, the serious comedy.'[10] In *The Guide,* he treats with extraordinary skill the stuff of tragedy in terms of comedy, and therein lies his 'unique achievement in Indian fiction.'[11]

In the characters of Sampath, Margayya and Raju, Narayan presents his serious ironic comedy remarkably well. His fine sense of 'tragicomic'[12] manifests itself in these remarkable novels. The element of fantasy, which is noticeable in *The Bachelor of Arts,* grows to be an integral part of his comic vision in almost all his novels.

The allegorical element finds its consummation in the 'puranic' mythical pattern of *The Man-Eater of Malgudi.* Using the puranic myth of Bhasmasura as the main plank, Narayan builds up a modern fable with Vasu as an embodiment of the demonic powers. His singular achievement consists in the texture of the novel that remains ironic and good-humoured in spite of its complexion of a crime thriller and a parable. Even the demonic character of Vasu, the 'Man-eater,' is not without an element of the comic and the grotesque. *The Vendor of Sweets* is richly comic in view of the incongruities of its central character,

Jagan, the ageing sweet-vendor. The theme of juxtaposition of tradition and modernity, a recurring source of comedy in Narayan's fiction, is treated here in a comical and fantastic manner. *The Painter of Signs,* the most topical of Narayan's novels, gives an unmistakable evidence of Narayan's comic fecundity that remains unimpaired by the passage of time. Its humour consists chiefly in his mocking treatment of sexual passion growing into an obsession. His stories also present to us a rich variety of themes and situations, comic, ironic, tragic, or supernatural.

Narayan's singular comic detachment suggests a personal endeavour to attain an equation with life, to overcome and rationalise the 'profound and unmitigated loneliness'[13] of life. The shock of his wife's death was so traumatic that he considered following her to the funeral pyre. *The English Teacher* expresses a profound personal realization. 'Living without illusions seemed to be the greatest task for me in life now ... The twists and turns of fate would cease to shock if we knew, and expected nothing more than the barest truth and facts of life.'[14] Narayan's great comic novels followed *The English Teacher,* and their comic thematic pattern is one of illusion–realization–disillusionment, or catastrophe–self-awareness–resolution.

His comic vision is, thus, a view of life with a frame of reference. It has its roots in a traditional ethos and scale of values. These values have a special reference to the institution of the family which constitutes Narayan's sensibility. Evolution of a 'proper detachment'[15] or dissociation while leading an embodied and temporal life has been the hallmark of the Indian philosophy of synthesis. Narayan has handled this philosophy in his novels in terms of comedy.

Narayan's humour is mild, not boisterous; he exposes the ills of society, and probes them too, but he does so neither for sadistic pleasure nor for causing disgust to his readers. It is intended to make the readers of his novels more and more aware of the contradictions of life. Neither is the past dead nor is the future clear; neither is anyone positively good nor downright bad; neither is a person completely civilized nor utterly primitive. The society of today is an amalgam of all such elements. If on the one hand there are simple villagers, on the other there are journalists with tape-recorders and microphones; if there are Swamis, the living anchorites, in modern India, there are unscrupulous sharks like Ramani and Vasu too in this country. The very spectacle of the age-old Indian sensibility trying to step in with the age of science and technology is grotesque but likable, if we have the eyes of a humorist and the sympathy of an artist.

A discussion of R. K. Narayan as a novelist cannot be complete without a consideration of his use of English language. Pointing to at least one aspect of Narayan's English, Khushwant Singh has remarked at a seminar at Jaipur that he has used words, like 'tiffin,' 'plantain' and 'brinjal,' which are no longer current in the U.K. or the U.S.A. It does not seem a valid objection because these words may not be in current use, but they have found their way into the English language. 'Tiffin' and 'plantain' are still in use in South India, and Narayan might have used them to convey the local flavour. Actually, Indian writers of English use this language as a vehicle of Indian culture to express culturally-determined networks of activities that are typically Indian. Narayan has been able to do it because of its 'siren-like charm and a lot of persistence.'[16] Singh further observes: 'English has proved that if a language has flexibility any experience can be communicated through it, even if it has to be paraphrased... .'[17] Therefore, Narayan rightly endeavours to express an Indian sensibility through a Western medium. Kamala Das also shares Narayan's views regarding the use of English by Indian writers:

> The language I speak
> Becomes mine, its distortions, its queerness
> All mine, mine alone. It is half English, half
> Indian, funny perhaps, but it is honest,
> It is as human as I am human, don't
> You see? It voices my joy, my longings,
> My hopes, and it is useful to me as cawing
> Is to crows or roaring to the lions, it
> Is human speech, the speech of the mind that is
> Here and not there, a mind that sees and hears and
> Is aware ...[18]

R. K. Narayan too subscribes to the views expressed by Kamala Das at a B. B. C. interview with William Walsh, and goes on to say that he has been using English all the time without being aware that it is an alien medium. R. K. Narayan has sometimes been accused of his conforming to the grammatical and linguistic norms of a language. V. Y. Kantak in his highly enlightening essay "The Language of Indian Fiction in English" expresses the view that

> he does not seem to be interested in exploring the fuller, deeper possibilities of the language he is using. The vocabulary has always a very modest range. Word or phrase rarely glints with compression or suggested meanings. They are just their own declared selves. The sentence has a certain structural monotony. It is always the same subject–predicate–object–complement ensembled with a few subsidiary appendages of phrases and clauses and occasional inversions. It seems all bone lacking the expected amplification of flesh.[19]

He does not hesitate to call his language 'one-stringed.'[20] Here V. Y. Kantak seems very convincing in making his points, but P. S. Sundaram takes Narayan's weaknesses as his strength: 'A great deal of his effect depends precisely on the unhurried pace, the even tone, the words which seem to be "just their own declared selves" and yet contain a world of irony.' [21] In fact, in spite of his being a good conformist he has been able to make a creative use of language successfully. In other words, we may say that he treats language like an absolute queen, obeys her laws, reasonable or unreasonable, but at times he acts as her acknowledged favourite to make her serve the purpose he intends to perform.

Narayan's craftsmanship in plot-construction does not reveal a consistent quality. He began in a tentative and episodic manner in *Swami and Friends,* but developed an artistic sense in his second novel, *The Bachelor of Arts*. His third novel, *The Dark Room,* reveals definite signs of technical maturity. His predilection for the fantastic, already suggested in *The Bachelor of Arts,* becomes quite prominent with *The English Teacher.* Generally, his plots split into two separate parts–the realistic and the fantastic. Uma Parameswaran also confirms it in her famous essay, 'Native Genius – R. K. Narayan': 'most of his plots break into two separate plots, the realistic view being carried alongside the fantastic and then dropped altogether.'[22] It is not always that he succeeds in fusing the two into an organic whole. He is notably successful in *The Financial Expert, The Guide, The Man-Eater of Malgudi* and *The Painter of Signs,* but not so in *Mr. Sampath, Waiting for the Mahatma* or *The Vendor of Sweets.* However, these technical inadequacies cannot detract him from its inventive ingenuity. Even the most loosely constructed plots, such as those in *Waiting for the Mahatma* and *Mr. Sampath,* are highly enjoyable in parts as most of Dickens's novels are.

Narayan excels as 'an artful delineator of character.'[23] Commenting on his mode of dealing with the character, K. R. S. Iyengar observes that

> ... he is content, like Jane Austen, with his "little bit of ivory", just so many inches wide: he would like to be a detached observer, to concentrate on a narrow scene, to sense the atmosphere of the place, to shape a small group of characters in their oddities and angularities; he would, if he could, explore the inner countries of the mind, heart and soul, catch the uniqueness in the ordinary, the tragic in the prosaic. [24]

R. K. Narayan is so much concerned about his character that he comments: 'my focus is all on character. If his personality comes alive, the rest is easy for me.' [25] Over the years he has created a rich portrait gallery of students, teachers, parents, grand-parents, half-hearted dreamers, journalists, cranks, movie-stars, *sanyasis* and women who are pious and suffering, excelling in household chores and also in seducing men.

Narayan's focus in his portraiture is steadily on the average. The extremes in life's scale do not interest him. His characters are ordinary men and women with human eccentricities, incongruities, oddities, follies and foibles. They are taken from the real world and are not abstractions of good or evil, virtues or vices. As a result, there are no 'heroes' or 'villains' in the conventional sense in Nayaran's world. Normally, Narayan avoids creating a character of epic dimension. Only once he ventured into this alien field when he attempted to draw the Mahatma, and the result was unhappy, if not disastrous.

His minor characters who crowd the world of Malgudi are almost as ageless as its familiar landmarks. They are fine cameos and, together, make a delightful bunch. They are mostly flat caricatures but very human and amusing in their idiosyncrasies and oddities. They impart colour and variety to the scene. The blacksmith burglar and his wife *(The Dark Room)*, the cart-boy and his companions *(Swami and Friends)*, the common run of people, the petty shop-keeper, the veterinary doctor and forest officials *(The Man-Eater of Malgudi)*, and those working at film-shooting with Sampath (*Mr. Sampath*), and Gaffur (*The Guide*), are some important specimens of the society.

R. K. Narayan, unlike the two novelists of the trio, Mulk Raj Anand and Raja Rao, believes in creating characters for their own sake. His characters do not fulfil any extraneous necessity. They are there by their own merits and for their own sake. Narayan presents, in his novels, a cross-section of varied humanity that may be found anywhere. He presents happy schoolchildren and their angry teachers *(Swami and Friends)* and a bachelor of Arts who enters the threshold of life rather in a frustrated manner *(The Bachelor of Arts)*. He portrays a happy English teacher whose happiness is soon eroded by the death of his beloved wife *(The English Teacher)*. His people include eccentric and harsh husbands as also their faithful wives, and mistresses with whom they flirt *(The Dark Room)*. He also presents the scheming adventurous moneymaking crooks and their superstitious clients (*The Financial Expert)*. We are introduced to a terrible human being who seems the very incarnation of a demon, and who like all demons, dies by his own hand *(The Man-Eater of Malgudi)*. We also come across a solicitous father who absorbs all the vices of an ultra-modern youth who is a challenge and a source of constant worry to him *(The Vendor of Sweets)*. We see a raw youth becoming a patriotic volunteer, under the leadership of a beautiful girl, with whom he has fallen in love. We also see the history-making Mahatma Gandhi and the life lived in his Ashram. The characters of his later novels are indeed more complex and more crooked. The later characters are roguish –Sampath, Raju, Margayya, Mali and others.

Among women characters, Narayan generally portrays two kinds of figures: typical Indian homemakers, and fashionable, social butterflies. His heroines, such as Susila and Savitri, are gentle, religious, and loving. Their only anxiety is the welfare of their husbands and children. Sometimes Narayan draws the more mature, experienced and aged varieties of these simple homemakers. Narayan also portrays a nagging woman in the form of the headmaster's wife in *The English Teacher*. This variety is rare in his novels.

Shantabai *(The Dark Room)*, Shanti *(Mr. Sampath)* and Rosie *(The Guide)* belong to the butterfly, vivacious sort of women. In Shantabai, Narayan has given a vivid description of this specie of artful and cunning flirts, whose only vocation is to satisfy their own caprices, and wreck the domestic life of indiscreet men. Rangi in *The Man-Eater of Malgudi* is very crude. Being a professional dancer, she is not ashamed of her antics and ways of life. She neither keeps any mask, nor abides by the norms of society. She has her own style of living, and is least concerned about what others say of her.

As is evident from these characters, Narayan is, largely, a traditionalist in the matter of characterisation. He does not give portraits of exceptional men and women among his characters. There are 'no Hamlets, no great intellectuals or statesman'[26] among his people. Still his personages are complex because of the diversity of Indian culture. The central, crucial dimension of his characters is their Indianness. It is because of their being the children of the soil that their way of living betrays the element of regionalism about them. Actually, Narayan never mutilates or disfigures his characters. His characters may be comical, or rather puny beings, and yet we develop a real affection for them. We may laugh at them, and still we cannot remain without loving them.

CRITICAL COMMENTS/REVIEWS

Narayan has been fortunate in respect of critics. However, their approaches to his works have been invariably through Western critical concepts because he has very successfully exposed the orient to the focus of the occident. V. Panduranga Rao is of the opinion that 'Narayan is a writer with a full commitment to certain spiritual and religious values and ideas, with which Indians are normally familiar.' [27] C. Paul Verghese confirms that 'it is above all Narayan's adherence to the Indian tradition reflected in the world-view he expresses through his novels that makes him an essentially Indian novelist.'[28] Anthony Thwaite finds him surprising 'not so much by his revelation of strangeness as his pictures of the common places of oriental.' [29] In the opinion of H.M. Williams, 'Narayan is essentially a humorous writer.'[30] Meenakshi Mukherjee also commends R. K. Narayan because he 'successfully achieves a universal vision'[31] through the provincial city of Malgudi.

Anita Desai in a reply to the question why Narayan's voice is taken as authentic in the West, records: 'it is "timeless,"... it has the unruffled calm of a civilization that has seen five thousand years pass before its eyes and endured all vicissitudes.'[32] P. S. Sundaram hails him as 'absolutely authentic.'[33] Nirmal Mukherji remarks: ' ... Narayan is neither a social pathologist nor a social reformer. He accepts life in totality.'[34] K. Venkatachari also shares N. Mukherji's observation: 'His novels in the main are variations on the theme of acceptance of life.'[35]

As regards Narayan's achievement, Rajeev Taranath states that 'Narayan's achievement could be described as the creative use of the ordinary'[36] and 'the uncompromising way in which he forces the ingredients of limitation towards evolving an authenticity which satisfies.'[37] Lakshmi Holmstrom endorses him as 'a comic novelist.'[38] She goes on to add that 'his attitude to comedy grows out of a whole view of man's condition in the universe.'[39] M. K. Naik acclaims him as 'the novelist of the individual man.'[40] Therefore, he discovers that 'the total fictional corpus of R. K. Narayan, presents a panorama of men and women in different life roles, ranging from the school boy indulging in his characteristic pranks in *Swami and Friends* to the old man about to renounce the world in *The Vendor of Sweets*.'[41] Uma Parameswaran announces that 'the most striking quality about both Narayan's work and Narayan himself is unpretentiousness.'[42] K. R. S. Iyengar gives a big hand to Narayan for his 'art of resolved limitation and conscientious exploration.'[43] He sums up the themes of Narayan's novel in an enlightening way: 'In Narayan's novels, there is generally a flight, an uprooting, a disturbance of order followed by a return–a renewal, a restoration of normalcy.'[44] William Walsh values his characters the most: 'Character is action, and action is plot, and it is by means of the actions of his character that Narayan summons up the world in which he lives.'[45]

Sometimes in the process of internationalizing Narayan, we forget that he is firmly rooted in his own culture. His novels really invite readers to enter and enjoy his South Indian world with all its different colours, enchanting smells and vital, vibrant people. The only critic who hesitates in absorbing Narayan in the Western novelistic tradition is V. S. Naipaul. Actually, Naipaul at first read his novels as social comedies and found them aimless and negative. He finds 'a contradiction between his form, which implies concern and his attitude which denies it.'[46] In his more recent writing, *India: A Wounded Civilization*, he corrects himself and says that both the content and the form of Narayan's novels are alien to the West and are intensely Hindu. Recording his impressions on re-reading *Mr.Sampath,* Naipaul says:

> ... What had seemed speculative and comic, aimless and "Russian" about Narayan's novel had turned out to be something else, the expression of an almost hermetic philosophical system. The novel I had read as novel was also a fable, a classic exposition of the Hindu equilibrium, surviving the shock of an alien culture, an alien literary form, an alien literary language, and making harmless even these new concepts it appeared to welcome.[47]

Naipaul's interpretation of Hinduism seems biased and wrong. G. S. Amur does not subscribe to his view that 'Narayan's novels are fables and not novels (after all, novels are fables).'[48] Yet Naipaul and John Updike find something almost similar about Narayan's writings. John Updike notices him 'immersed in his material'[49] and V. S. Naipaul finds him operating 'from deep within his society.'[50]

Narayan's long span of writing fiction has fetched him a faithful following and a distinguished reputation in not only India but outside India too. In the West, perhaps his greatest admirer is Graham Greene who rationalizes his liking for Narayan: 'Narayan, more than any of them, wakes in me a spring of gratitude, for he has offered me a second home.'[51] Whatever be his achievement in the opinion of the critics, his books have necessarily 'the ring of true India in them.'[52]

Though many critics have devoted a lot of time and energy to study R. K. Narayan's creative works, Narayan himself dislikes his critics: 'They (scholars) always try to read meanings into my books, trace a theme, relate this character to that, make a connection between hero and hero. I wish they would leave my books and me alone.'[53] Narayan may be right in developing some sort of antipathy to his critics, but there are valid reasons for his widespread popularity among his commentators. These reasons may be traced to his uniqueness, his subtle irony, his sincerity, and his bright humour. P. S. Sundaram elaborates Narayan's excellence:

> What makes Narayan the writer he is, and makes it worth our while to write about him is the zest he so obviously has in life and all his creatures, his modesty, his irony, his sense of humour, the complete absence of pomposity and pretence.[54]

Narayan has been very lucky with his critics but some critics have tried to highlight his limitations and shortcomings. Shashi Tharoor is one such critic who does not consider him one of the greatest Indian novelists wholeheartedly. He compares R. K. Narayan to Jane Austen and remarks:

> Like Jane Austen, his fiction is restricted to the concerns of a small society portrayed with precision and empathy; unlike Austen, his prose could not elevate those concerns beyond the ordinariness of its subjects. Narayan wrote of, and from, the mindset of the small-town South Indian Brahmin, and did not seem capable of a greater range.[55]

Tharoor is deeply concerned about Narayan's style too:

> His metronomic style was frequently not equal to the demands of his situations. Intense and potentially charged scenes were rendered pathetic by the inadequacy of the language used to describe them. ... In much of his writings, stories with extraordinary possibilities unfolded in flat, monotonous sentences that frustrated rather than convinced me.... At its worst, Narayan's prose was like the bullock-cart: a vehicle that can move only in one gear, is unable to turn, accelerate or reverse, and remains yoked to traditional creatures .... [56]

Even Shashi Deshpande does not want to place Narayan at the highest pedestal in spite of considering him as an important link among Indo-Anglican Writers:

> was Narayan a great writer? To my mind, he was a very good writer, for his time a remarkable one but to me he was not a great writer.... English writers in this country today could not have written the way they do if it had not been for R. K. Narayan. Each writer is a link in a chain, each generation of writers takes a step, making more things for those who follow.[57]

In spite of the caustic remarks by Shashi Tharoor, R. K. Narayan occupies a very important place in the galaxy of Indian novelists writing in English. He may be called the pioneer of the regional novel in the field of Indo-English fiction. In his novels and short stories, he has depicted the life and activities of the various categories of people of Malgudi. Actually, he has developed a spatial symbol to give a definite location and setting to his characters. The city of his imagination is miniature India. Its complexion, its variegated life makes one feel that life is almost the same everywhere. The novels present a picture of Malgudi that has gone on growing from the early thirties to the nineties. A closer study of the novels reveals that Malgudi is a compromise between the oriental age-old traditions and the modern Western civilization. As Western modernity comes to Malgudi in due course of time, its own indigenous values are corroded. In *Swami and Friends,* Malgudi is a semi-agricultural town, surrounded by the three natural landmarks–the Sarayu, the Mempi Hills and the Forest, but Malgudi in *The Dark Room* presents itself as a civilized and a commercial centre where corrupt practices of sorts are also in vogue.

Being a novelist of the thirties, he came under the impact of Mahatma Gandhi, but he never actively participated in any political activity. He focused his attention on the ironies of life rather than on the history of India. That is why he did not write a single political novel in his life. Even *Waiting for the Mahatma* is not a political novel. It describes a love-story against the political background of pre-independent India. In *The Vendor of Sweets,* he presents a sociological analysis of the two generations that find it difficult to live together. In *The Guide*, he juxtaposes traditional India with the modern India of sophisticated culture.

A serious study of the novels of R. K. Narayan gives us the impression that he subscribes to a particular philosophy of life. In his opinion, what makes life delightful or sad does not depend on the real texture of life itself, but on the way one lives or on the attitude that one has towards it. His novels suggest that one who lives with caution, sincerity, good sense, intelligence and understanding as does Srinivas in *Mr. Sampath* or Bharati in *Waiting for the Mahatma* or Nataraj in *The Man-Eater of Malgudi,* sails her or his way through the wide ocean of life smoothly and finds life full of delight; but one who brings much sentimentality and selfishness stumbles and undergoes innumerable hardships and difficulties like Chandran or Margayya or Sriram and sometimes like Ravi or Raju.[58]

Each one of R. K. Narayan's novels is a full circle. In the majority of Narayan's novels, there seems to be the recurrent movement of characters – 'from average to the extraordinary and back again to a more poignant state of average.'[59] For instance, Swami, Chandran, Savitri and Margayya's son-Balu-run away, but later come back or are brought back by some agent. Srinivas returns to his paper, Margayya to his knobbly trunk, and Nataraj to his office. Sriram and Bharati once again seem to be back in Malgudi, and Susila herself falls in a nice relationship again with Krishna. Uma Parameswaran also subscribes to Taranath's view: 'his main characters are like the weighted, inflatable toys that bob up on their feet no matter how they are pushed.'[60] Narayan sees some sort of balance operating all the time in the world, wrong-doers and policemen keeping one another properly engaged, light and shadow playing hide and seek with each other, hope and failure embracing each other and again taking different paths. This balance has been more beautifully and successfully portrayed in R. K. Narayan's latest novels.

Reading Narayan's novels is an event. While reading them we feel like riding a country bus through rural India. It is a kind of journey in which we meet different kinds of people with their different customs and value systems. However, the bus moves so smoothly that it neither bumps nor jerks. Even if a tragedy, melodrama or crisis occurs, it leaves the familiar landscape unscarred. It is surely R. K. Narayan's control and effortless driving of the somewhat ancient vehicle that makes the ride so smooth.

One of the most convincing reasons behind R. K. Narayan's authenticity in the West is that his novels transcend the colourful and exotic setting in India and make it a part of universal human experience. Some very highly perceptive scholars regard him as the best Indian writer in the English language. Though his novels are widely read in the West, he never chooses his themes nor does he develop them to suit the Westerners' sensibility. His themes are authentically Indian and he discusses them in a vein any self-respecting and self-assured Indian would do.

MALGUDI: A MICROCOSM OF MIDDLE CLASS SOUTH INDIAN SOCIETY

Malgudi, a small South Indian town has become the universe for all Narayan's works, though Malgudi does not exist physically. It is Narayan's creation as Wessex is Hardy's creation or Yoknapatawpha is the imaginary creation of William Faulkner. R K Narayan describes his conception of Malgudi:

> Malgudi was an earth-shaking discovery for me, because I had no mind for facts and things like that, which would be necessary in writing about Lalgudi or any real place. I first pictured not my town but just the railway station, which was a small platform with a banyan tree, a station master, and two trains a day, one coming and one going. On Vijayadasami I sat down and wrote the first sentence about my town: The train had just arrived in Malgudi Station.[61]

The recurrence of the same place serves to put together the various novels into an organic whole and can be labelled as Malgudi novels just as Hardy's novels are called Wessex novels. Anoop Sarkar stretches the importance of Narayan's world and finds it a miniature India:

> Narayan creates his fictional world of Malgudi as an essentially Indian society or town. The Indianness and Indian sensibility pervaded the whole place. Narayan's Malgudi is also a microcosm of India. It grows and develops and expands and changes, and is full of humanity, drawing its sustenance from the human drama and is enacted in it.[62]

Uma Parameswaran considers Malgudi a living being, as she firmly believes, 'Malgudi is the only character that grows, changes, reacts to time and circumstance, has a spirit, a soul.'[63] Narayan further justifies the reason for Malgudi's being an essentially South Indian town:

> I must be certain about the psychology of the character I am writing about, and I must be equally sure of the background. I know the Tamil and Kannada speaking people most. I know how their minds work and almost as if it is happening to me. I know exactly what will happen to them in certain circumstances. And I know how they will react.[64]

Thus, Narayan's choice of Malgudi starts an issue of Malgudi remaining intertwined with its inhabitants (i.e. characters). In fact, the customs, beliefs and thought patterns of people are deeply rooted in the place they come from. Naturally, the identity and ethos of the place are reflected in its characters. Malgudi affects the psychology and behaviour pattern of characters over a period of time but somehow Narayan emphasizes the importance of age-old tradition and the solace and peace it provides to its people in time of crisis and emergency. Reading Narayan's novels in chronological order suggests Malgudi to be a combination of the old and the new, the primitive and the modern, and the Eastern and the Western. Sometimes, these opposites (like the primitive and the modern) are shown to remain in peaceful co-existence but on other occasions, they enter into a conflict with each other. Just like the growth of a living entity, the Malgudi of *The Bachelor of Arts* has not been presented in the same way as it has been painted in *Talkative Man*. In *Talkative Man*, Malgudi witnesses many modern facilities, like a night club, Nalli's Hardware, the modern sanitaryware with its porcelain products, a number of studios and a hire-purchase system besides a changing attitude of people towards women regarding their education and empowerment. Further, we find a new face of Malgudi in *The World of Nataraj*. Because of dramatic changes in the town, this novel talks about the new methods of farming, the gobar gas plant, the new bar and restaurant in the town called Kismet with a dress code. '... Malgudi is a place where change is leisurely and incremental.'[65] As this leisurely and incremental transformation has been perceived mostly by Narayan's characters, so, we have tried to explore the characters more than any other elements of a novel. Even Susan Ram and Narasimhan Ram find Narayan rich with the variety of his characters:

> To wander any street, peer through a window or push open a door is to encounter a character: Swami, the undistinguished, cricket loving boy; Savitri, the put-upon, and briefly rebellious, housewife; Krishna, the college lecturer traumatised by the loss of his wife; Margayya, the financial expert at his questionable business beneath the banyan tree; Raju, the tourist-seeking guide.[66]

Narayan's expertise lies in the fact that through his characters and their social, moral, and financial predicaments, he tries to reveal the universal in the particular. This very universality of these characters give life, colour and momentum to Malgudi and keep it pulsating always and this universality has come into focus in this book.

REFERENCES

1. R. K. Narayan, *My Days* (Mysore, 1975), p. 53.
2. *My Days*, p. 116.
3. *My Days*, p. 119.
4. B. S. Goyal (ed.), *R. K. Narayan: A Critical Spectrum* (Meerut, 1983), p. 101.
5. Graham Greene, Introduction to *The Bachelor of Arts* (London, 1978), p. v.
6. *R. K. Narayan: A Critical Spectrum*, p. 101.
7. *Ibid.*
8. *R. K. Narayan: A Critical Spectrum*, p. 101.
9. R. K. Narayan, *Swami and Friends* (Mysore, 1971), p. 9.
10. William Walsh, *Indo-English Literature*, ed. K.K. Sharma (Ghaziabad, 1977), p. 129.
11. C.D. Narasimhaiah, *The Swan and the Eagle* (Simla, 1969), p. 150.
12. *R. K. Narayan: A Critical Spectrum*, p. 102.
13. R. K. Narayan, *The English Teacher* (Mysore, 1970), p. 203.
14. V. Panduranga Rao, 'Tea with R. K. Narayan,' *The Journal of Commonwealth Literature* (June 1971), pp. 79-80.

15. Shriley Chew, *Readings in the Commonwealth Literature,* ed. William Walsh (Oxford, 1973), p. 60.
16. R. K. Narayan, *Next Sunday* (Mysore, 1956), p. 15.
17. M. K. Naik (ed.), *Aspects of Indian Writing in English* (Delhi, 1979), p. 22.
18. Kamala Das, *The Golden Treasury of Indo-Anglian Poetry* 1828-1965, ed. V.K. Gokak (New Delhi, 1970), p. 240.
19. M. K. Naik, S.K. Desai and G.S. Amur (eds.), *Critical Essays on Indian Writing in English* (Dharwar, 1968), pp. 148-49.
20. *Ibid.*, p. 150.
21. P. S. Sundaram, *R. K. Narayan* (New Delhi, 1973), p. 135.
22. Uma Parameswaran, *A Study of Representative Indo-English Novelists* (New Delhi, 1976), p. 62.
23. *R. K. Narayan:* A *Critical Spectrum,* p. 105.
24. K. R. S. Iyengar, *Indian Writing in English* (New Delhi, 1984), p. 360.
25. *R. K. Narayan: A Critical Spectrum*, p. 105.
26. G. N. Agnihotri, 'R. K. Narayan, The Pure Artist,' *Indian Life and Problems in the Novels of Mulk Raj Anand, Raja Rao and R. K. Narayan* (Meerut, 1984), p. 93.
27. V. Panduranga Rao, 'The Art of R. K. Narayan,' *The Journal of Commonwealth Literature,* 5 (July 1968), p. 19.
28. C. Paul Verghese, *Problems of the Indian Creative Writer in English* (Bombay, 1971), p. 138.
29. Anthony Thwaite, 'The Painter of Signs,' *Times Literary Supplement,* 20 June 1976, pp. 6-7.
30. H. M. Williams, *Indo-Anglian Literature* (1800-1970): A Survey (Bombay, 1976), p. 49.
31 Meenakshi Mukherjee, *The Twice Born Fiction* (New Delhi, 1971), p. 25.
32. Anita Desai, 'Timeless Tales,' *India Today,* No. 20, 16 Nov. 1985, pp. 152-53.
33. P. S. Sundaram, *R. K. Narayan* (New Delhi, 1973), p. 144.
34. Nirmal Mukherji, 'Some Aspects of the Literary Development of R. K. Narayan,' *The Banasthali Patrika,* Vol 5, No.13 (1969), p. 87.
35. K. Venkatachari, 'R. K. Narayan's Novels: Acceptance of Life,' *Osmania Journal of English Studies* (1969), p. 51.
36. *Critical Essays on Indian Writings in English,* p. 294.

37. *Ibid.*, p. 306.
38. Lakshmi Holmstrom, *The Novels of R. K. Narayan* (Calcutta, 1973), p. 122.
39. *Ibid.*, p. 122.
40. M. K. Naik, *The Ironic Vision* (New Delhi, 1983), p. 1.
41. *Ibid.*
42. *A Study of Representative Indo-English Novelists,* p. 45.
43. *Indian Writing in English*, p. 360.
44. *Ibid.*, p. 385.
45. William Walsh, *R. K. Narayan: A Critical Appreciation* (New Delhi, 1983), p. 135.
46. V. S. Naipaul, *An Area of Darkness* (Harmondsworth, 1968), p. 216.
47. V. S. Naipaul, *India: A Wounded Civilization* (New York, 1977), p. 19.
48. R. K. Dhawan (ed.), *Explorations in Modern Indo-English Fiction* (New Delhi, 1982), p. 124.
49. John Updike, 'R. K. Narayan, A Writer Immersed in his Material,' *Span* (April 1975), n. p.
50. *An Area of Darkness*, p. 216.
51. Introduction to *The Bachelor of Arts*, p. v.
52. Ved Mehta, *John is Easy to Please* (Harmondsworth, 1974), p. 109.
53. *Ibid.*, p. 120.
54. *R. K. Narayan*, p. 144.
55. Shashi Tharoor 'Comedies of Sufferings,' 2 Oct. 2008 <http://www.hinduonet.com/2001/07/08/stories/13080675.htm>.
56. *Ibid.*
57. Shashi Deshpande, 'R. K. Narayan: A Personal view,' *The Journal of Commonwealth Literature*, 42.65 (2007), p. 71.
58. Harish Raizada, *R. K. Narayan: A Critical Study of His Works* (New Delhi, 1969), p. 159.
59. Rajeev Taranath, *Critical Essays on Indian Writings in English* (Dharwar, 1972), p. 296.
60. *A Study of Representative Indo-English Novelists*, p. 51.
61. Ved Mehta. 'The Train had just arrived at Malgudi Station' in *John is Easy to Please* (London, 1971) p. 55.
62. Anoop Sarkar, 'R. K. Narayan: A Profile,' 20 Oct. 2008 http:// tamilnation .org/hundredtamils/rknarayan.htm.

63. *A Study of Representative Indo-English Novelists*, p. 50.

64. R. K. Narayan, in an interview given to S. Krishna, quoted by Hilda Pontes in *R. K. Narayan*, ed. Nissim Ezekiel (New Delhi, 1983).

65. Susan Ram and Narasimhan Ram, 'R.K.Narayan: India's Greatest writer, Illuminating the Human Condition through Small-town Life,' 4 Oct. 2008 <http://www.guardian.co.uk/news/2001/may/14/guardianobituaries.books/print>.

66. *Ibid.*

2

A JOURNEY FROM INNOCENCE TO EXPERIENCE: SWAMI AND FRIENDS AND THE BACHELOR OF ARTS

Experience, which destroys innocence,
also leads one back to it.

—James Arthur Baldwin

SWAMI AND FRIENDS

R. K. Narayan's first novel *Swami and Friends* was first published in 1935 by Hamish Hamilton, London, on the recommendation of Graham Greene. This book has since gone through several Indian and American editions. It is 'a very innocent and delightful picture of a young boy baffled by a half-westernized school system'.[1] The novel attracted many prominent writers and critics all over India and abroad. According to K. R. Srinivasa Iyengar 'in some respects, *Swami and Friends* is the most enjoyable of the novels'.[2] Lakshmi Holmstrom finds it 'an episodic comedy which first of all sees the world and its different patterns of loyalties and authority through the eyes of a child'.[3] A. V. Krishna Rao discovers the novel typifying 'the middle-class school boy in the British India with his incoherent thoughts, playful moods and sentimental inter-personal relations at home as well as at school'.[4] Joseph Hitrec in *The Saturday Review of Literature* comments: ' it is a sort of South Indian opposite number of *Huckleberry Finn*, but with a texture that is peculiarly and charmingly Indian'.[5]

The main character of this novel is a child named Swaminathan. The entire plot moves round the activities of Swaminathan, a south Indian schoolboy and his friends who are the students of the first form at Albert Mission School at Malgudi. His first friend is Somu, the monitor, who is more or less 'the uncle of the class'.[6] His second friend is Mani, 'the mighty Good-For-Nothing'.[7] Then there is Sankar, 'the most brilliant boy of the class'.[8] His fourth friend is Samuel, known as 'the Pea'[9] on account of his size, with whom he has only the bond of laughter. His fifth and the dearest friend is Rajam who happens to be the son of a superintendent of police. He is good at study, and is highly admired for his being elegantly dressed and mannered.

Swami shudders at the very thought of school. The Headmaster with his thin long cane, the ugly and fire-eyed Vedanayagam, the arithmetic teacher, and Mr. Ebenzer, the fanatical scripture-master, are objects of fear for Swami. He hates Ebenzer for his tirades against the Hindu idol-worship. Swaminathan's childish retort enrages the scripture-master and consequently, his left ear is wrenched off. Swami complains to his father against the teacher and takes revenge against the teacher by lodging his father's complaint to the Headmaster. His close friend, Mani, who habitually bullies every newcomer, does not spare even Rajam, a newcomer. They plan to fight against each other to assert one's supremacy over the other, but luckily, the fight is averted and both end up being good friends. Swami's other friends feel unhappy with him because of his excessive intimacy with Rajam, and start calling him 'the tail'[10] of Rajam. Once he slaps Samuel and Sankar for passing remarks over him and naturally, there is pandemonium in the class. The Headmaster's timely intervention settles the issue temporarily. Nevertheless, the incident causes bitterness among old friends, and they are in search of a chance to take revenge upon one another. Rajam intervenes, and thus, all the differences among friends melt away. Meanwhile, the approaching examinations make them burn midnight oil. The examination comes to its close making all the examinees relaxed and happy for the summer-vacation.

The school re-opens and Swami's innocent participation in the freedom movement and the consequent damage of furniture leads to his expulsion from Albert Mission School. He gets admission in Board High school, but from the very beginning has an aversion to the strict discipline arid drill classes. The drill class compels him to absent himself from participating in Malgudi Cricket Club (MCC) chores started by himself and his friends.

His love for the club makes him indifferent to the drill classes. This invites the Headmaster's severe beating. He runs away in desperation. Afraid to go home, he drifts aimlessly on the outskirts of the town and finally gets lost in the Mempi forest. Hungry and terrified by the ghosts and wild animals, he faints. He is rescued by a forest officer and is sent to his parents. He feels sorry for his non-participation in the match against young Men's Union. Rajam becomes angry at his betrayal, but when his father is transferred somewhere else, he forgets his old score with Swami and waves back his hand at the time of parting from him.

Swami and Friends, The Bachelor of Arts and *The English Teacher* are three independent novels; but for all practical purposes, they form a trilogy. Here is traced the development and growth of an average Indian intellectual in the pre-independence period. If *Swami and Friends* presents the school days of Swaminathan, *The Bachelor of Arts* tries to capture the feelings of Chandran, a young man of twenty-one, and *The English Teacher* portrays the life and elaborates the propensities of a teacher of thirty years. If the names of the heroes were not different, one would very easily take it that the trilogy was autobiographical and was distanced to generalise the growth of an Indian mind in a period seething with discontent. Through the character of Swami, Narayan depicts the first of the three stages in a man's life in the above-mentioned three early novels. Like Wordsworth, Narayan is at his best when he presents childhood and boyhood scenes.

A brief survey of the novel highlights the different dimensions of Swami's character and one comes to conclude that Swami is the central figure of the novel. Almost all the actions have been presented from his point of view. This statement may be illustrated in various ways. The opening lines of the novel reflect Swami's attitude towards his school and, incidentally, the impending psychological tension:

> It was Monday morning. Swaminathan was reluctant to open his eyes. He considered Monday specially unpleasant in the calendar. After the delicious freedom of Saturday and Sunday, it was difficult to get into the Monday mood of work and discipline. He shuddered at the very thought of school: that dismal yellow building.[11]

He retorts to his Christian teacher who is out to abuse Hindu gods and goddesses by putting a question mark on the godhood of Christ, as he was a non-vegetarian:

> 'If he was a God, why did he eat flesh and fish and drink wine?' As a brahmin boy, it was inconceivable to him that a God should be a non-vegetarian.[12]

Swami is very much impressed by Rajam's carefree conduct and manners and by his brilliance as a student. Rajam is spoken of highly because of being well-dressed, his coming to school in a car and his ability to speak chaste English. He is considered rich with miniature trains and motors, mechanical marvels and a magic lantern with slides.

Swami's sense of observation is remarkable when his mother is about to deliver a baby. He notices his mother's relief from cooking and listens to whisperings that start with the lady doctor's arrival in the house, all members of the family being at her command. He wakes up early in the morning only to find that the commotion during the previous night has come to a grinding halt. To his utter surprise, he finds a new arrival in the house so small, plump and red like a chilly. He describes the kid in a remarkable way:

> He shut his eyes, compressed his lips, folded his hands on his chest, protruded his tongue, and tilted his head from side to side.[13]

He also learns from his friend that a kid grows so fast that one would hardly believe that one is meeting the same child.

Swami, like little boys and girls, takes life very seriously. An examination is not a joke and preparation for it starts with a detailed list of the stationery that is required:

Unruled white paper	20 sheets
Ruled white paper	10 Sheets
Black ink	1 Bottle
Clips	~~3~~ – ~~6~~ –12
Pins	~~6~~ – 12 [14]

We may notice that any alteration of requirement is in the upward direction. In Swami's opinion, if he does not get these items, heaven may fall down. When Swami's father advises him only to put urgent items, Swami gets disappointed because buying fewer items may tell upon his total performance in the examination.

Swami has many misconceptions about the source of the questions set for the examination. He believes that the clerk of the school is the real custodian of question papers and therefore, he may tell him the questions in advance. When Mani approaches the clerk, the clerk very wisely gives him the guidance for the examination. Mani shares it with Swami. Swami takes pride in having the guidance and believes that this will have a miraculous effect on his result of the examination. Several times a boy's imagination enlarges and exaggerates. Swami's imagination magnifies the powers of the coachman's son beyond all proportions. He believes that he is out to destroy him and drink his blood. Swaminathan, having got his father's permission to accompany him to the club, does indeed feel delighted, though the appearance of the coachman's son in the club makes him grief-stricken:

> Swaminathan was seized with cold fear. He moved away fast, unobtrusively, to his former place, which was at a safe distance from his enemy.[15]

Later on, he musters his courage:

> This was the safest place on earth. There was father and any number of his friends, and let the coachman's son try a hand if he liked.[16]

However, after some moments, as the light advances, fear grips him again. The reason is that he becomes aware of the possibility of the coachman's son coming with a gang of criminals. Swami waits for him in the darkness. Swami does not feel safe in the car either, as it takes a great time to start. He anticipates the rascal's arrival and thinks that he (the coachman's son) may finish him after pulling him out. Anyway, the car starts and he heaves a great sigh of relief because the mobility of the car means a fresh gush of life to him:

> When its engine rumbled, it sounded to Swaminathan's ears like the voice of a saviour.[17]

The above-mentioned incident makes us peep into Swami's soul and see the whole episode from his point of view.

Swami is introduced to Indian freedom struggle through a fiery speech by Gaurishankar, a prominent political worker of Bombay:

> Let every Indian spit on England, and the quantity of saliva will be enough to drown England.[18]

Swami has been enthused by patriotic feelings. At a simple cry for the boycott of imported cloth, he removes his cap, flings it into fire with a feeling that he is saving the country. Later, he discovers from his father that the cap was made of Khadi. Nonetheless, he joins the agitation and breaks chairs and tables and smashes windowpanes. All these observations on his part are taken into account and he is expelled from Albert Mission School.

He is an immature child, and so, his responses are undisciplined and uncontrolled. His expulsion from the school stems from his failure to weigh and balance the consequences of his actions. As Swami is a fresher in Board High School, he is happy because of his being popular among his mates at the new school. At the same time, he enjoys the company of all his friends who were on roll in Albert Mission School. Swami, after the establishment of the M.C.C., wants to get a ball immediately from a sports company. The sports company delays the supply. Therefore, finding no other way out he makes three bats out of the bottom of a wood case. He also obtains three old tennis balls from the club of his father. Swami is also over-enthusiastic about the founding of M.C.C. He inaugurates the club with his first bowling and gets the title of 'Tate'. On a close analysis of the above-mentioned two events, that is, the foundation of the cricket club and the actual inauguration of the club with three improvised bats, we come to know the boy's ways of thinking and acting. They might seem to be ridiculous for the grown ups, but are quite serious matters for Swami and his friends.

Swami's overall experiences at Board School are also not pleasant. He has to study for a longer period to save his skin. His opinion about the school is a balanced reflection on the public school system that pays more attention to the making of the exterior and almost no attention to one's interior. He has to make excuses to stay home during the day and to attend the practice class at Malgudi Cricket Club in the evening. When his excuses do not go a long way in relieving him of drill classes, he approaches a doctor for a medical certificate to get a permanent relief from these classes. The doctor, instead of obliging him by issuing a certificate, promises to convince the principal of Swami's inability of taking part in drill and scout classes. The doctor does not keep his words and Swami's predictable absence from drill classes makes the principal furious. Naturally enough, a merciless beating starts. Swami, unable to bear the burning, tingling, stinging pain, snatches the cane and runs away from the school never to come back. His state of mind, his psychic condition at this point has been remarkably painted:

> He had left the school to which he would never go back as long as that tyrant was there. If his father should hear of it, he would do heaven knew what. He would force him to go back, which would be impossible ... He had got out of two schools in this fashion. There were no more schools in Malgudi. His father would have to send him to Trichinopoly or Madras. But probably Board High School Headmaster would write to all the schools, telling them who Swaminathan was. He would not be admitted to any school. So he would have to work and earn ... He might get some rupees –and he could go to hotels and buy coffee and tiffin as often as he pleased.[19]

There is an instinct of confession in every child. Swami is no exception to it. When beaten by the Headmaster of Board High School, he decides to leave Malgudi. Meanwhile he remembers Rajam and confesses before him and then he decides to leave the place secretly. Again, when he lands into the Mempi forest by mistake he, being tired, hungry, and helpless, imagines that all sorts of monsters and devils are after him. His feeling of dread, terror, and hallucinations are quite understandable:

> Every noise entered Swaminathan's ears. For some time he was conscious of nothing else. His feet said pish–pish–pish–pat–pit–pat–swish and crackled. These noises streamed into his head, monotonously, endlessly. They were like sinister whispers, calling him to a dreadful sacrifice. He clearly heard his name whispered. There was no doubt about it. 'Swami... Swami... Swami... Swami... Swami... ,' the voice said, and then the dreadful suggestion of a sacrifice. It was some devil, coming behind him noiselessly, and saying the same thing over and over again, deep into his ears. He stopped and looked about. There the immense monster crouched, with its immense black legs wide apart, and its shadowy arms joined over its head. It now swayed little. He dared not take his eyes off it for fear that it might pounce upon him.[20]

Swami after some time comes to his senses. He is all the time anxious to know if it is Saturday or Sunday, Saturday being a day for the match.

When he discovers that it is Sunday, he gets a shock for unknowingly betraying his M. C. C. . Rajam becomes furious at his treachery. Swami tries to assuage his feeling by presenting him Anderson's *Fairy Tales* and by presenting himself at the station to see Rajam off when his father is transferred to some distant place. Rajam's waving of his hands at the time of his departure again brings him very close to Swami emotionally. We feel that boys do also have a tendency to live in the present and thus live a life of totality.

The above discussion lends herohood to Swami for his occupying a pivotal position in the novel; however, a close reading of the novel declares him an 'unheroic hero'. Really, he has nothing heroic in his character. Mostly he is a passive character, like Railway Raju in *The Guide,* a character who does not act, but is acted upon, who has no control over his circumstances, but is controlled by them. The result is that he drifts passively about. He is involved in difficulties from which he is rescued by the timely help of his father. Swami gets a severe beating from the Headmasters of Albert Mission School and Board High School for no fault of his own. His running away from school and from Malgudi and from home is again a sign of passivity. Unable to face harsh realities, he takes the much easier course of escape, and when hunger, fatigue, and terror of the forest are too much for him, he decides to return home. He is told to believe that his country is a slave to the British who treat Indians savagely. As such, one must boycott imported clothes. He becomes over-enthusiastic about the crowd that collects to damage the school and its furniture. He joins it and mechanically picks up a stone and breaks the windowpanes of the Headmaster's room. When police arrive at the scene, he becomes a victim of lathi-charge and gets injured. Thus, we find that his initiatives, too, depend on the other's triggering him off. Sometime he acts on the suggestions and persuasions of his friends and sometimes a particular situation tempts him to fall into it.

Swami's character cannot be understood fully without taking into consideration his life at the school, his life at home and his life among his friends. Of these, his life at the school is the most forbidding. He trembles at the very thought of the dismal yellow building of the school. Perhaps, the colour of the school connotes Swami's status (in growing pale) on every Monday that comes after the delicious freedom of Saturday and Sunday. He is afraid of the teachers and the Headmaster of his school. However, when one of his teachers makes an attack on his religion, he retorts.

Swami's educational career is, however, a tragic failure. His innocent participation in the nationalistic demonstration and the ugly scenes of violence result in school's building and furniture damaged, and finally lead to his expulsion from Albert Mission School. His career at Board High School too is not very happy because of his defiant attitude towards the discipline of the scout training and the drill classes. In contrast, Swami's domestic life is more stable and happy. He is blessed with a considerate father and a likeable mother, besides an affectionately caring Granny who influences Swami's formative years.

Swami is attached to his friends on two levels. He has a liking for Somu, and Pea. However, his liking is purely scholastic, and as the school closes for the vacation, his concern for them also ceases. His attachment to Rajam and Mani is more human and lasting. A. V. Krishna Rao observes about this friendship:

> ...Swami's association with Mani, 'the mighty good for nothing' and Rajam, the son of the superintendent of police grows deeper, together, they found the M. C. C., (Malgudi Cricket Club); and perform a few heroic deeds that recall the exploits of Tom Sawyer and Huck Finn. Mani is probably the Indian version of Mark Twain's Huck Finn, while Swami resembles Tom Sawyer.[21]

The cricket match between the M. C. C. and the Y. M. U. is of great importance for Swami because it is associated with Rajam's prestige. Swami's friendship with Rajam grows to the extent of an obsession. Swami prefers cricket to school. That is why when he is not exempted from drill classes, he runs away from the school, gets lost in Mempi forest and consequently his non-participation in the match alienates him from Rajam.

The story of Swami appears to be a school story of boys for boys. For instance, Swami's friendship, his quarrels, his teachers, his idleness, his homework, his examinations, and his running away make up the materials of a school story. Graham Greene puts a sensitive finger on the right point when he speaks of Swami in his introduction to *The Bachelor of Arts*. 'Swami is the story of a child written with complete objectivity, with a humour strange to our fiction, closer to Chekov than to any English writer, with the same underlying sense of beauty and sadness'.[22] William Walsh in his famous book, *R. K. Narayan: A Critical Appreciation,* points to a remarkable distinction between a boy and a child: 'A boy is a recognized figure in a given pattern obeying certain conventions. A child is an individual human creature, improphesiable, unlegislated for, enjoying spontaneously an unrehearsed autonomy.'[23] Actually Swami is a boy of ten; still he has all the attractiveness of a child of his age. Harish Raizada also subscribes to this view when he says that nothing is ordinary for Swami; everything/everyone encountered is unique for him:

> To him the birth of a baby in his house, or the delivering of father's letter to the principal, or seeking an interview with him or riding in a car or going to the club with his father are very extraordinary and thrilling events. He very earnestly thinks of giving a joy ride to an ant and when it is dead, prays for its soul. In his world, an air gun or a pen-knife is enough to arouse cold fear in one's heart and imaginary apprehensions in one's mind.[24]

David Cecil's idea also sounds apt in the delineation of a child's psychology of seeing the extraordinary in the ordinary when he says:

> Children are instinctive, they have strange imagination, vivid sensation; they see life as black or white, and bigger than reality, their enemies seem demons, their friends' angels, their joys or sorrows absolute and eternal.[25]

Swami's child-like behaviour also becomes known when he is asked to solve a sum by his father. While solving the sum he seems wiser than a scientist. He sees a gap between the concrete poetic truth and the formidable abstract arithmetical dryness he is supposed to be mastering. A look at the passages reveals Swami's vision of life:

> Father held the arithmetic book open and dictated:
> "Rama has ten mangoes with which he wants to earn fifteen annas. Krishna wants only four mangoes. How much will Krishna have to pay?"
> Swaminathan gazed and gazed at the sum, and every time he read it, it seemed to acquire a new meaning. He had the feeling of having stepped into a fearful maze.... His mouth began to water at the thought of mangoes. He wondered what made Rama fix fifteen annas for ten mangoes.
> 'Have you done the sum?' father asked, looking over the newspaper he was reading. 'Father, will you tell me if the mangoes were ripe?'

> Father regarded him for a while and smothering a smile remarked: 'Do the sum first. I will tell you whether the fruits were ripe or not, afterwards.'
> Swaminathan felt utterly helpless. If only father would tell him whether Rama was trying to sell ripe fruits or unripe ones! Of what avail would it be to tell him afterwards? He felt strongly that the answer to this question contained the key to the whole problem. [26]

Here, for a mathematician it is simply irrelevant whether the mangoes in question are ripe or unripe, once the price of a given number of mangoes is known and the price of another number is asked for. Swami does not feel comfortable with abstractions, and there is something more to a mango than the number viz. its sweetness. This can neither be counted nor weighed, but is the most important aspect of the fruit. Thus, Swami who is puzzled at these different aspects of mangoes definitely seems wiser than a mathematician does.

A child moves and acts in the miniature world. All events happening in an adult's world also do happen in a child's world on a smaller scale. Like adults, children do withdraw all diplomatic relations when they quarrel. Swami acts as a third party, as it generally happens at the international level, when Mani wants to talk to Rajam, like a grown-up person. He also prays for the salvation of the ant which meets the boat tragedy. He is not distracted by sex or ambition. Thus, he is a whole and integrated person. He has developed enough to be an individual.

Swami's environment is also remarkable. He lives in a world of Edwardian mixture of sweet mangoes and malt vinegar, a world where the East and the West meet. He plays on the bank of Sarayu and gets his schooling in Albert Mission School. He has a fascination for the M. C. C. (which stands for both the Malgudi and the Marylebone Cricket Club). The Lord of Thirupathi, a god of South India, saves his life, in the opinion of Granny. While at school, he wrestles with English Reader; at home, he faces simple interest sums. He tries to collect articles eg. bats and balls associated with cricket and is easily deceived by the Coachman's son who assures him to turn copper into silver and even into gold.

R. K. Narayan deserves appreciation for surveying the world from the standpoint of Swami and here he follows the tradition of Charles Dickens, William Blake, Thackeray, Charlotte Bronte, R. L. Stevenson,

Katherine Mansfield, Fielding and others. In the history of English literature, Dickens firmly established the tradition of choosing the child as a principal character for its emancipation from the prevailing contemporary ills. It is said that Thackeray, Charlotte Bronte, R. L. Stevenson, Katherine Mansfield and others, with all their understanding of child psychology, could not draw a better portrayal of early childhood as Dickens could do in his famous novels *David Copperfield* and *Great Expectations.* R. K. Narayan deserves cheers for his thorough and perfect understanding of child psychology. He does not miss anything about child life. Like Wordsworth, Narayan may also say, 'The fullness of your bliss, I feel–I feel it all.' [27]

There is a Swami story in *Lawley Road* entitled 'A Hero'. In this story, the father persuades Swami, a student of Second Form to sleep alone. He weeps and cries, as he is afraid of sleeping in isolation. However, in spite of Granny's sympathy for his case he is made to sleep in the office. He spends almost a sleepless night as he feels that ghosts and spirits are after him. While daydreaming, he really witnesses some image that advances towards him. Further, in sheer nervousness, he catches hold of it and is declared a hero by the members of the family, as he has been able to catch a great thief. Nobody in the family takes into consideration his restlessness during the previous night.

As far as minor characters are concerned, they are Swami's Granny, his father, teachers and his friends. Swami's grandmother is representative of thousands of Indian grandmothers, who uphold values of the Indian joint-family, guard the family prestige, insist on the observance of caste conventions, and, above all, shape the mental attitudes of the youngsters. She is old, 'too old' like any other grandmother. She is indispensable to Swami and Swami to her. She prays to Lord Thirupathi for his speedy return to his place. When she does not understand the intricacies of cricket, Swami delivers a short discourse on 'the principles, ideals, and the philosophy, of the game of cricket.'[28] She is almost an archetypal character. Swami's father is a bit fussy. He insists on Swami's studying even during the vacations. He forbids him to move in the company of his friends in the hot summer afternoon, though he loves him, thinks about his welfare and comes to his help when things go wrong. He allows Swami to use his room during Rajam's visit, searches for him when he runs away from home, and sets matter right with Board School so that Swami can be admitted there again.

Swami's mother is kind and affectionate, but does not allow him to go the wrong way. She complains against him to her husband when he goes wrong. Even when the baby brother arrives, Swami is not neglected. She cries with grief when he disappears from the school. She attends to the needs of the whole family.

Swami attends two schools, and the headmasters of both the schools are harsh and unsympathetic. Instead of understanding his child psychology, they humiliate and cane him. Swami, unable to bear the tyranny, flees away. At Albert Mission School, Ebenzer, the Scripture teacher, criticizes Hindu gods. At Board High School, too, the drillmaster is always ready to thrash the boys at the slightest provocation.

Swami's friendship with Mani and Rajam is deeper than his friendship with Somu, Sankar and the Pea. Swami's friends are also fascinating and charming. Somu, the monitor, sets about his business with absolute confidence and calmness. He is envious of Swami and, therefore, calls him 'Rajam's Tail'. He fails at the examination and is excluded from the group. Sankar, the most brilliant boy, solves any problems within five minutes, and knows all the rivers, mountains and countries. He is also very bright at grammar and history. Like Somu, he also grows hostile to Swami's growing friendship with Rajam. Samuel, called the Pea because of his short stature, is very ordinary and bad at arithmetic. He is promoted to the higher classes, but he abstains from coming to school for several months because of his illness. Mani, the "Mighty-Good-for-Nothing," towers above all the other boys of the class and seldom brings any book to the class. Mani bullies every stranger. He tries to bully even Rajam. Rajam accepts his invitation for a fight, though they do not fight and become friends. Mani always stands up for Swami. He takes courage to fight against the coachman's son, and later realises his incapability. Rajam's father is an S. P. and so, Rajam has innate qualities of leadership. He brings reconciliation between Swami and his former friends–Sankar, Somu and the Pea. He takes the initiative to go and talk to the headmaster to secure exemption for Swami from the drill and scout classes. As an S. P's son, he is angry with Swami for taking part in political movement. Later, he forms a bad impression of Swami for his betrayal by not playing the match, but when his father is transferred to some other place, they are united.

We may sum up the discussion with K. R. Srinivas Iyengar's comments '... the story of Swami and his friends would be true anywhere. It is as though everyday actuality has taken Narayan's pen and written out the universal epic of all our boyhood... that are now no more.'[29]

THE BACHELOR OF ARTS

R. K. Narayan's second novel, *The Bachelor of Arts,* was first published in 1937 on the recommendation of Graham Greene. It is a more mature work than *Swami and Friends.* It deals with a later stage in a young man's career, when he is about to leave college and join worldly life. It is the story of a person who is neither a boy nor an adult, but somewhere in-between. A reviewer finds it as the story of 'a young man growing out of adolescence and into maturity.'[30] Edward M. Case remarks that it is the story of 'a young man's emergence from the agonies and miseries of late adolescence.'[31] He further adds: 'In *The Bachelor of Arts,* Mr. Narayan has managed a most difficult feat — he has written of the pangs of youth without either condescension, satire or excessive dramatisation. In other words, he has written with art and understanding.'[32] The book has drawn the attention of many critics, and different critics appreciate it differently. In the opinion of A. V. Krishna Rao, The *Bachelor of Arts* is a 'conglomeration of the old values and the new ideas.'[33] V. Panduranga Rao discovers it to be 'the most popular with young people. Yet its formal structure is certain to attract older readers.'[34] Lakshmi Holmstrom hails this novel because 'it anticipates the cyclic view of the universe which is Narayan's main theme in his later novels.'[35] Shirley Chew considers it a 'story of Chandran's struggle to meet the constraining influences of his life with a measure of sobriety and steadfastness.'[36] H. M. Williams recommends it because in this novel, 'the techniques of narrative and characterisation are more subtle.'[37] M. K. Naik declares that the novel is 'cast in the same mould as his first.' [38] There are also some critics who try to find fault with the novel, such as Joseph Hitrec who observes that 'its theme is infinitely complex and Mr. Narayan allows his reportorial sense, lilting though it is, to skim away from the potential of his subject matter.... This absence of emotion, ... becomes expressive of the placid, well-trodden way of life under Hinduism, which does not give an individual enough room to thrash about in order to express himself.'[39] V. Panduranga Rao appreciates this novel because it 'implies a vision which stresses that life must be gratefully accepted and joyously lived.'[40] A. V. Krishna Rao approves of this novel because it 'presents yet another type of the Indian middle class, still struggling to find an inner harmony in the fast changing world of India, that is, Malgudi.'[41] He attaches great importance to the novel because of its 'artistic seed-plot containing the germinal ideas of the succeeding novels.'[42]

The whole novel has been neatly divided into four parts. Part I gives us a clear account of the college life of the hero, Chandran. The story starts with a college debate. He identifies himself as a brilliant speaker, and consequently, he is appointed the secretary of the College Historical Association, by Ragavachar, the Professor of History. His indulgence in extra-curricular activities tells upon his studies, and he has to struggle hard to pass the B.A. examination. Part II describes the young man's pursuit of a job and his frustration and depression resulting from unemployment. He passes time by aimless wanderings on the bank of the river, Sarayu, where he encounters a beautiful girl of about fifteen years, falls instantly in love with her without being at all aware of her interest in him. He convinces his parents to start negotiations with the girl's parents. The girl's parents agree to his proposal, but the horoscopes do not tally and naturally, the proposal is dropped. Disappointed and upset by this incident, Chandran falls ill, recovers and goes to Madras for a change. Part III presents him as an aimless wanderer in Madras and other parts of South India. He stays in a hotel and once visits a prostitute's house in the company of a degenerate friend. He gets disgusted with the atmosphere and runs away from that place. He is charmed by the magnificence, grandeur and peace of Kapaleeswar temple and takes refuge in that very place. He now likes the life of a sanyasi as he is respected by the entire village. Neverthless, he keeps on feeling guilty for deceiving the villagers. Part IV recounts Chandran's marriage and his settling down in life. On his return to Malgudi, he finds a sea change there and discovers all his friends either employed or settled in life. He is persuaded to go in for a job and is appointed agent to *The Daily Messenger.* He gets so much absorbed in his work that he forgets Malathi, and marries another girl, Susila and lives a very prosperous life.

R. K. Narayan, a novelist of the individual man, is primarily preoccupied with man's filling of the life role entrusted to him by tradition and environment. For instance, Chandran educates himself, craves for a job, and gets it. He is married to Susila and thus, he settles down in life.

Swami in *Swami and Friends* has been painted as a schoolchild, unfamiliar with the many formalities and responsibilities of later life. His life is made of joy and laughter and there is little scope for sobbing and sniffing. Chandran in *The Bachelor of Arts* starts his life with a feeling that he is made to live a very happy and prosperous life. Only after sometime, he feels that his world has been threatened with the wrath of God.

Chandran, the young hero of the novel, finishes his graduate study at Albert Mission College, a natural extension of Albert Mission School. The novel opens with a dialogue between Chandran and Natesan:

> Chandran was just climbing the steps of the College Union when Natesan, the secretary, sprang on him and said, "You are just the person I was looking for. You remember your old promise?"
> "No," said Chandran promptly, to be on the safe side.[43]

We immediately catch the tone of the undergraduate's concern in Albert Mission College. At the same time, we sense the flavour of Chandran's personality. He appears to be tender, tense, sharp, self-protective, and informed. Chandran's brilliant speech makes Ragavachar appoint him Secretary of the History Association. As a secretary, his involvement increases and naturally, he is not left even with the sufficient time to do his courses. He decides to change his habits and makes several resolutions for making thorough preparation for the final examination:

> On November the first Chandran left his bed at 5 a.m., bathed in cold water, and sat at his study table, before even his mother, the earliest riser in the house, was up. He sat there strengthening himself with several resolutions. One was that he would get up every day at the same hour, bathe in cold water, and get through three hours of solid work before starting for the college. The second resolution was that he would be back home before eight in the evenings and study till eleven-thirty. He also resolved not to smoke because it was bad for the heart, and a very sound heart was necessary for the examination.[44]

On the eve of the examination, the entire atmosphere of the college campus is charged with a peculiar seriousness. The preparatory leave starts and Chandran leaves the campus with a sad and depressed heart, as he is not likely to return to the college:

> Chandran was aware that he had passed the very last moments in his college life, which had filled the major portion of his waking hours for the last four years. There would be no more college for him from tomorrow. He would return to it a fortnight hence for the examination and (hoping for the best) pass it, and pass out into the world, forever out of Albert College. He felt very tender and depressed.[45]

Anyway, Chandran becomes a graduate, and it is then that his real predicaments start. He does not get a job and naturally, he takes recourse to aimless wanderings, and once while wandering at the bank of Sarayu, comes across Malathi, a beautiful girl of about fifteen, gets infatuated and falls in love with her. Being persuaded, his parents approach the girl's parents. Malathi's parents agree, but her horoscope does not agree with his and the marriage does not take place. This brings about a crisis of consciousness for Chandran, but Chandran's own excitement at the beginning takes wings:

> How old was she? Probably fourteen. Might be even fifteen or sixteen. If she was more than fourteen she must be married. There was a touch of despair in this thought. What was the use of thinking of a married girl? It would be very improper. He tried to force his mind to think of other things...
>
> Suppose, though unmarried, she belonged to some other caste? A marriage would not be tolerated even between sub-sects of the same caste. If India was to attain salvation these watertight divisions must go—Community, Caste, Sects, Sub-sects, and still further divisions. He felt very indignant.[46]

Chandran's illusions become more and more colourful as the marriage negotiation proceeds:

> He had every reason to believe that the girl had told her parents she would marry Chandran and no one else. But how could she know him or his name? Girls had a knack of learning of these things by a sort of sixth sense. How splendid of her to speak out her mind like this, brave girl.[47]

R. K. Narayan, like D. H. Lawrence and Graham Greene is an autobiographical writer. Chandran's falling in love with Malathi so very instantly is a reflection of Narayan's encounter with Rajam. In an interview with Ved Mehta, Narayan paints his real life situation:

> I escorted my elder sister Janaki from Mysore to nearby Coimbatore, where her husband was a practising advocate. While I was standing at the corner of the equivalent of a big city hall there, I saw a girl about eighteen. She was tall and slim and had classical feature: her face had the finish and perfection of sculpture. She walked past me as in a dance. I kept looking for a gargoyle or some such perfection, but there was none. It was spring and I was twenty-eight. I suppose that had something to do with my falling completely and instantly in love with her... Rajam's parents, realizing that I was from a good and large family, and that whatever happened to me, she would always be taken care of, gave into the marriage.[48]

The only difference between Narayan's affair and Chandran's is that Narayan is able to marry Rajam, in spite of his horoscope not tallying with hers, whereas Malathi's marriage does not materialise because of the horoscopes of Malathi and Chandran disagreeing with each other.

Malathi is married to some other person, and now Chandran's romanticism turns into cynicism. His cynicism, however, is as much an aspect of his self-deception as his romantic love was earlier. Chandran, reflecting on the affair, feels:

> It was a silly infatuation. Little sign did she show of caring for a fellow; she couldn't say that she had no chance. She had plenty of opportunities to show that she noticed him. Where there was a will there was a way. She had only been playing with him, the devil. Women were like that, they enjoyed torturing people. [49]

He grows cynical, owing to the frustration arising out of the failure to marry Malathi, so much so that all friendships become meaningless expressions:

> He then explained his new philosophy, which followed the devastating discovery that Love and Friendship were the illusions. He explained that people married because their sexual appetite had to be satisfied and there must be somebody to manage the

> house. There was nothing deeper than that in any man and woman relationship.[50]

Disillusioned in his relationship with Malathi, he gets terribly sick, but when cured, leaves for Madras for a change. In Madras, he indulges in aimless wanderings and accidentally happens to visit a prostitue's house. He goes into the prostitute's house only to run away from there.

He chooses to be a *sanyasi* when charmed by the peace of a temple. He is supporterd by the alms he gets by begging. He strays into the country and sits under a banyan tree. News spreads of a holy man under the vow of silence for the years sitting and spending his time in rigorous meditation under the banyan tree. C D Narasimhaiah appropriately comments upon Chandran's status as a sadhu:

> The appearance, the place, the gullible peasants–all help achieve the effect. The situation is very similar to what makes the Railway Guide a Swami in Narayan's later novel, *The Guide.* But whereas the guide, a hardened scoundrel, could hold on and become a swami in spite of himself, the inexperienced Chandran with the idealism of a youth fresh from the university, retrieves himself from the undeserved role of the ascetic foisted on him by others– and goes away with remorse for 'humbugging through life.'[51]

Finally, the cycle of Chandran's life takes a complete turn, and he comes back to his parents, but everything changes in Malgudi including dresses and addresses. Finding all his friends settled in life, he also acquires the agency of *The Daily Messenger.* When he gets a suitable proposal, he is married to Susila. Here the irony does not lie as much in his return to his native village (for the return happens instintinctively because of his failure in his mission), as it lies in his present willingness to marry Susila, a girl chosen by his parents. The retreat into romantic illusion is so swift and total that his mind is now full of nothing but his wife, the fragrance of jasmine and sandal-paste:

> Susila, Susila, Susila. Her name, music, figure, face and everything about her was divine. Susila, Susila–Malathi, not a spot beside Susila; it was a tongue-twister; he wondered why people liked that name.[52]

In addition, the state of mind of young Chandran, now newly married, conclusively proves that in spite of his brief life as a *sanyasi*, he still aspires for the romantic dream as enthusiastically as ever.

The novel ends with an optimistic note. Now life is flowing on in spite of some of the great setbacks that threaten to block its way. Chandran, once a forlorn and dejected youth ready to commit suicide, turns into a sadhu, renouncing the world and finally coming back to the world and living his life without any memory of the old wounds. Malathi who becomes the be-all and end-all of his life goes totally into oblivion and an irresponsible and carefree graduate of olden days is now a respectable man with a job to provide him sustenance in life and a wife to look after his household affairs.

Actually, Chandran is an extension of Swami's personality. The only difference is that while Swami's world is a world of inexhaustible joy and shooting ambitions, a world of sparkling and eternal sunshine in which even a wayward cloud never throws its shadows, Chandran's paradise is, at times, on the verge of being lost, but finally it is saved. At times, he seems to succumb to the ruthless fury of life, but his dauntless and indomitable spirit asserts and he wins over the obstacle:

> Thunders and clouds pass away, leaving the sky clear, but the trees are burnt and scalded, the plants consumed and withered. The sun shines again in the heart of the disillusioned young man, but now he is less confident though more bold, less care-free though more responsible, less zealous though more sober, less violent though more thoughtful.[53]

William Walsh examines Chandran's dual personality, and comments:

> Chandran's two worlds, college and home, chime in contrast and agreement. In one, life is cerebral and relationships intense but fundamentally indifferent; in the other, life is instinctive and shut-in, and relationships are intimate and relaxed. Each part of the composition points up the other: on one side, the angular dons humming with abstract passion about the incompetence of Bradley or the necessity for inaugurating an Historical Society at the College, without which, it seems, society and history itself would crumble away; on the other side, the distinct temperaments of the family–dry, generous father; bustling, grumpy mother; small brother and pampered Chandran–rubbing against each other in innumerable tiny irritations, but united by and safe in a basic serenity .[54]

In *The Bachelor of Arts,* we see the world through Chandran's eyes and Chandran and the world through Narayan's. Besides, it is Narayan's perspective that yields most of the irony in *The Bachelor of Arts.* 'This good-humoured irony lays bare some archetypal failings of young Chandran. Several episodes reveal the enormous self-importance and self-centredness of callous youth'.[55] For example, when the debate is over, he tries desperately for the compliment, but when he finds the Secretary appreciating only the Principal's speech, a frustrated Chandran retorts by calling the Principal a humbug. At last while parting away from the Secretary, he does not avoid asking: 'How did you like my speech today?' Further, when the Secretary pays a fulsome compliment and also adds that even the Principal has a high opinion of his performance, he suddenly discovers that the Principal is a 'great scholar.'

Decidedly, Chandran's capacity for self-deception matches his self-centredness. When the examination approaches, he has a revelation of his deficiency and to compensate he takes a firm decision of getting up at 5 A.M., sitting up reading until 11.30 at night, calculating the total number of preparation hours now available. His capacity for self-centredness and self-deception makes him an easy prey to the illusions of romantic love. He imagines he has found his soulmate in Malathi, but the irony is that she is not even aware of his infatuation for her, nor does she exchange even a single word with him. Yet we cannot say that his whole life is a series of self-deceptions. On occasions, we witness the high point of awareness in Chandran's life. While he is living the life of a saint, people have great faith in him and his divinity. They offer ample gifts to him, but Chandran is always aware that he has not even a grain of saintliness in him:

> He moved away from the gifts; still the light shone on them. He even blew out the lantern–he did not deserve the light.[56]

Sometimes he has a fleeting awareness of the larger irony of life and its ways. The first such moment is when Chandran is at the Head Office of 'The Daily Messenger,' trying to secure its agency. As he looks at the decision-taking men, he thinks:

> "My life is in these fellows' hands! Absolute strangers. Decision of my fate in their hands, absolutely! Why is it so?" [57]

The second occasion is Chandran's visit to his college years after he left it:

> Chandran... stood looking at some group photos hanging on the wall. All your interests, joys, sorrows, hopes, contacts, and experience boiled down to group photos, Chandran thought. You lived in the college, thinking that you were the first and the last of your kind the college would ever see, and you ended as a group photo; ... He met so few of his classmates, though they had been two hundred strong for four years. Where were they? Scattered like spray... all at grips with life, like a buffalo caught in the coils of a python.[58]

In his essay, 'The Average as the Positive' Rajeev Taranath rightly says:

> From average to the extraordinary and back again to a more poignant state of average–this seems to be the recurrent movement in terms of interacting characters in the majority of Narayan's novels.[59]

Chandran is no exception to the above rule. He moves from a state of busy normalcy, through infatuation, to dejection. He also tries sanyasa for a short time and settles down finally into a sober state of regained ordinariness, happily looking forward to his marriage with Susila. Lakshmi Holmstrom holds more or less a similar view when she writes:

> Chandran never leaves the orbit of social norms: this is why he does not become a true *sanyasi*. He chooses Sanyasa in preference to the other alternative because of the 'social stigma' attached to suicide; he returns to the world because he has neither earned 'nor deserved by virtue of spiritual worth' the gifts of food he is given by the villagers.[60]

Minor characters of the novel also deserve mention. Natesan, the Secretary of the Union, is petty and corrupt. Chandran's relation with him is strictly limited to the college. His relationship with Mohan, who writes poetry in English on a wide variety of subjects–from a Roadside Grass-seller to the planet in its orbit–is more lasting. The loquacious revolutionary, Veeraswami, is more volatile than enduring Chandran's best friend, however, is Ramu with whom he shares all his leisure outside the college. The witty Principal, the scholarly and stern-looking Ragavachar stand apart from the self-opinionated Gajapathy with all his knowledge of the principles of literary criticism and the English Grammar. We also encounter the holy and dignified thief who steals flowers to lay them before the gods. One cannot ignore the Principal's peon, Aziz who only allows an entrance to the Principal's office after his palm is greased. We also have the company of Kailash who despite having two wives cannot prevent himself from going to prostitutes. The novel presents us a postmaster who is tired of being pestered with talks about s*anyasis*. With such characters and with an all-pervading genial humour, the novel turns out to be a charming and amusing work of fiction.

REFERENCES

Swami and Friends

1. Nirmal Mukherji, *The World of Malgudi: A Study of the Novels of* R. K. *Narayan* (Louisiana State Univ, 1960) Unpublished Dissertation, p. 75.
2. K. R. Srinivasa Iyengar, *Indian Writing in English* (New Delhi, 1984), p. 364.
3. Lakshmi Holmstrom, *The Novels of* R. K. *Narayan* (Calcutta, 1973), p. 36.
4. A. V. Krishna Rao, *The Indo-Anglian Novel and the Changing Tradition* (Mysore, 1972), p. 68.
5. Joseph Hitrec, 'Hindu Huckleberry,' *Saturday Review of Literature,* 37 (6 November 1954), p. 27.
6. R. K. *Narayan, Swami and Friends* (Mysore, 1971), p. 8.
7. *Swami and Friends,* p. 8.
8. *Swami and Friends*, p. 8.
9. *Swami and Friends,* p. 9.
10. *Swami and Friends*, p. 30.
11. *Swami and Friends*, p. 3.
12. *Swami and Friends,* p. 6.
13. *Swami and Friends*, p. 49.
14. *Swami and Friends,* p. 58.
15. *Swami and Friends*, p. 91.
16. *Swami and Friends,* p. 91.
17. *Swami and Friends*, p. 92.
18. *Swami and Friends*, p. 94.
19. *Swami and Friends,* pp. 144-45.

20. *Swami and Friends*, p. 158.
21. *The Indo-Anglian Novel and the Changing Tradition* (Mysore, 1972), p. 70.
22. Graham Greene, Introduction to *The Bachelor of Arts* (London, 1951), p. vii.
23. William Walsh, *R. K. Narayan: A Critical Appreciation* (New Delhi, 1983), p.28.
24. Harish Raizada, *R. K. Narayan: A Critical Study of His Works* (New Delhi, 1969), p. 9.
25. David Cecil, *Early Victorian Novelists* (Ludhiana, 1972), p. 50.
26. *Swami and Friends*, pp. 86-87.
27. William Wordsworth, *The Complete Poetical Works* (London, 1930), p. 359.
28. *Swami and Friends*, p. 128.
29. *Indian Writing in English*, p. 365.

The Bachelor of Arts

30. Review, *Retail Bookseller*, 57 (November 1954), pp. 69-70.
31. Edward M. Case, 'Critic says New Novels Show Indian Truly Great Writer,' *Buffalo Evening News* (New York), 13 November 1954, Sec II, p. 10.
32. *ibid.*
33. *The indo-Anglian Novel and the Changing Tradition*, p. 102.
34. V. Panduranga Rao, *The Journal of Commonwealth Literature, No 5* (July, 1968), p. 31.
35. *The Novels of R. K. Narayan*, p. 39.
36. Shirley Chew, *Readings in Commonwealth Literature* (London, 1973), p. 60.
37. H. M. Williams, *Indo-Angian Literature: A Survey* (Bombay, 1975), p. 51.
38. M. K. Naik, *The Ironic Vision: A Study of the Fiction of R. K. Narayan* (New Delhi, 1983), p. 11.
39. Joseph Hitrec, 'Hindu Huckleberry,' p. 27
40. 'The Art of R. K. Narayan,' p. 31.
41. *The Indo-Anglian Novel and the Changing Tradition,* p 70.
42. *ibid.*, p. 71.
43. *The Bachelor of Arts*, p. 1.
44. *The Bachelor of Arts*, p. 18.

45. *The Bachelor of Arts*, p. 51.
46. *The Bachelor of Arts*, pp. 55-56.
47. *The Bachelor of Arts,* pp. 78-79.
48. Ved Mehta, *John Is Easy To Please* (Harmondsworth, 1974), pp. 115-16.
49. *The Bachelor of Arts*, pp. 111- 112.
50. *The Bachelor of Arts,* p. 123.
51. C. D. Narasimhaiah, *The Swan and The Eagle* (Simla, 1969), pp. 142-43.
52. *The Bachelor of Arts*, p. 162.
53. Harish Raizada, R. K. *Narayan: A Critical Study of the His Works* (New Delhi, 1969), p. 17.
54. William Walsh, R. K. *Narayan: A Critical Appreciation* (New Delhi, 1983), p. 39.
55. *The Ironic Vision: A Study of the Fiction of* R. K. *Narayan*, p. 11.
56. *The Bachelor of Arts*, p. 111.
57. *The Bachelor of Arts*, p. 138.
58. *The Bachelor of Arts,* pp. 144-45.
59. M. K. Naik, S. K. Desai and G. S. Amur (eds.), *Critical essays on Indian Writings in English* (Dharwar, 1972), p. 296.
60. *The Novels of* R. K. *Narayan,* p. 41.

3

SEARCH FOR IDENTITY: THE DARK ROOM AND THE ENGLISH TEACHER

For years, copying othr people, I tried to know myself. From within, I couln't decide what to do. Unable to see, I heard my name being called. Then I walked outside.

—Rumi

THE DARK ROOM

The Dark Room was first published by Macmillan in 1938 on the approval of Graham Greene. This novel brings to the forefront the trials, tribulations and torments of a traditional Hindu homemaker who finds courage to walk out on her tyrannical husband. Recalling the genesis of the novel, R. K. Narayan says in *My Days:*

> I was somehow obsessed with a philosophy of Woman as opposed to Man, her constant oppressor. This must have been an early testament of the "Women's Lib" movement. Man assigned her a secondary place and kept her there with such subtlety and cunningness that she herself began to lose all notion of her independence, her individuality, stature and strength. A wife in an orthodox milieu of Indian society was an ideal victim of such circumstances. My novel dealt with her, with this philosophy broadly in the background.[1]

Though Narayan has written more than a dozen novels, this novel is unique from many points of view. In the opinion of Shiv K. Gilra, 'the darker shades of moral aberration are first noticed in *The Dark Room*.'[2] Ron Shepherd finds 'an absence of laughter'[3] in the novel. Harish Raizada finds this novel unique from some other angle:

> It is only in *The Dark Room* that the narrater shifts his focus on different characters viewing them from an equal distance... He presents a detached approach to life by perceiving the wrong and right actions of the characters with certain equanimity .[4]

It may also be looked on as a speciality of this novel that either it has been denounced on several scores by its critics or it has not received as much attention as it deserves. William Walsh ignores this novel by simply mentioning it in the bibliography. While writing on Narayan, C. D. Narsimhaish is highly critical of *The Dark Room*:

> One may without loss skip the intervening *The Dark Room* which for all its pathos develops melodramatically and has a didactic ending.[5]

A. N. Kaul takes it as a 'weak and insignificant novel'.[6] K. R. Srinivas Iyengar observes that the novel has a 'cynical conclusion.'[7] V. Y. Kantak does not find any 'serious probing of the tragical consequences of passion' [8] in it. These critics, we see, have not been able to do justice to this novel. If their statements are judged at the touchstone of the facts pertaining to the novel, it seems that perhaps they have misread it or have not delved deep into it.

C. D. Narasimhaiah associates the novel with pathos, melodrama and a didactic ending. If his observation is examined minutely, it appears that what he says does not carry conviction. This novel is not melodramatic in the accepted sense of the term, for what we find in this book is true of a society where the old double standards are still in vogue and where women are economically so helpless that they just have to take to something odd which they do not like. Again, the novel does not have quite a didactic ending. Actually, Narayan, unlike Mulk Raj Anand, is essentially an artist, and naturally, he does not labour a point to load his novel with preaching. R. K. Narayan himself asserts this view in an interview with *The Telegraph:*

> Everyone thinks he's a writer with a mission. Myself, absolutely not. I write only because I am interested in a type of character

> and I'm amused mostly by the seriousness with which each man takes himself.[9]

As for the element of pathos in *The Dark Room,* we may say that it is Savitri who suffers most, and, to quote M. K. Naik, 'Savitri's plight fails to evoke even pathos, for she is shown to be a bundle of changing moods and conflicting responses and made to talk and act in turns like an orthodox Hindu wife, and an ardent feminist, a brooding fatalist and a bold activist.'[10] V. Y. Kantak's contention that the novel lacks serious probing of the tragical consequences of passion[11] does not point to any weakness in the novel. His search for passion in *The Dark Room* is a search for something impossible. P. S. Sundaram's views may be seen as an answer to Kantak's observation:

> There is no "passion" in Ramani's feeling for Shantabai, still less is hers for him. It is just an "affair" in which Ramani indulges as he sees no reason why he should not, this being a man's privilege: and Shantabai, living on her own, is out to exploit him to the maximum.[12]

In fact, some critics regard this novel as a pioneering work. Harish Raizada considers it one of the most successful of his novels. He says:

> From the point of view of the structure, it still remains unexcelled among all the novels by its author.[13]

Dr. Hari Mohan Prasad feels that '*The Dark Room* like a many-coloured glass, displays myriad hues of Narayan's art. It reveals his basic stands, and points towards the emerging contours of his craft. The liet motif of his fictional corpus has been to explore human relationships, to articulate the awareness of Indian culture and heritage.'[14] Uma Parameswaran appreciates this novel from the point of view of characterization. She states:

> The characterization is stronger in this novel than in most others because Narayan shows a casual sequence in the character's interpersonal relationship and in the outcome of their behaviour.[15]

The Dark Room dramatizes the psychological tragedy of a conventional homemaker. Her redemption is achieved not through her husband's love but through the affirmation of her own motherhood. The novel exposes the demeaning dichotomy between Ramani's utter insensibility and Savitri's fine sensibility. This dichotomy inevitably results into suffering.

The story of *The Dark Room* revolves, in the beginning, round Ramani, Secretary of the Engladia Insurance Company, his wife, Savitri, and their three children–Sumati, Kamla and Babu. Later, one more character, Shantabai, a probationer in Engladia Insurance Company, is introduced. With the introduction of this new character, Shantabai, and her growing illicit relationship with Ramani, the already prevailing discordent notes of Savitri's domestic orchestrea can now be heard loud and clear. The atmosphere of the entire household hinges on Ramani's moods, and his affairs with Shantabai do indeed make Savitri's life more and more miserable. She reacts and revolts against his relationship with Shantabai. Besides, she tries to win him over by charming him, but fails. She leaves the house, attempts to commit suicide by throwing herself into the Sarayu River, but is saved by Mari, the burgler and tinker. She is pressed into an employment at the Murugan temple in Sukkur village with the help of Mari and his wife, Ponni. However, her deep concern and anxiety for her children and for home, where she has her roots, compel her to go for a retreat–perhaps a glorious one.

Savitri is one of the few women characters in Narayan's novels who represent the main points of view in them. She is placed carefully in the book along with some other women who, by contrasting themselves with her, provide us with a complete picture of women in an orthodox Indian society.

At this point, we may refer to 'savitri's treatment by William Walsh, as he takes into account the different shades of her personality:

> Savitri is a middle class but not highly educated woman, who is burdened by the immense weight of the Indian past, by her caste, her religion and her role as a wife and mother... . She is an ordinary, amiable housewife; not deeply dissatisfied with her allotted part, given on occasion to boredom with its pointlessness, but increasingly oppressed by her loud, assertive and exigent husband.[16]

Savitri is the very symbol of traditional Indian womanhood. She is beautiful and deeply devoted to her husband. She has been married to Ramani for fifteen years, but, unfortunately, she has seldom been the centre of her husband's love and attention. The only gift she receives from her husband is his temper. Even the children are accustomed more to their father's rebuke than to his fitful love and affection. Savitri is a capable homemaker who knows how to deal with unexpected guests. 'She had a genius for making the existing supply elastic and transforming an ordinary evening course, with a few hurriedly fried trimmings into a feast.'[17]

Savitri is intelligent enough to understand the changing moods of her husband by such minute things as the varying pitch of the hooting of the Chevrolet horn. When Ramani grows unreasonably amorous, her strategy never fails. She is also efficient enough to divert his attention by bringing him into a professional mood. In spite of all these, the rhythm of the family seems to be halting and broken from the very beginning. Even the opening scene of the novel is a reflection of the disharmony between the husband and the wife. *The Dark Room* opens with a conversation between Ramani and Savitri over Babu's sudden illness and his consequential absence from the school.

> "What is the matter with Babu?"
>
> "He is not well."
>
> "You are too ready with your medical certificate. Babu, get up! Don't miss your school on any account."
>
> Babu turned on his mother a look of appeal.
>
> She said, "Lie down, Babu. You are not going to school today."
>
> Ramani said, "Mind your own business, do you hear?"
>
> "The boy has fever."
>
> "No, he hasn't. Go and do any work you like in the kitchen, but leave the training of a grown up boy to me. It is none of a woman's business."[18]

In the very first confrontation with her husband over the simple question if sick Babu should attend school, she is not only denied her right, but is also humiliated.

Ramni's tyranny continues, and Savitri swallows it with feeble grudges. Whenever she is hurt deeply, she confines herself to the dark room as a mark of protest against the rude behaviour of her husband. Narayan deserves credit for preserving the dark room as part of the age old Indian tradition, 'like the mummified curiosities of ancient Egypt'.[19] She takes to the dark room twice. Her first confinement is the result of Ramani's beating of Babu on the ground that he is the man behind the failure of the coloured electric lights at Navaratri, an annual festival celebrated with dolls, lights and gifts. She reacts in the spirit of an ideal wife, and her confinement to the dark room is 'a symptom of the eminent collapse of the psychic system which has sustained Savitri in her life as wife and mother.'[20] The distressed and frightened children call in Savitri's friend, Janamma, sensing the gravity of the situation and taking their mother's state as 'more than a mere tantrum.'[21] Janamma advises and helps Savitri to get over her depression and sheepishly asserts the classical Indian concept of wife's devotion and loyalty to her husband that Savitri finds increasingly difficult to live up to:

> "There is no quarrel. I never uttered a single word." "That makes it worse. You should either let your words out or feel that everything your husband does it right. As for me, I have never opposed my husband or agreed with him at any time in my life. I might have occasionally suggested an alternative, but nothing more. What he does is right. It is a wife's duty to feel so."[22]

Savitri's second and grimmer recourse to the dark room stems from her unsuccessful attempt to commit suicide when her husband takes to another woman, Shantabai, a young recruit in his office. She is rescued from the water by the lock-repairer and umbrella-mender who finds her a job at the Murugan temple where the priest commands her to live in the shanty at the corner of the temple's corridor. It is a kind of store where the pedestal meant for installing and carrying out the image in procession is kept. It is very dark, air and light admitted only by the chinks in the joints of the iron-sheets. The two dark rooms have some underlying implications for Lakshmi Holmstrom. She believes that 'the two dark rooms–one in the home and one in the temple are used symbolically and reflect directly the limits of free choice and the implications of individuality.'[23] She discovers a striking difference between the two dark rooms:

> The one [dark room] in the house implies limited privacy within known conditions, the one [dark room] in the temple implies a final and frightening choice of individuality .[24]

The two dark rooms of the novel also point to Savitri's assertion of independence and her failure because of her lack of inner sources to sustain it. Whenever she takes shelter in the dark room, she withdraws from all domestic chores and responsibilities generally associated with the mistress of a house.

We may compare Savitri with Nora (a character in lbsen's famous drama, *A Doll's House)* who turns out to be a rebel against her debased position in domestic life. For fifteen years, Savitri has also been a doll wife, living in a doll's house, and playing with her doll children. Nonetheless, suddenly, she reacts against her humiliating position she has endured all through when her husband takes delight in flirting with a woman with impunity. 'She becomes disillusioned and the revelation comes to her as it does to Nora Helmer that her whole life with her father and her husband has been a doll-life in which her own personality has been suppressed and her worth as an individual ignored.'[25] She says in despair:

> "Things? I don't possess anything in this world. What possession can a woman call her own except her body? Everything else that she has is her father's, her husband's or her son's."[26]

Like Nora, she too feels: 'I believe that before all else I am a reasonable human being just as you are–or at all events, that I must try and become one'.[27] Savitri realizes her dignity as a human being, and apprehending her husband's affair with Shantabai, she bursts out:

> "I'm a human being,"... "You men will never grant that. For you we are playthings when you feel like hugging, and slaves at other times. Don't think that you can fondle us when you like and kick us when you choose."[28]

Savitri's use of 'us' twice in the last sentence shows her deep yearning for the redemption of the whole woman race from the tyranny and unjust behaviour of the male towards the female. She attributes her sufferings to her dependence on other male members of the society. She feels that in this materialistic world 'no one who couldn't live by herself had a right to exist.'[29] She does not accept charity from anyone and goes hungry till she earns her bread. When she is offered food by Ponni, she announces emphatically: "I am resolved never to accept food or shelter which I have not earned."[30]

The only difference she has with Nora is that Nora does not come back and that the reader remains guessing about her destiny, whereas Savitri's concern for her children and home leads to her homecoming, though she knows that she is going to breathe in that very old house. This awareness makes her cry in a fit of utter despair:

> "What despicable creations of God are we that we can't exist without a support? I am like a bamboo pole which cannot stand without a wall to support it."[31]

It would not be out of place to mention here Raizada's viewpoint regarding the difference between the approaches of Ibsen and Narayan:

> Ibsen's approach is revolutionary and radical; Narayan's more realistic and practical. Savitri's decision to submit to the inevitable may be sad but it is more true to life–specially Indian life. The difference between the two authors is of their countries and their environments.[32]

We may also compare Savitri with Gauri, the heroine of Mulk Raj Anand's *The Old Woman and the Cow.* Both desert their respective homes because of their neglect in the family. While Savitri quietly comes back, Gauri does not think of committing suicide or of coming back home. Instead, she joins Dr. Mahendra's clinic as a nurse. Narayan's hero is an average Hindu homemaker who can only sulk in the dark room, whereas Anand's hero is more courageous. Isn't it a pity that only a few Hindu homemakers have such a good fortune and such protecting heavens as Gauri has?

Savitri's revolt and her retreat have received the attention of many scholars, and they have tried to explain them in different ways. In the eyes of Harish Raizada, 'Savitri's revolt gives a magnificent suggestion and hint of the strength of women.'[33] Hari Mohan Prasad illuminates this point by saying that 'Savitri does not submit to Ramani; she submits to her obligations. It may be a failure on the material plane, but spiritually she comes triumphant... It is in keeping with both her character and her cultural heritage.'[34] However, Hari Mohan Prasad does not clearly spell out the obligations to which Savitri feels inclined to submit. A.V. Krishna Rao in his thought-provoking essay, 'R. K. Narayan and the Novel of Affirmation,' tries to enlighten us on the point where Hari Mohan Prasad remains silent:

> Savitri's defiance, and defeat and even the detestable dark room seem to be trivial in the light of her motherly fulfilment. Ramani's libertine uncouthness may be there to drive her again to the dark room; but the supreme beatitude of a mother illumines the darkest of the dark rooms.[35]

V. Panduranga Rao thinks that 'Savitri's acceptance of duty and response to instinct' are no doubt 'qualified by the bitter recognition of the helplessness of her sex in general and her own unavoidable dependence on her husband.'[36] William Walsh does not consider her return a transformation, but takes it as 'the Indian habit or gift for acceptance'[37] of life as it offers itself to one.

Savitri's running away from home and her futile attempt to commit suicide may be looked upon as the different facets of her personality. Narayan's Savitri, unlike the mythological Savitri, grows into an ardent feminist when she is neglected and betrayed by her husband. It is only natural that in view of the crisis she has to undergo, she says:

> What is the difference between a prostitute and a married woman? – the prostitute changes her men, but a married woman doesn't; that's all, but both earn their food and shelter in the same manner.[38]

We find Savitri to be 'an individual with pride and with a soul'[39], and not unexpectedly, she refuses to submit to anything hereafter. When she is advised by Ramani to keep the ring, the necklace and the stud with herself because they happen to be her father's gift to her, she shrinks from them as almost from pollution: 'Take them away, they are also a man's gift.'[40] At this point P. S. Sundaram rightly comments:

> No champion of "Women's Lib" could have put more venom into a single sentence summing up the intolerable situation in which an educated middle class woman of India finds herself.[41]

Savitri's revolt is the revolt of a modern woman who is on the look out for her independent human identity. After all, how can she be content with her status as a mere appendage, a slave to her husband? She rebels against the society full of Ramanis who lay down one law for themselves and another for their wives and sisters. Savitri's abortive attempt to commit suicide is a reflection on the Indian social ethos. An Indian woman who is always dominated by fear from the cradle to the funeral pyre and who is always afraid of walking alone even a hundred yards from the house unescorted, can only embrace death if she is granted freedom.

Savitri's homecoming, we may infer, has been prompted by multiple considerations: a feeling of abject helplessness and despair; an emotional void sapping all her vitality, and her greater concern for her children. Shiv K. Gilra also subscribes to an almost similar view when he emphasizes the point that 'Malgudi is steeped in tradition and that its inhabitants are men and women with their roots in family and religion.'[42] Naturally, Savitri's retreat is a search for the lost root.

Savitri's life is a veritable journey. She starts with an acceptance of her role as a submissive wife and doting mother, and switches over to her rebellious abandonment of her husband's house in search for the meaning of life. However, even with her terrifying awareness of the futility of a lonely woman's life, she finally accepts and gets back to the old house.

As the importance of light can be better judged against the background of darkness, we can examine Savitri's character better if she is juxtaposed against other female and male characters of the novel. The contrast between Savitri and Shantabai is implicit throughout *The Dark Room.* Shantabai, an educated and self-made woman, is a product of Western civilization, and naturally, we become aware in her case of the artful movement of her lips, the tossing of her head and her humming of a tune all to herself. Narayan presents this specie of artful and cunning characters only at two other places, in the form of Shanti in *Mr. Sampath* and of Rosie in *The Guide.* At a very young age, Shantabai is married to her cousin, a gambler and drunkard, who refuses to change. However, unlike Savitri, Shantabai does not even hesitate to desert him. She may find it difficult to maintain her economic independence, but she does enjoy her emotional freedom. Referring to her great admiration of Omar Khayyam and Fitzgerald, she says to Ramani:

> "1 cannot exist without a copy of The Rubaiyat;... Dead yesterday and unborn tomorrow... The cup of life must be filled to the brim and drained; ..."[43]

At yet another place, she explains her own philosophy of life:

> "Tonight I feel life pacing the whole earth up and down. I won't sleep. I feel like roaming all over the town and the whole length of the river. I will laugh and dance. That's my philosophy of life ..."[44]

Lakshmi Holmstram in her seminal essay, 'Women Characters in The Novels of R. K. Narayan,' says that Shantabai and Savitri 'balance each other, each losing out in one way; both are victims. Savitri can manage a minimal economic independence, but emotionally she is still bound. Shantabai apparently enjoys her emotional independence, but economically she is still not free.'[45] We may also compare Savitri with Gangu and Janamma. But thse three ladies stand at the two extremes. Gangu's ambitions range from film stardom to political leadership. She talks irresponsibly and is dismissed by Janamma, who, in turn, is stigmatised as "temple chariot."[46] However, in the opinion of Savitri, 'she (Gangu) was interesting; with all her talk, she was very religious, visiting the temple regularly, and she was not immoral.'[47] She (Gangu) is eccentric, and her husband claims her to be a champion of women's rights. Janamma is proud of having never opposed her husband or argued with him. Lakshmi Holmstrom places Savitri somewhere between the two:

> She (Savitri) is "fascinated by" Gangu, on the other hand, it is Janamma she obeys. Unlike Gangu, her life is ordered and arranged around her family, but unlike Janamma she has her own forms of protest against her husband, Ramani.[48]

A discussion of Savitri's character cannot be complete without a consideration of the character of Ponni who brings a new hope in her life. She has a clear philosophy of husband management:

> Keep the men under the rod, and they will be all right. Show them that you care for them and they will tie you and treat you like a dog.[49]

She declares that she cannot be coaxed into believing that any husband could be unmanageable in this world.

At this point, a discussion of Ramani's character seems appropriate because it is Ramani who is responsible for all the unsavoury events in the novel. Ramani is an utterly self-centred and self-indulgent man who takes pride in making his whole family dance to his tunes. The treatment that he accords to his wife swings between the two extremes of blandishment and browbeating. He is a tough man at home and in his office, but he is meek like a lamb before Shantabai. He is the representative of that vicious coterie of husbands who look upon their wives as toys, to be fondled or kicked at their own sweet will. Still, Ramani deserves our pity and sympathy when his best intentions, unfortunately, produce the worst results. For instance, his insistence on Babu's carrying a tiffin packet to school sounds incongruous because the school code prohibits him to do so.

Savitri's portrait, we have to admit, cannot be complete without her children–Sumati, Kamla and Babu. The quarrels among these children, their petty rivalries and vanities, their innocent complaints against each other, their unending demands of notebooks, their excitement and enthusiasm on the eve of festivals, and their anxiety for their sad mother contribute to the beauty, grandeur and depth of R. K. Narayan's novel *The Dark Room.*

THE ENGLISH TEACHER

The English Teacher was first published abroad in 1944. In 1945, Indian Thought Publication brought out its native edition, and later in 1953 the Michigan State College Press made it available to the Americans with a new title, *Grateful to Life and Death*, appended to it by Lyle Blair, the Press Chief. Unfortunately, this title has not been approved of by many scholars. Anyway, this novel is a work of immense value – both thematically and technically.

The English Teacher has received words of both praise and censure from critics. P. S. Sundaram does not find it 'everybody's cup of tea'[50] because of its metaphysical content. Anthony West, considers it 'an excellent novel filled with the remarkable vitality.'[51] Margaret Parton reviews this book in the *New York Herald Tribune Book Review*: 'Every page of it is Grateful to Life and Death.'[52] A journal entitled *Special Libraries* observes: 'The simple eloquence of this moving tale transcends its richly colourful and exotic setting in India and makes it a part of universal human experience.'[53]

However, some writers and reviewers have disputed its literary worth. On the contrary, for Lyle Blair it is Narayan's 'greatest work and enough achievement for a lifetime.'[54] A. N. Kaul views it as 'one of the author's weakest works.'[55] Nevertheless, its uniqueness cannot be ignored. Lakshmi Holmstrom places it as 'a link novel, coming between Narayan's earliest and later works.'[56]

The English Teacher is the last novel in which R. K. Narayan uses the theme of romantic love. *The Vendor of Sweets* uses it as a minor theme and that too, between a father and a son. One of the greatest specialities of the novel is its autobiographical content. Almost the whole of this novel confirms the facts of Narayan's life, and has very little of fiction. Narayan himself confesses in *My Days:*

> More than any other book, *The English Teacher* is autobiographical in content, very little part of it being fiction. The English Teacher of the novel, Krishna, is a fictional character in the fictional city of Malgudi; but he goes through the same expereince I had gone through, and he calls his wife Susila, and the child is Leela instead of Hema. The toll that typhoid took and all the desolation that

> followed, with a child to look after, and the psychic adjustments, are based on my own experience ...The dedication of the book to the memory of my wife should to some extent give the reader a clue that the book may not be all fiction ...[57]

One special feature of this novel is that perhaps this is the only Narayan novel that speaks of parapsychology and the world beyond. It is also a little unusual that the narrator of this novel is also the protagonist in the novel. Uma Parameswaran comments on this type of narrative:

> First-person narration usually gives a certain measure of authenticity to an experience, but the authenticity of *The English Teacher* stems from the deeper sense of autobiography. [58]

Readers are fortunate that they get an adequate idea of the genesis of this novel from the author himself. Narayan recalls that the novel sprang out of the sudden demise of his wife, Rajam, in 1939. It is only natural that the author was steeped in despair; to him life had become meaningless, and it was getting increasingly difficult to write again. Two of his close friends, Graham Greene and Dr. Paul Brunton, wrote to him that the creative artist in him would outlive this state of depression. Ttruly enough, after some years he started writing again, and surprisingly wrote all through, even in his extreme old age.

The English Teacher may be divided into three sections–Krishna's lifestyle before Susila's arrival; Krishna's life in company with his wife; and his experiences of life after his wife's death. It is the third part that makes the novel controversial. Harish Raizada looks upon this part as 'comparatively its dullest and weakest portion.'[59] He goes on to add that this part is so irrelevant to this story that it does not contribute to its evolution. In his opinion, this part is so cut off from the first two parts that the scheme does not lead to a convincing denouement of the earlier parts of the story, and as such, he comments that *The English Teacher* is perhaps the most incoherent of all the novels of R. K. Narayan. C. D. Narasimhaiah also censures this novel: 'But for the second half he [Narayan] would not have written the novel at all.'[60] Arthur Conan Doyle in his famous book *History of Spiritualism* and Stanley De Brath in *Physical Phenomena of Spiritualism* testify the reliability of occult practices. M. K. Naik examines this novel in the light of these two famous books. He says, 'Narayan's entire account of the spiritualistic experiment agrees in all essential details with accounts of well-known cases of occult practice described by authorities on the subject.'[61] M. K. Naik warns us that 'the second half of *The English Teacher* is neither pure autobiography nor a scientific treatise on spiritualism but a work of fiction, and must be judged as such.'[62] K. K. Sharma has to say something interesting about the second half of this novel:

> Perhaps those, who resent the spiritualism and psychic experiences in the novel, do not understand the philosophic mind and do not have any interest in matters beyond this world of time and space. As Narayan confesses it is through psychic adjustments that he was able to attain "an understanding of life and death", and of his own self which are the primary obsessions with every thoughtful man.[63]

Uma Parameswaran has her own explanation in respect of the supernatural element in this novel. She observes that 'familiarity with the Indian background is an important requisite in the understanding of these fantastic events as seen in reviews of *The English Teacher.*'[64] At this point, Narayan's interview with Ved Mehta may persuade us to reevaluate the elements of those reviewers who are critical of this novel. Mr. Mehta says:

> 'The reviewers did not realise that the whole story was autobiographical–that I myself have been a witness to the experiments.'[65]

The story of the novel is about Krishna, an English teacher, at the Albert Mission College. He lives in the college until his wife Susila reaches Malgudi with their baby daughter, Leela. They live in a house in Sarayu Street. Three years later, Krishna and Susila go to inspect a house in Lawley Extension where they hope to shift. Susila comes back, falls ill of typhoid, is nursed with great care, but dies. Krishna continues to live in the old house with his daughter. Once he receives a message from a man in contact with the dead Susila. Through this medium Krishna receives messages from his wife, and later communicates with her directly. Krishna finally agrees to let Leela go to his parents. Being dissatisfied with teaching English at the college, he decides to join Leela's former nursery school headed by a dedicated but eccentric headmaster. He resigns from the college to do some experiments in nursery education.

All of Narayan's central characters are of great significance to both the writer and the reader. Krishna is also the central character in *The*

English Teacher. As Narayan views that 'character in situation' [66] holds the primary place in his composition, Krishna has also been thrown into different situations, and, therefore, we encounter the different facets of his personality as and when he faces those situations with varying degrees of courage and tactfulness. Krishna in this novel begins where Chandran in *The Bachelor of Arts* ends. Chandran stands on the threshold of married life, while Krishna is already mature enough to start a married life.

The English Teacher, as Raizada also believes, is in line with the first two novels, *Swami and Friends* and *The Bachelor of Arts.* These three novels form a trilogy as they depict three consecutive stages in the life of a man. In the first novel, we find the picture of a boy studying in lower classes; in the second, there is a portrait of a young man winding up his college career and facing the shocks of life, while in the third, we find the story of a man of the world bearing sweet and bitter fruits of life. Though the names of the heroes vary, they are the same person, perhaps the incarnations of the writer himself, as shown in the different stages of his life.

As the novel opens, we witness the mechanical life of Krishna, a lecturer in English at Albert Mission College in Malgudi. He is a young man of hardly thirty, but his life as lecturer seems dull, drab and monotonous. He reads Milton, Carlyle and Shakespeare repeatedly, takes his meals, dresses himself up, and hurries to the college. At the college, he admonishes, cajoles and browbeats his students to make them mug up Shakespeare and Milton. He tries his best to make them able to fetch high marks and, thus, to save himself from any adverse comments from his chief at the end of the year. He discharges his duties, comes back to his room, chats with his colleagues and takes rest in the hostel. Being a poet by nature, he sometimes writes nature poems.

However, soon he decides to leave the hostel because he gets a letter from his father advising him to find a good house for his wife and daughter who are to settle down with him. At first he is taken aback by the very thought of living with a baby of barely seven months. He shivers with the thought of his sister's children crying the whole night and his mother rubbing them with oil. It seems surprising that a man who shrinks from the thought of living with his unmanageable daughter also has a desire to settle down and be comfortable with his wife and daughter at the earliest. This ambivalence or contradiction in his character is a reflection of the fickleness of his mind. Actually, Krishna is still to attain the maturity of an experienced householder. Naturally he longs for the ideal house and states, 'I must have a house... which faces south, for its breeze, keeps out the western sun, gets in the eastern, and admits the due measure of northern light that artists so highly value.'[67] On inspection he finds a clear contrast between expectation and reality. The description of the available house is itself an ironic comment on his immaturity. Krishna remarks about the house: 'The builder of this house must have been dead-drunk while doing the latter portion of the house. This is a house evidently intended for monkeys to live in. This house must have been designed by a tuberculosis expert so that his business may prosper for the next hundred years.'[68] Krishna's expectations with respect to the house do not end at this point. He prays as well for good neighbours and invokes the divine grace to be able to remain far, far away from the bad ones. Krishna dreams of getting a house close to his college for comfort, to be able to enjoy his domestic life free from professional interference. Finally, he finds a house in Ellaman Street belonging to an old man who is a 'typical Narayan eccentric.'[69] When asked, 'are you the owner of the house?' he replies, 'God is the owner and I am his slave.'[70] Krishna, luckily, discovers the old man's weakness for education:

> "College teacher!" He gave a salute with both hands and said, "I revere college teachers, our *Gurus.*"... "Everybody knows how good we are, and how cultured our family is!"... I added: "Don't mistake me for an ordinary person!"... He was tremendously impressed. His face beamed with relief: ....
>
> ... I said "What shall I have to pay you?"
>
> "Twenty-five on the fifth of every month. It must reach me on that day at Bellary."[71]

This lively encounter is a mark of sustained growth of Krishna's personality within the framework of an arranged marriage. William Walsh sounds apt in his observation when he says, 'Narayan in this novel is the poet of Indian domestic life.'[72] He finds a striking similarity between Katherine Mansfield and Narayan's description of domestic life. Mansfield also explores and analyses what has happened to her: 'she is the poet of a family with young children, and the material of which her poetry is made is New Zealand life.' [73]

Krishna's anxiety over receiving his wife and child at the station makes 'a delightful example of comic irony.'[74] He absurdly imagines all kinds of eventualities such as, (a) the baby's head banging against the carriage door, while alighting from the train and (b) his wife's luggage being left on the train owing to its stoppage for a very short duration. Overjoyed on receiving his kins, he offers the porter three times his normal wages.

Krishna starts living in a small family. His mother guides and initiates his wife into domestic work. Later when Susila is able to prove her excellence in it, Krishna's mother leaves for home. Now his life has become more meaningful. Received by his wife and daughter in the evening, he takes a bath, puts on fresh clothes, takes coffee and shares college affair with Susila. He feels relieved by handing over his salary to his wife who prepares the monthly budget carefully. In short, by joining his family he has joined 'the world of genuine response'[75] where he is not in a danger of drying up 'in a society of formal relationships, abstract preoccupations and waspish egotisms.'[76] Suddenly Krishna's paradise is lost when his wife falls ill, never to get back her health and life.

We find a close connection between his profession and ensuing fate. He asks his students to write an essay on *Man is the Maker of His own Destiny* while he is unaware of the fact that this question applies to him too. Once he remarks, 'she was a phantom of delight.'[77] Perhaps some inner voice convinces him of her potentiality of being transformed into phantom soon. Susila does not survive in spite of the best treatment she gets. Krishna is shocked, and his whole life gets upset. He loses his peculiar gaiety of temperament. Leela provides him strength and meaning for his survival. After the death of his wife, he becomes receptacle of condolence and sympathy. Unlike Ramani in *The Dark Room* who believes in concupiscence, Krishna is all for monogamy. At present, his only concern is a life without illusions. He drops the idea of buying a new house because his present house links his mind with a happy past worthy to be cherished.

We can notice Krishna's psychic development in his occult communion with the spirit of his dead wife. Informed by a stranger about his being in touch with his wife, he (Krishna) becomes witness to this event. Later, he is able to make contacts with her spirit independently. During this very experience, he learns about Leela's frequent visits to a children's school. He meets the headmaster, talks to him, explains his views on education, resigns his lectureship at the Albert College, entrusts Leela to the care of his old mother, and settles down to lead a life of detachment in the true spirit of *karamyogi*.

Professor A. V. Krishna Rao asserts that in *The Serpent and The Rope* Raja Rao propagates the philosophy of *Advaita*. But Krishna's psychic perception of Susila's spirit finds favour with the traditional belief of the *Visistha-Advaitha,* the monotheistic creed of Ramanuja, which recognises, like other Indian systems, the individual salvation as freedom from this mundane existence, but with a difference. [78] Krishna's intense esoteric experience corroborates the fact that the band of spirits 'strive to help the imperfect souls of this world by removing the barrier of Death, not in the physical sense, but in the transcendental sense of supra-mental development.'[79]

In the beginning, Krishna does not believe in life after death, but in due course, he comes to realize that a meeting with a spirit is possible when the subjective consciousness merges with the pure objective consciousness. In fact, this occult experience assures him that death is not the end of everything because human personality has many other planes of existence. Narayan clearly confesses: 'This outlook may be unscientific but it helped me survive the death of my wife... I could somehow manage to live after her death and, eventually, also attain a philosophical understanding.'[80] This changed philosophy of his life helps him to discover a meaning in everything. He finds a supreme joy dawning upon him: 'The boundaries of our personalities suddenly dissolved. It was a moment of rare, immutable joy–a moment for which one feels grateful to Life and Death.'[81] In the light of all these, Lyle Blair's discovery of the new title *Grateful to Life and Death* seems justified.

P. S. Sundaram also confirms, 'Life has taught him a little, but death has taught him more, and he has reason to be grateful to life and death'.[82] Judged from Rajeev Taranath's standard, Krishna does not come within the preview of his definition of Narayan's characters. Taranath believes that in almost all Narayan's characters there is a similar pattern of development– 'from average to extraordinary and back again to a more poignant state of average.'[83] Krishna who is concerned about trifles like the safe arrival of his baby, grows mature enough at the end to pronounce some sort of Upanishadic truth:

> We come together only to go apart again. It is one continuous movement... The law comes into operation the moment we detach

> ourselves from our mother's womb. All struggle and misery in life is due to our attempt to arrest this law or get away from it, or in allowing ourselves to be hurt by it... A profound unmitigated loneliness is the only truth of life.[84]

Krishna's attitude to education is also noteworthy. He is aware of the absurdities of the kind of education being imparted to students. He condemns the 'grim tolerance'[85] with which students have to learn everything from their teacher. For Krishna, discipline grows from within and cannot be imposed from outside. He has absolute faith in 'The Leave Alone System' [86] which will transform children into 'wholesome human beings' [87] by providing them with an opportunity for the natural growth of 'the original vision.'[88] Perhaps, he wants the revival of the old Indian tradition of education, and naturally, opposes modern education imparted in convent and mission schools: 'This education had reduced us to a nation of morons; we were strangers to our culture and camp followers of another culture, feeding on leavings and garbage.'[89]

By way of conclusion, we may say that Krishna looks like a tragi-comic hero of Narayan. He is an intelligent man of artistic taste and fine sensibilities. He is brooding and introspective, and does not hesitate in taking to self-criticism. A man of minute observations, he discerns even the slightest aberrations of man.

There are three types of homemakers in the novel–Krishna's mother, his wife and the headmaster's wife. Krishna's mother is old and experienced, and a staunch supporter of the philosophy of housekeeping. Always 'wrapped up in her duties,'[90] she gets satisfaction from domestic chores and looks violent where she meets slovenliness: 'If a woman can't take charge of a house and run it sensibly, she must be made to get into man's dress and go'.[91] She is religious and superstitious, and observes all the Indian customs handed down to her from time immemorial. Susila, being the last child of her parents, seems initially a little inexperienced as homemaker, but achieves excellence in running a household soon thereafter. She spends her time in reading, knitting, embroidery, or nurturing a garden. Narayan has drawn a fine and elaborate portrait of Susila by endowing her with a separateness and distance, and by the use of the first-person narrative. Her devotion to her gods and her unsophisticated trust in tradition lend her a particular kind of innocence and individuality. Susila is 'an ideal Hindu wife, steeped in the cultural traditions of the country.' [92] Her attachment to Krishna is not merely physical as explained by Coomarswamy: 'In India, the conditions of human love... have seemed spiritually significant... physical union has seemed to present a self-evident image of spiritual unity.'[93] Even after her death she makes him feel her radiant presence and she assures him of her ever watchful eyes from a higher region. William Walsh tries to squeeze her character in a single sentence: 'Above all, she possesses that serenity of psyche which seems so powerfully a part of the mature Indian sensibility, achieving a point of equilibrium between the unavoidable accommodations with, and the necessary responses to, the rhythm of life.'[94] The novel also introduces us to a quarrelsome, bitter-tongue and petty-minded wife of the good-natured headmaster. She harasses her husband by her constant nagging and mismanagement of domestic affairs. The husband, unable to find the atmosphere congenial for him, leaves the house, and finds peace in the company of children.

Narayan's skill is at its height when drawing the picture of children. We witness the houseowner's grandson whose pockets are always full of fried nuts. We encounter affectionate Leela who is innocent, carefree, eager and sensitive. Children's quarrels are simply wonderful for Narayan:

> The most enchanting thing among children is their quarrels. How they carry it on for its own sake, without the slightest bitterness or any memory of it later. This is how we were once, God help us: this too is what we have turned out to be! [95]

The eccentric schoolmaster has an idea of child psychology and claims that children are invaluable to society. He finds them a source of knowledge for him: 'Children have taught me to speak plainly, without the varnish of the adult world. I don't care if it strikes anyone as odd'.[96]

The minor characters also contribute much to the charm of the novel. The most interesting of them are Krishna's father, his brother, Shastri, Dr. Menon, Gopal, Gajapathy, Principal Brown and Singaram. Krishna's father, a Bachelor of Arts of olden days, is devoted to the works of Carlyle, Scott and Browning, and is particular about correct use of language. Krishna's brother, a henpecked husband, is always worried about his twelve children. Shastri is straightforward and liberal-minded. Dr. Menon is never forgetful of his student days at the Columbia University, America. Gopal is bright at mathematics, but otherwise very stupid. Gajapathy is a mechanical teacher of English.

Principal Brown is proud of his pivotal role in Indian awakening. Singaram, an old man with wrinkles on his face, is an admixture of rudeness and servility.

In short, Narayan has been able to present a lively, entertaining and valuable portrait-gallery of characters very skillfully.

REFERENCES

The Dark Room

1. R. K. Narayan, *My Days* (Mysore, 1975), p. 119.
2. Atma Ram (ed.), *Perspectives on* R. K. *Narayan* (Ghaziabad, 1981), p. 40.
3. Bhagwat S. Goyal (ed.), R. K. *Narayan: A Critical Spectrum* (Meerut, 1983), p. 79.
4. *Perspectives on* R. K. *Narayan*, p. 40.
5. C. D. Narasimhaiah, *The Swan and the Eagle* (Simla, 1969), p. 143.
6. A. N. Kaul, 'R. K. Narayan and the East-West Theme,' *Indian Literature*, Arbind Poddar [ed.] (Simla 1972), p. 223.
7. K. R. Srinivas Iyengar, *Indian Writing in English* (New Delhi, 1984), p. 372.
8. C. D. Narasimhaiah (ed.), *Indian Literature of the Past Fifty Years: 1917-1967* (Mysore, 1970).
9. *The Telegraph* (Calcutta: 11 May, 1986), p. 11.
10. M. K. Naik, *The Ironic Vision: A Study of the Fiction of* R. K. *Narayan* (New Delhi, 1983), p. 20.
11. Kantak, V. Y. 'The Achievement of R. K. Narayan,' Narasimhaiah, C. D. (ed) *Indian Literature of the Past Fifty Years*, 133-146.
12. P. S. Sundaram, R. K. *Narayan (New* Delhi, 1973), p. 48.
13. *Perspectives on* R. K. *Narayan*, p. 75.
14. *Ibid.*, p. 92.
15. Uma Parameswaran, *A Study of Representative Indo-English Novelists* (New Delhi, 1976), p. 51.
16. William Walsh, R. K. *Narayan: A Critical Appreciation* (New Delhi, 1983), p. 43.
17. R. K. Narayan, *The Dark Room* (Mysore, 1986), p. 13.
18. *The Dark Room*, p. 1.
19. *Indian Writing in English*, p. 291.

20. R. K. *Narayan: A Critical Appreciation*, p. 45.
21. *Ibid.*, p. 45.
22. *The Dark Room*, p. 59.
23. Lakshmi Holmstrom, *The Novels of* R. K. *Narayan* (Calcutta, 1973), p. 43.
24. *Ibid.*, p. 45.
25. Harish Raizada, R. K. *Narayan: A Critical Study of His Works* (New Delhi, 1969), p. 26.
26. *The Dark Room*, p. 113.
27. H. Ibsen, *Three Plays* (New York, 1966), p. 75.
28. *The Dark Room*, p. 110.
29. *The Dark Room*, p. 120.
30. *The Dark Room*, p. 157.
31. *The Dark Room*, p. 189.
32. R. K. *Narayan: A Critical Study of His Works*, p. 28.
33. K. *Narayan: A Critical Study of His Works*, pp. 27-28.
34. *Perspectives on* R. K. *Narayan* (Ghaziabad, 1981), p. 88.
35. A. V. Krishna Rao, *The Indo-Anglian Novel and the Changing Tradition* (Mysore, 1972), p. 74.
36. V. Panduranga Rao, 'The Art of R. K. Narayan,' *Journal of Commonwealth Literature, 5* (July 1968), 39-40.
37. R. K. *Narayan: A Critical Appreciation*, p. 46.
38. *The Dark Room*, p. 120.
39. *The Dark Room*, p. 133.
40. *The Dark Room*, p. 114
41. P. S. Sundaram, R. K. *Narayan* (New Delhi, 1973), p. 45.
42. *Perspectives on* R. K. *Narayan*, p. 39.
43. *The Dark Room*, p. 151.
44. *The Dark Room*, p. 89.
45. *Perspectives on* R. K. *Narayan*, p. 66.
46. *The Dark Room*, p. 20.
47. *The Dark Room*, p. 19.
48. *Perspectives on* R. K. *Narayan*, p. 63.
49. *The Dark Room*, p. 136.

The English Teacher

50. *R. K. Narayan,* p. 50.
51. Anthony West, 'I is Love, I is Love' *New Yorker,* 29 (31 October 1953), 126.
52. Margaret Parton, 'A Novel from India, Shimmering Between Laughter and Tears' *New York Herald Tribune Book Review,* 29 November 1953, p. 7.
53. 'Publications Received,' *Special Libraries,* 44 (December 1953), 417.
54. R. K. Narayan, *My Dateless Diary* (New Delhi, 1969), p. 171.
55. 'R. K. Narayan and the East-West Theme,' p. 230.
56. *The Novels of R. K. Narayan*, p. 49.
57. *My Days*, pp. 134-35.
58. A *Study of Representative Indo-English Novelists*, p. 53.
59. *R. K. Narayan:* A *Critical Study of His Works*, p. 38.
60. *The Swan and the Eagle,* p. 147.
61. *The Ironic Vision*: A *Study of the Fiction of* R. K. *Narayan*, p. 28.
62. *Ibid.*, p. 28.
63. *Perspectives on* R. K. *Narayan*, p. 96.
64. A *Study of Representative Indo English Novelists,* p. 63.
65. Ved Mehta, *John is Easy to please* (Harmondsworth, 1974), p. 118.
66. R. K. Narayan, 'Replies to the Questionnaire,' *Kakatiya Journal of English Studies, III*, 1978, p. 35.
67. R. K. Narayan, *The English Teacher* (Mysore, 1970), pp. 21-22.
68. *The English Teacher*, p. 22.
69. *The Ironic Vision: A Study of the Fiction of* R. K. *Narayan*, p. 24.
70. *The English Teacher*, p. 23.
71. *The English Teacher*, pp. 25-26.
72. R. K. *Narayan: A Critical Appreciation*, p. 51.
73. *Ibid.*, p. 51.
74. *The Ironic Vision: A Study of the Fiction of* R. K. *Narayan*, p. 24.
75. R. K. *Narayan: A Critical Appreciation*, p. 53.
76. *Ibid.*, p. 53.
77. *The English Teacher*, p. 49.

78. *The Indo-Anglian Novelists and the Changing Tradition*, p. 77.
79. *Ibid.*
80. *My Days*, p. 135.
81. *The English Teacher*, p. 213.
82. R. K. *Narayan*, p. 45.
83. M. K. Naik, S.K. Desai and G.S. Amur (eds), *Critical Essays on Indian Writings in English* (Dharwar, 1972), p. 296.
84. *The English Teacher*, p. 203.
85. *The English Teacher*, p. 7.
86. *The English Teacher*, p. 168.
87. *The English Teacher*, p. 168.
88. *The English Teacher*, p. 168.
89. *The English Teacher*, p. 205.
90. *The English Teacher*, p. 29.
91. *The English Teacher*, p. 29.
92. *The Indo-Anglian Novelists and the Changing Tradition*, p. 76.
93. Anand K. Coomarswamy, *The Transformation of Nature in Art* (New York, 1956), p. 44.
94. R .K. *Narayan: A Critical Appreciation* (New Delhi, 1983), p. 53
95. *The English Teacher* (Mysore, 1970), p. 156.
96. *The English Teacher*, p. 165.

4

NOVELS OF UPHEAVAL: MR. SAMPATH AND THE FINANCIAL EXPERT

> The sea is dangerous and its storms terrible but
> these obstacles have never been sufficient
> reasons to remain ashore.
>
> —Annonymous

MR. SAMPATH

Mr. Sampath, first published in 1949, has earned not only words of appreciation in plenty, but also earned rebukes from some quarters. John Haverstick appreciates Narayan's honesty in portraying his milieu in this novel:

> Mr. Narayan is an Indian writer, who sees his own country from an Eastern point of view, not, as has frequently been the custom of novels about India that appear in the United States, over the shoulders of a Westerner. [1]

Donald Barr discovers 'something more than charming'[2] in it. Christine Weston acknowledges that 'the novel is recognizably Russian in its compassion, its humor, its pathos and its force.'[3] Anne Fremantle also eulogizes the novel: 'Mr. Narayan most deftly weaves for his readers a story that gives them something of the immense complexity of a civilization, over five hundred years old.'[4] Margaret Palmer Beals endorses the book by saying that it has 'a wholly delightful story well worth reading.'[5] Welford Inge approves the balanced view of the novelist:

'writing in a gently satirical vein, the author presents an India neither muffled in mysticism nor depressed by poverty.' [6] A. V. Krishan Rao holds a very high opinion of the novel:

> It is, in the first place, a novel of education, embodying the traditional spiritual images: and secondly, a picaresque story of a scoundrel, typical of a war-torn world with its floundering values even in such a quiet town as Malgudi.[7]

H. M. Williams makes a revelation about the uniqueness of the novel: '*Mr. Sampath* starts where his previous novels leave off, pursuing the effects of modernization on the sleepy old community."[8] Lakshmi Holmstrom takes delight in announcing: '... in *Mr. Sampath,* Narayan works with a whole network of human relationships, showing how they are precariously held in balance."[9] P. S. Sundaram aptly observes: '... from *Mr. Sampath* onwards Narayan seems to depend more on invention; and it would seem that the starting point is not a plot but a character, in every sense of that latter term.'[10] Perhaps only V. Panduranga Rao seems critical of this book when he announces, '*Mr. Sampath* is a book of sins and woes.' [11]

Mr. Sampath is full of autobiographical elements. For instance, Narayan himself edits a Journal named *Indian Thought* as Srinivas edits *The Banner.* Narayan's experience of the film-industry is similar to that of Srinivas while the commercial version of *The Guide* is made. Narayan also encounters a preacher in his life and he puts this real experience in this novel. Further, Narayan's book *My Days* is also a witness of some of his real life experiences mentioned in the novel. In reality, Sampath was a printer. We get a revelation of this fact in *My Days:*

> 'Mr. Sampath who was my printer (and who became a character in one novel and two film stories) ...'[12]

Narayan also discloses:

> In a novel of mine, Mr. Sampath became a Film Director. Today I find that Sampath in real life too has become a very busy film personality, with a shooting schedule almost every day at studios in Mysore and Madras.[13]

In the famous essay entitled 'The Ambivalance of R.K Narayan,' P. S. Sundaram also states that in *Mr. Sampath* there are many autobiographical elements connected with the printing business. For instance, he identifies Srinivas' attitude towards life with that of Narayan:

> His mind perceived a balance of power in human relationships. He marvelled at the invisible forces of the universe which maintained this subtle balance in all matters: it was so perfect that it seemed to be unnecessary for anybody to do anything.[14]

Harish Raizada introduces the novel mentioning its specialities: 'With his novel *Mr. Sampath*, R. K. Narayan starts portraying human life in more complex circumstances and probing more intricate human relationships than he has done in his earlier novels.'[15]

The plot of the novel primarily centres round the activities of a mysterious character, Mr. Sampath from where the novel takes its name. Srinivas arrives at Malgudi in order to start an idealistic magazine, *The Banner*. Sampath undertakes to print it, but the venture comes to a halt temporarily when Sampath starts the production of a mythological film depicting the story of the temptation of Shiva on Mount Kailash. Srinivas is assigned the role of a scriptwriter in the new enterprise. Srinivas' all friends including Ravi, an artist of acknowledged talent, are drawn into the film production in various capacities. Ravi encounters Shanti during the shooting of the film, identifies her as the long lost love of Malgudi and therefore, grows very possessive of her. Sampath also develops deep intimacy with her, invents an opportunity to play opposite her when the scene of temptation is being shot, Ravi goes mad with envy and brings disaster to the studio. He is declared mad and is taken off on a pilgrimage. Srinivas joins his old occupation of bringing out a magazine. Finally, Sampath is also abandoned.

The plot of the novel is very loose and incoherent because it lacks natural growth and seems to have been formed by linking different types of incidents. These diverse types of episodes do not provide the novel a well-knit plot. Further, Narayan's unrestricted love for details leads him to incorporate several events that a successful storyteller would have safely avoided. For example, does the story suffer if he dispenses with Srinivas' interview with Edward Shilling and his conversation with the old "jutka-man" while going to Sampath's house?

In spite of its defects in the plot and storytelling, the novel is rich and great in the portrayal of living characters and their dynamic relationship with one another. As far as the decision of identifying the main character is concerned, many scholars go in for Mr. Sampath and some for Srinivas too. There are still others who are either not clear about it or avoid the trouble of making a right decision. Harish Raizada is not clear about this issue. At one place he asserts: 'The most important of all the characters in the novel is the versatile and mysterious Mr. Sampath.'[16] At other place in the same book he grants herohood to Srinivas: 'Srinivas, the hero of the novel, is a typical hero of R. K. Narayan.'[17]

Similarly, initially, William Walsh attaches equal importance to both characters because of their dominance in different parts of the novel: '... the first part devoted to running the newspaper and organised round Srinivas, the second to the film industry in which Mr. Sampath is the more significant figure.'[18] Later, he draws a conclusion favouring Mr. Sampath: '...each of the significant decisions about the production, the continuance and finally the dissolution of *The Banner* is taken by Mr. Sampath, the printer.'[19] Donald Barr, *The New York Times* reviewer, also considers him as a superhuman being for he 'moves among the imagination of his friends like some minor deity.'[20] Nirmal Mukherji also confirms Sampath as a hero: 'The moment he enters the novel, he not only takes charge of the publication of the weekly, *The Banner,* but also takes the novel itself from the hands of Srinivas. It no longer remains the story of an editor; it becomes his story, the story of the printer of Malgudi.'[21] She also adds, 'Sampath dominates the rest, even our editor Srinivas.'[22] If we take all these opinions into consideration, Mr. Sampath deserves the treatment of a hero.

Mr. Sampath is the most mysterious and versatile character in the novel. He is introduced to us as a printer. He has his own way of doing business. He is expert in buying customers by his oft-quoted persuasive statement that they cannot get that finish in the whole of South India. Mr. Sampath has not always been a printer. Narayan drops a hint that he was attached to a theatre before starting his career as a printer. The portrait with side-whiskers... with a long pipe, sticking out of a corner of his mouth, hung on the walls of his room speaks volumes about his character. Even as a printer, he is always well versed in make-up, costumes and stagecraft. That is why when Sampath is on his way to another adventure, his theatrical experience of his early days helps him considerably. Actually, Sampath is so confident of his ability that he can fit in any role–from director to actor and dancer.

Sampath is a case for psychological study because we find polar opposite elements in him. At one end, he is the most amusing, talkative, ingenious, witty, resourceful and exceptionally social. At the other end, he is so secretive and mysterious that to get a secret from him or to read his mind is not everyone's cup of tea. These qualities have their effects on his physical existence too. He does not allow anyone to look through the curtains dividing him from his staff. Even Mr. Srinivas could not gather enough courage to peep into the sanctum since he always notices Mr. Sampath announce with a considerable force: 'That is the one point on which I'm always very strict – the best of my friends and relations have not seen inside there.'[23] Srinivas instead of grudging his mysterious character, fully accepts it. In spite of his mastery in the printing business, his administrative capability, his extraordinary way of persuasiveness, and his opting for the film-world also go in making his character somewhat mysterious. William Walsh sounds apt here: Mr. Sampath's personal life also showed this discrepancy between surface and inwardness.[24]

We observe this duality in his character in his relationship with several characters too. He prints Srinivas's newspaper without receiving any payment and makes a clean breast of his way of treatment with his customer: 'When a person becomes my customer he becomes a sort of blood relation of mine: do you understand?'[25] Nonetheless, he offers a job to Srinivas and at his request arranges for Ravi's employment too. Moreover, he does not complain of Ravi's indecent behaviour. However, the same generous and considerate Sampath deceives Somu and Sohan Lal, leaves his wife in the lurch, causes Shanti's ruin and is perhaps responsible for the houseowner's death. All these merit his condemnation:

> Mr. Sampath has got a wonderful capacity to blend truths with lies. At one occasion when Srinivas looks at him doubtfully after hearing the story of his holiday at Mempi Hills, he remarks: My editor knows me too well; nothing short of absolute truth will pass with him.'[26]

He is many entities rolled into one–a printer, a connoisseur of art, a musician, a dance-master, an actor, a make-up man and a film director. Even in real life, he changes his lifestyle in such a rapid sequence that people have difficulty in identifying the real man in him. He feels as happy in moving on foot as in travelling in a brand new car. Now he is wearing a faded tweed coat and the next moment he appears in a silk shirt, muslin dhoti and lace-edged upper-cloth with a golden belt shining on his wrist. As far as his ingenuity is concerned, Narayan has hardly been able to create another such ingenious character. He has been portrayed as an achiever. He can make the court sanction a newspaper easily; he can print it all by himself; he can have pride in holding the position of a film-producer without making any investment. He can also persuade and influence a charming girl to marry him in spite of his living a happy married life with his wife and children.

He can cope with any situation and is always ready with a convincing reply. When inquired by Srinivas about the red polish on his nails, he replies instantly, 'Oh that cousin of mine; she must have played some joke on me when I was not noticing.'[27] He has reasons for not printing Somu's speech as the President of the District Board. He even rationalises his love for Shanti:

> Some people say that every sane man needs two wives – a perfect one for the house and a perfect one for the social life... I have the one. Why not the other? [28]

His magnetic personality and extraordinary power of persuasion win him a friend easily. Srinivas strongly feels that 'there are no strangers to Sampath.' [29] It sounds strange but true that under his influence Soma Sundaram, Sohan Lal and his greedy house-owner part with a considerable amount of money for starting the production of a film. His elocution simply charms everyone. This ability makes him oldman's successor to rejuvenate his dilapidated property:

> We are all gathered today to honour the memory of a noble master...
> I have had the special honour of being in his confidence.
> I must acknowledge my indebtedness to our Srinivas, our editor, for introducing me to the old gentleman....
> Let us now pull together–his relations and sons and friends– and do something to cherish the memory of this great soul...[30]

We find different facets of Mr. Sampath's character. In the beginning, Srinivas is the employer of Mr. Sampath and the resource of his printing work. When the publication of *The Banner* is stopped in favour of the production of a film, Mr. Sampath employs Srinivas as a scriptwriter. Here the relationship between Mr. Sampath and Srinivas turns topsy-turvy. "The master modulates into servant, the servant into master."[31] William Walsh rationalizes these qualitative reversals in character:

> We see the same people from different points of view and are aware in them of contrary and co-existing personalities, functions, and modes of being. No one of these identities is the absolutely true one, since all of them are equally true and equally illusory.[32]

The dualism in Mr. Sampath's character can also be noticed in his relation with Shanti. Mr. Sampath calls her his cousin in public, but acts as her lover in private. They exchange 'side glances,' [33] drive always in a car 'sitting close,'[34] almost touching and 'are always together.'[35] Though, in spite of his carnal relationship with Shanti he does not overlook the fact that he has to support a family of his own consisting of his wife and five children. We find him playing the role of her guardian, but at the same time treating her as his exclusive possession. When his blind passion for Shanti brings rebuke from Srinivas for his unseemly conduct, he justifies his love for Shanti and his intention to marry her:

> I have married according to Vedic rites: let me have one according to the civil marriage law.[36]

Here Sampath's development appears temporary and is not of much significance. There may be a change in social status for some time, but a closer look at his whole life reveals that he remains the same in spite of his changing situations and professions. Rajeev Taranath finds a similar pattern of development with Narayan's almost all characters– 'from average to the extraordinary and back again to a more poignant state of average.'[37] And Sampath fits in this pattern. He 'starts as a printer, becomes a producer-actor, finds disaster overtaking his film company, and… his relation with Shanti, the actress, and ends as a forlorn person whose real job is only to be a printer.'[38] H.M. Williams also subscribes to Taranath's view of Mr. Sampath's homecoming:

> With the film at an end, Sampath runs off to the jungle with Shanti, but like many a rebel in Narayan's novels, he soon sickens of her and returns to his family, comparatively normal once again.[39]

To Nirmal Mukherji, 'Sampath turns out to be one of the most fascinating characters that Narayan has ever created.'[40] His character is fascinating because of the complexity of his character. His tricks make us laugh, but there is an undercurrent of sadness beneath that laughter. Moreover, he poses to be a big optimist. 'But when this apparent optimism is studied against the drab, ill-fitting background of his family life–the outhouse with a gabled front and two small rooms, sickly children, the bundles of unwashed clothes pushed into a corner–his whole personality gains an inexpressible depth.' [41] This is the reason why he never allows anyone to peep into his private world having more sorrow than happiness. Infact, he is always creating a world of illusion. Sampath may have several weaknesses and lapses in his character, but his witty and eloquent dialogues and his ability to win friends, his adventurous risk-taking spirit and his undying optimism make him a likeable fellow.

Srinivas, like most other heroes of R. K. Narayan, is simple, intelligent, helpful, considerate and witty. He is a journalist who seeks his self-knowledge through, his weekly *The Banner. The Banner* proclaims that 'it is only concerned with war that is going on between man's inside and outside.' When the Second World War was to begin, *The Banner's* immediate concern was to attack the high handedness of the municipality and arouse humanity to live life more seriously. P. S. Sundaram also contributes to the same view:

> [Srinivas] would like to wield his paper *The Banner* less as a flag than as a broom to sweep the many cobwebs that have taken possession of every nook and corner of our land.[42]

Here Narayan's observation on his ambitious project is worth mentioning. He beleives that within twelve pages of foolscap, it attempts to set the world right. In the opinion of M. K. Naik, Narayan's comment is 'an ironic thrust entirely typical of the author.'[43]

Srinivas sets a two-fold task for *the Banner:* 'on the one hand attacking ruthlessly pig-headedness wherever found, and on the other prodding humanity into pursuing an ever-receding perfection.'[44] Its achievements are not in conformity with its big claims. His brother's evaluation exposes its (*The Banner's*) hollowness and pettiness:

> You are showing yourself to be a pugnacious fellow. Almost every line of your paper is an attack on something. You give a page for politics–and it is all abuse; you don't seem to approve of any party or any leader. You give another page for local affairs, and it

> is nothing but abuse again. And then a column for cinema and arts–and even here you deal hard knocks. Current publications, the same thing–what is the matter with you? [45]

Mr. Sampath is out and out a religious man. He never starts his day without first invoking the blessings of the Godhead in the image of Nataraj. This divine image, an invisible consciousness, has been well explained by one of the famous cognoscenti of Indian traditional art, Anand K Coomaraswami:

> He wraps about Him as a garment, the tiger-fury of human passion. He wears Him as a 'necklace'; and beneath his feet is for ever crushed the embodiment of evil.[46]

Actually *The Banner* has been designed to reflect his spiritual leanings because he is of the view that the inanities of the materialistic world and the spiritual quest for lasting peace are the only panacea for the suffering humanity. Though, *the Banner* for some reason, could not achieve its aim fully.

Srinivas drifts along the current of life, pushed by Sampath's whimsical and flippant temperament. He is appointed scriptwriter by Sunrise Pictures. However, the shooting of the mythological film 'The Burning of Kama' for some obvious reason turns into a fiasco. He learns his life's lesson that there is no sense in interfering in other people's life. However, A. V. Krishna Rao establishes the superiority of his character:

> His experience of the vastness and the multi-valence of life resolves his spiritual ambivalence... he now lives his spiritual life with a sense of detachment, like his counterpart in *The English Teacher*. It is interesting to note that both reach the equal state of equilibrium by different ways: Krishna through psychic development and Srinivas by self-education in the school of life.[47]

V. Panduranga Rao makes a comparative study of Krishna and Srinivas and places Srinivas at a higher pedestal as he (Srinivas) is preoccupied with himself:

> Krishna is not concerned with self-realization or Moksha; his preoccupations are mundane. Srinivas is an improvement over Krishna...[48]

K. Venkatachari also lends superiority to Srinivas as he has a more developed sense of sensibility and greater awareness of his situation:

> … while Krishna undergoes psychic discipline unquestioningly with a view to achieving contact with his dead wife, Srinivas asks:...who am I? This is for a more serious problem than any I have known before. It is a big problem and I have to face it. Till I know who I am, how can I know what I should do? [49]

Srinivas understands the true detachment only by becoming involved in 'the chance of human relationships and activities' without losing personal identity. He, like a philosopher, is always preoccupied with some existential problems. He spends most of his time reading the Upanishads and seems least concerned about earning a livelihood. Even his wife's and father-in-law's letters go unattended because of his lack of interest in worldly affairs. When he is asked 'who are you' by his property owner, Srinivas instead of introducing himself answers back: 'It is a profound question. What mortal can answer it?'[50]

Lakshmi Holmstrom also confirms his being a philosophical person. He is antithetical to the importance of social obligation in a universe where 'the perfect and the imperfect are all the same.'[51] Srinivas understands that these opposites balance each other and form a total picture that may not be clearly perceived by man:

> If only one would get a comprehensive view of all humanity, one would get a correct view of the world: things being neither particularly wrong nor right, but just balancing themselves.[52]

Lakshmi Holmstrom further finds a visionary in him:

> In *Mr. Sampath*, Srinivas speculates that the wheel of existence and the round of birth and rebirth have meaning only in so far as a man moves towards his true nature.[53]

Srinivas' character is important because much of the humour in the novel results from his witty conversations with other characters. Even the slightest oddity in other people's behaviour and character makes him burst with his witty remarks when his houseowner castigates the hairy towels of the modern age:

> ...Do you know, I used to buy twenty towels to a rupee, the Malayalam variety? I'm still using some of them I bought in those days.[54]

Srinivas outwits him by his remarks:

> It was due to bargains like yours that no industry ever found it possible to raise its head in our country. [55]

Srinivas is not only humorous, but he is very humane, full of the milk of human kindness. He helps Ravi and his family and is remembered for his warm hospitality to his houseowner. He belongs to the school of idealistic Narayan characters, and is like Chandran in *The Bachelor of Arts* and Krishna in *The English Teacher*. Therefore, he is 'afflicted with the same uncertainty of purpose and mild hopelessness about the future.'[56] In the beginning, he suffers from Hamlet's indecisiveness, but slowly he develops a firm will that becomes considerably appreciable in the second part of the novel.

Srinivas appears an elevated soul to V. Panduranga Rao because 'with inner harmony, he is able to reconcile the opposites and fulfil his duties to himself, society and God.' [57] Shirley Chew makes almost the same observation about Sampath:

> A desirable balance must be found between his various roles as editor, husband, father, friend, just as amidst 'the multitudinousness and vastness' of life a 'subtle balance in all matters is maintained by 'the invisible forces of the universe.' [58]

As Srinivas' actual experience and understanding of life grow, his profundity as a writer increases. He has many remarkable revelations about truth, death, rebirth and the sufferings of humanity. His detachment from worldly affairs lies in his awareness of the centuries of wisdom, but his detachment cannot be equated with his forgetfulness towards the calls of humanity and herein lies the beauty of his character.

The character of Shanti whose astonishing beauty has its effect even on a balanced man like Srinivas, has not been described in detail. Still we come to know enough of her amazing beauty and people's reaction to it: she has 'a perfect figure, rosy complexion and arched eyebrows and almond shaped eyes – everything that should send a man especially an artist, into hysterics.'[59] Srinivas, charmed by her beauty, is compelled to think: 'Surely God does not create a person like this in order to drive people mad.'[60] She also consciously adorns herself with infinite care. However, we do not know much about her conduct and actions. Still this much is certain that she appears to be 'the butterfly type of woman–a type which is so very different from homely and domestic housewives and which is getting very common now in modern India owing to the impact of Western civilization.'[61]

Both Harish Raizada and Lakshmi Holmstrom find a resemblance between Shantabai and Shanti. Shanti resembles Shantabai for her wanton ways and flirtations. Here Lakshmi Holmstrom makes a concession: She is 'the victim of her circumstances or she is a heartless manipulator.'[62] O. P. Saxena too observes her negligence of conventional propriety. Hence, it does not surprise us that she allows Sampath to call her his cousin, but acts as his mistress in private. 'Their living ironic remarks against each other, their vision of things and people, their mutual agreements and disagreements, their ogling at each other, all these things prove the intimacy between them,'[63] but towards the end of the novel we feel that Shanti is always acting as Sampath's mistress without any genuine feeling of love for him. Saxena has an enlightening remark about their relationship: 'she succumbs, in fact, to an economic need and not to any genuine feeling of love.'[64] He also analyses the situation wherein Shanti refuses Sampath's proposal for marriage because she keeps relations with Sampath for earning her bread and not for the ecstasies of marriage.

It is a pity that almost all critics have taken up the negative aspect of her character and have been blind to her brighter aspect. O. P. Saxena glorifies the mother in her and thus indirectly eulogies her concern for our cultural value which places motherhood at a higher pedestal than being in love with someone. Therefore, in spite of her glamour, she remains a mother. The thought of her son salvages and purges her and 'she thus returns to family and tradition, which offer the proper place to a woman.'[65]

Ravi is one of the most tragic characters of R. K. Narayan. He first rots as a petty clerk in a bank and then the infatuation for a girl drives him mad. He appears a tragic character also because in spite of his being born in a very rich family, he is compelled to wind up his studies and shoulder all the family responsibility when his father suffers from paralysis. He supports his invalid father, old ailing mother and a vast crowd of brothers and sisters with a very poor amount he gets as salary in the bank.

> He finds peace in painting, but even that peace is transitory. A beautiful girl receives his attention and he is maddened by her divine beauty. He starts drawing her picture, but suddenly she

> disappears. He gives up painting in utter desperation and again takes to it only when he meets Srinivas. On being highly praised by Srinivas for drawing a pencil sketch of his love he remarks: 'She is the real artist and not I. A picture is produced only when she appears. A flash of her eyes can make a picture.' [66]

His love for the girl rekindles at the sight of the same girl in the role of Parvathi in the film company where he also works. His abnormality increases and finally he turns mad when he finds his beloved being embraced by Mr. Sampath. Thus, an artist is ruined forever.

The character of Srinivas' old property owner is interesting and valuable because it lessens the seriousness of the story and amuses the audience by creating some comic situations in the novel. The property owner is a greedy and miserly rich man with several sons and daughters with whom he is not on speaking terms. In spite of his being a very moneyed man, he bathes at the street tap and takes cooked rice distributed as charity in a nearby temple. Still he finds a novel way to rationalise his miserliness: 'the true Sanayasi has no need to live on anything more than the leavings of God.' [67] He loves to quote from scriptures and Mr. Sampath takes advantage of his love and respect for the holy books is encashed by Mr. Sampath. He owns a dilapidated mud house, but is not of the view to replace its walls and roofs by the cemented ones. His orthodoxy comes in the way of his liking even toothbrushes, hairy towels and combs. He only likes his granddaughter, amasses wealth for her dowry and makes a frantic search for a suitable groom. Dr. Ram Sewak Singh evaluates his character aptly:

> The landlord of Srinivas is a class by himself for he is a miser though rich in every sense, and a self-styled *sanyasi* with a full interest in the worldly life and its pleasures.[68]

Howsoever miser or conservative or short-tempered he may be we feel sorry at his mysterious death which is perhaps caused by his intimacy with Mr. Sampath.

Ravi's father is a cantankerous old man. Ravi's father feels desperately sorry at Ravi's association with film stars and dancing girls. That is the reason when Ravi's mind gives way he does not take pity on him.

Soma Sundram, the District Board President, is a ridiculous character. We feel sorry because he cannot use the bridge opening lecture because the ceremony never materializes. He has to relinquish the office also because 'it is too hard a life for a conscientious man.' Nirmal Mukherji comments: 'who could be more conscientious than the honorable president?' [69] He seems ridiculous because after saying good-bye to the presidentship he joins a new film company with a very strong desire to serve the country. Nonetheless, he considers himself a very authentic critic of issues related to a film as plot, action, dances and so on. R. K Narayan has skillfully portrayed Sundram's picture in some detail. That is why by the end of the novel we come to know all likes and dislikes of Soma Sundram, the ex-president of the District Board and this gives us a better understanding about his character.

THE FINANCIAL EXPERT

The Financial Expert was first published in 1952. This novel has been highly acclaimed by great scholars and critics. M. K. Naik finds this novel along with *The Guide* and *The Man-Eater of Malgudi* as 'the cream of Narayan's fiction'. [70] Kripal Singh also holds almost the similar view: 'the four novels which are considered to be his best–*The Financial Expert(1952), The Guide(1958), The Man-Eater of Malgudi(1962)* and *The Vender of Sweets (1967)*–are without exception, flawless.'[71] William Walsh finds the novel with 'three hallmarks–arrangement, scheme, composition.'[72] Bhagwat. S. Goyal perceives in it 'the typical charm of Narayan's unadorned prose, along with the expression of a characteristically naive and simplistic philosophy: the futility of man's forays into unaccustomed paths of quick gains and easy prosperity and the necessity of his turning back to the same point where he began, for this cycle of experience embodies the only worthwhile wisdom that a man can find in this life or in the lives to come.'[73] For Ram Sewak Singh it is 'a delightful novel for the gentle irony used to bring out the rise and fall of Margayya, the financial wizard.'[74] V. Panduranga Rao maintains that 'in form and structure which are rarely weak in Narayan's work, *The Financial Expert* is perhaps his best novel.'[75] Nirmal Mukherji hails it as 'a successful book from the point of view of organization'.[76] Uma Parameswaran discovers the novel as an example of 'Narayan's excellence at reportorial description'[77] and 'his compressed cataloguing of fraternal animosity and the sharing of patrimony'.[78]

Not only literary critics but reviewers also are very much sympathetic to this novel. Rumer Godden states in *New York Herald*

Tribune Book Review: 'It is a gentle ironic book written with a humour that comes naturally from the typically Indian inconsequential mixture of revered tradition and modern ideas.'[79] Frank Getleen commends this novel because of its 'powerful though delicately held grasp of life'.[80] Anthony West gets charmed by the 'deceptively effortless narrative'[81] style of the novelist. Booklist eulogises it for having 'an authentic ring and appeal'.[82]

This novel has not only received appraisals but also condemnation from some quarters. John Frederick Muehl feels that characters are so 'amoral and unreal that when the crude forces of justice and reality enter, they seem a wholly unwarranted, if inevitable, intrusion.'[83] Even Rumer Godden has a point for denouncing this novel: '... there is a curious aridity, a flatness as if it had no depth. Why? Because it is overtold.'[84] However, in spite of its several weaknesses the novel has 'a form, a rare thing among Indian writers writing in English today.'[85]

The Financial Expert is the story of the rise and fall of Margayya, the main character. He expands and adjusts keeping the audience's interest sustained. P. S. Sundaram finds three strains in the novel: 'Margayya's determination to acquire wealth so that no one dare look down upon him: his love for his son Balu and anxiety that he should turn out well: the curious ambivalent relationship with his brother and sister-in-law, whose kinship tradition comes into conflict with modern individualism and the traditional holds.'[86] In spite of these diverse notes the novel sounds musical.

Margayya, an adviser of forty-two, makes his living by advising the farmers intending to take loans from the Central Co-operative Land Mortgage Bank. He embarks upon a long course of prayers and puja to Laxmi, the Goddess of Wealth, in order to be a very rich and respectable man. His desire to acquire wealth brings him into contact with Dr. Pal, the author of an erotic manuscript 'Bed-Life or The Science of Marital Happiness.' Dr. Pal discloses him a secret of growing rich overnight by publishing this book. He accepts his proposal and thus earns a lot of money, but sticks to his old profession of advising peasants on a grand scale with his new office in Market Road. He also raises a big fund by borrowing money at a high rate of interest just to create the impression that he did not earn money by publishing an erotic book, though after a short time he develops differences with Dr. Pal who persuades people to get their money back from Margayya. Thus, he ruins himself and returns to the same banyan tree to advise the peasants in the old style again.

Margayya is the central figure of the novel. His character passes through five phases of life. We first notice him sitting under a banyan tree in front of the Central Co-operative Land Mortgage Bank in Malgudi advising peasants. His profession wins him bread but not wealth. After his insult at the hands of the Secretary of the Bank like Thomas Sutpen in Faulkner's *Absalom,* he decides to improve his financial condition to get prestige, strength, courage and confidence in society. Phase II records his accidental meeting with Dr. Pal and the meeting changes his entire course of life. Pal's association brings him wealth. In the third phase, we come across the vicissitudes in the career of Margayya's son, Balu. The fourth phase witnesses him again as a financial adviser but of a greater status. He collects a sea of wealth by borrowing money from others, arranges his son's marriage and thus has a satisfaction of seeing his son nicely settled in life. In his last phase, he moves like a celebrity, but suddenly his smooth-going life gets a jerk when he parts with Dr. Pal. Many things follow and finally he comes back to his old self.

Margayya's character is different from that of the heroes of Narayan's earlier novels in that he 'controls action with an emphasis more pressing than before.'[87] Margayya does not set out like earlier heroes 'in quest of spiritual improvement.'[88] He is attached to the world and worldly values. For him 'money was men's greatest need, like air or food.'[89] His conviction grows stronger and he introspects:

> If I have money, I need not dodge that spectacle dealer. I need not cringe before that storesman. I could give those medicines to my wife. The doctor would look at her with more interest, and she might look like other women. That son of mine, that Balu – I could give him everything.[90]

As regards money, his opinion keeps on changing. In the beginning, he always comes up with a patent answer to all the queries of his submissive wife: 'Take any money you want. Only leave me alone.'[91] In due course, he grows more close-fisted and rationalizes the philosophy of money in a somewhat extremist way. He considers 'money as something to accumulate and not to be spent.'[92] It seems ironical that Margayya–who showed way to others–is himself lost in this mirage of money. Therefore, it is not surprising that he even undertakes some censurable works. For example, he undertakes the publication of an erotic book and collects money from different persons at a high rate of interest. He, perhaps, stoops low because of 'the power and dynamism of money, its capacity to make people to do strange deeds.'[93] His basic philosophy of life appears to be centred on the subtle scale of values–money, riches, wealth and fortune. When rebuked by the bank-manager because of his being poor, his self-contempt convinces him:

> It's money which gives people all this. Money alone is important in this world. Everything else will come to us naturally if we have money in our purse.[94]

Later, Margayya claims to be the connoisseur of making and using money:

> Money is the greatest factor in life and the most ill-used. People don't know how to tend it, how to manure it, how to water it, how to make it grow, and when to pluck its flowers and when to pluck its fruits. What most people now do is to try and eat the plant itself.[95]

In his opinion, man would not have been civilized if money had not been present in the world. It can tell upon one's family peace also: 'He that hath not (money) is spurned even by his wife.'[96] His madness for money makes him seek some novel way to acquire it after his account book has been thrown by Balu. He takes pride in being a man of value and importance owing to the money he earned by publishing a pornographic book:

> He knew that he had a scheme somewhere at the back of his mind, a scheme which would place him among the elect in society, which would make people flock to him and look to him for guidance, advice and management...[97]

Margayya is an example of archetypal fantasy of money. He has an inflated ego that sets Margayya on his great financial adventure.

Money, no doubt, is the requirement of life, but, if not used and understood judiciously, it can turn to be a great curse and is liable to put one's life in danger. Suresh Nath finds this theory applicable to Margayya's life:

> The rise and fall of Margayya is a case in point. His contact with the printer Mr. Madan Lal provides the necessary nutritive manure to the already embedded seed of his lust for money. Soon, the seed sprouts up into a full-fledged plant solely depending on the diet of more and more money. The corrupting power of excessive money is evidenced in the novel by the growth of his son into a frustrated corrupt young man. Once set in, the love of money becomes irresistible and continuous. The disbursement of his whole money to depositors and declaration of insolvency thrust the father and son to the harsh but sound realities of life. The elusive realm of treacherous gold in which they had been meandering is lost with a stroke. Like the magical web of the Lady of Shallot, the paradise of unreality is blown up.[98]

Shirley Chew also shares Suresh Nath's views regarding the damaging role of money in Margayya's life:

> Margayya's wealth is monstrous because it affords his family so little happiness. It spoils his son, isolates him from his wife, and ruins his own health.[99]

Margayya may have an excessive lust for money, but what strikes most is the fact that he is 'a full-blooded character'.[100] He looks authentic because of his expertise in mortgages, his desire for wealth and motor cars, his wish to please goddess Laxmi and because of his rapport with police and income-tax officials. Margayya's authenticity also stems from Narayan's real-life experience. In 1940, he met a financial expert in Bangalore who collected big deposits and promised high rates of interest. Margayya's name is suggestive of his nature and temperament. It is purely derivative:

> 'Marga' meant 'The Way' and 'Ayya' was an honorific suffix: taken together it denoted one who showed the way.[101]

Therefore, Margayya is from time immemorial the financial guide to the needy people. 'Like a master magician he casts a spell on all those who approach him. The naive villagers are easily taken in by the glib tongue of this financial adviser. It does not take him long to hook a new customer, his stock-in-trade is the technique of "persuasion"that lends credibility to the sordid transactions.'[102] He aims at dissolving the co-operative spirit among his clients. 'The twin objects of the co-operative movement–thrift and the elimination of the middlemen– are constantly flouted by Margayya, for his life is dependent on the consumption of 'the loan application forms of the Co-operative Bank'.[03]

The rise and fall of the financial wizard affect his son's progress. Margayya celebrates his son's schooling ceremony with great enthusisam. Balu holds a special status in the school because of his being rich. Though an ardent worshipper of goddess Laxmi, he brings the image of goddess Saraswati for his son. He nourishes dreams of his being educated, but those dreams are shattered. He could not pass even Matriculation examination in spite of several efforts. Still his concern for his son does not lessen. He engineers his homecoming when he flees away to Madras. He remains, nonetheless, seriously preoccupied with the question of his marriage. Balu's engagement to Brinda, the daughter of a tea-estate's owner ends his worry. Moreover, his attachment to his son prevents Dr. Pal from wrecking the family life of his innocent daughter-in-law Brinda. Nirmal Mukherji rightly observes that 'the whole book is as much a study of Balu's growth as of Margayya's mind perceiving this growth.'[104]

It sounds paradoxical, but it is a fact, that wealth could not bring father and son very close to each other, but poverty united them at the end. Further, it is his love to Balu which makes him survive the terrible sting of poverty and advises his resurrected son to join his old business in a somewhat pathetic way:

> You see that box there... Its contents are intact as I left them years ago–a pen and inkbottle. You asked for my property. There it is, take it: have an early meal tomorrow and go to the banyan tree in front of the Co-operative Bank. I hope the tree is still there. Go there, that is all I can say: and anything may happen thereafter .[105]

Uma Parameswaran in her famous essay 'Native Genius–R. K. Narayan' presents an indepth study of father-son relationship in *The Financial Expert.* She discovers Margayya's love, like Jagan's in *The Vendor of the Sweets,* growing into imprudence: 'The first part of the novel is a fine delineation of the wonderful experience of fatherhood.' [106] All the scenes between father and son evoke genuine feelings. For instance, the child's enthusiastic reception of his father every evening, his cunning balckmail of his parents when he is hurt, his stubborn tantrum resulting in the loss of Margayya's precious account books make the reader share these moments sincerely. Margayya's love, anxiety and ambition for his young son can be depicted with the help of only one paragraph:

> His mind gloated over visions of his son. He would grow into an aristocrat. He would study, not in a Corporation school, but in the convent, and hobnob with the sons of the District Collector or the Superintendent of Police or Mangal Seth, the biggest mill-owner in the town. He would promise him a car all for himself when he came to the College. He could go to America and obtain degrees... He would buy another bungalow in Lawley Road for his son, and then his vision went on to the next generation of aristocrats.[107]

When Margayya achieves success and riches, Balu is only thirteen. At that time, the relationship is very warm. Margayya does not even scold his son at his failure at Matriculation examination. He always tries to cover up his failure or mistake:

> What is there in Matriculation? People can learn nothing in schools. I have no faith in our education, who wants all this nonsense about A squared plus B squared... Boys must learn things in the rough school of life.[108]

Marriage does not correct Balu. In fact, Margayya remains so preoccupied with moneymaking that he remains oblivious of his son's affairs. Balu gets completely spoilt in the company of Dr. Pal. Naturally, Margayya hates him. His paternal love is restored again when he turns a pauper. Thus, the cycle is complete–the beginning becomes the end. Uma Parameswaran also shares Taranath's view of a presence of 'a cyclic order'[109] in this novel. Nonetheless, she does not find any 'altered and enriched kind of awareness'[110] in him:

> Margayya has not, after all, learnt anything from several other experiences; his self-imposed discipline of worship did not improve him..., because it was not a discipline at all but merely ritual; the rise to wealth did not affect him, and his reflections about money automatically bringing recognition and status turn out untrue; money can bring him nothing because he does not know how to use money; he still lives in his bare, old-fashioned little house with its single file of four rooms, and the small room he builds upstairs houses dust and currency notes.[111]

Really, he does not take any lesson from Balu's flight and return. Instead, his spirit dampens and is now more willing to keep Balu nearby parting with more money. In Rajeev Taranath's opinion, Margayya conforms to the recurring pattern in the novels of R. K. Narayan:

> ... Margayya is in the beginning a petty money-lender, having his office under a tree in front of a Co-operative Bank. Coming under the influence of Dr. Pal and Madan Lal he becomes successively a prosperous publisher, and rich and influential banker and philanthropist–his business is shady. Getting involved in a scrape with Pal, he is scandalised by the latter as a heartless villain, his banking business collapses and at the end, he is left a sorrier edition of his original self.[112]

The same critic, further, attempts to philosophise Margayya's averageness:

> Margayya as a human entity has preserved all through his changing fortunes as a financial expert, by his unchanging slightly awkward tenderness towards his wife, son and later daughter-in-law and grandson. His affection of the family is the constant which keeps the other constant of his as an average person, alive...[113]

M. K. Naik also confirms that he remains the same man throughout because he feels that even after witnessing several twists and turns 'he is still hopeful that the next turn of the wheel of fortune will again restore his dream.'[114]

V. Panduranga Rao, contrary to Taranath's theory of Narayan's characters, experiences a marked change in the total mental make-up of Margayya:

> He punishes Pal and thunderously exhibits his resentment against lewd life but the beating he administers to Pal is something more: It is a revolt against a world that keeps him unhappy.[115]

Uma Parameswaran disagrees with Rao because in her opinion, 'Margayya is blissfully happy in his profession right from his bunyan tree to his financial wizardry.'[116] We also agree with M. K. Naik, Uma Parameswaran and R. Taranath with regard to the pattern of Margayya's character. V. Panduranga Rao, perhaps, wants to thrust his own meaning to Margayya's behaviour. Margayya's fight with Dr. Pal is a reflection on his attachment to his son and not a revolt against his materialistic venture.

V. Panduranga Rao feels that Margayya is amusingly simple:

> He is at once among people of his own kind but greatly handicapped by a want of sophistication when exposed to the modern world. Inspite of his crude methods, he works with the stubbornness of a thorough schemer. Margayya fails in his career and in bringing up his son, because he cannot adapt himself to a changing world. (His failure lies in his being) caught between the two civilizations of modern India, involved in a tension that at once provides the comedy and the pathos of this remarkable novel.[117]

Margayya deserves our sympathy not because he is caught between two civilizations, but because of his helplessness to maintain a balance between his love for money as well as family. Ironically, his capacity for love and affection sustains him through the odds of his life. His very affection for his grandson saves him from breaking up at the end of the novel:

> Now get the youngster here. I will play with him. Life has been too dull without him in this house.[118]

Margayya professes a humanitarian concern for his brethren:

> 'I want to do so much for you fellows, do you know why? ... It is because I want you all to get over your money worries and improve your lives. You must all adopt civilized ways. That's why I am trying to help you to get money from bastard office.' [119]

The relationship between Margayya and his brother is a reflection on the bonds of kinship in an Indian family. On the one hand, division of the ancestral home by erecting a wall within the house makes the relationship between the two bitter, on the other, the brother is there to help Margayya in the event of his financial bankruptcy.

Many critics have compared Margayya with different characters of Narayan's own novels and other novels to highlight the real worth of his character. Nirmal Mukherji finds him 'as fascinating as Mr. Sampath.'[120] Uma Parameswaran makes a wonderful comparison between Margayya and Jagan:

> Both are essentially misers who have hoarded a huge fortune and do not wish to spend a penny of it. For both, their only child is a

> child of many prayers. Both express their gratitude to the deity of their prayers by making an offering of their son's weight in gold and silver; ... Both have inordinately high hopes for their son and heir. Both are ruined by the son they have spoilt ... Both, Margayya and Jagan, have a core of romanticism, and repeatedly go back to pleasant memories... Both men are themselves the product of fundamental change in the traditional family pattern; the joint family system, so basic to the Hindu way of life, has been broken in their youth, and each lives with his immediate family in a relatively isolated domestic world. [121]

Margayya is comparable to Raju and Natraj too because each one of them is worldly. His character also comes closer to Barabas (*The Jew of Malta* by Christopher Marlowe) who embodies a person all out for wealth and gold. Margayya may further be associated with Mr. De Barral, the banker father of Flora, the hero of Joseph Conrad's novel *Chance*. De Barral's financial kingdom gives way because of his dishonesty and foolishness in investments and so does Margayya's due to his over-ambition and dishonesty. 'Margayya in *The Financial Expert* is comparable to Silas Marner if only in respect of his inordinate love of money.'[122]

P. S. Sundaram appreciates Margayya's childlike innocence:

> He is in many ways like a child, surprised by everything that happens to him, and unhappy and bewildered that he could not establish a better relationship with the son who means much to him. His financial triumphs and disaster has taken in his stride: he is not particularly elated or depressed. There is a certain childish vanity when, after the insult by the Secretary and Arul Doss, he takes out his old lace *dhoti* and wears it to show the people of the Land Mortgage Bank that he is not a man to be despised.[123]

Margayya's character is strong, forceful and magnanimous because 'the imaginative powers of Narayan reach their expressive best in developing the common Indian type of a village banker into a universal prototype in the *Financial Expert* on an epic scale.'[124] In fact, 'He is, in a special sense, Narayan's Micawber–not a sanguine idler but a dynamic financial expert'.[125] The popularity of the novel very largely rests on Margayya who, in the opinion of Graham Greene, 'is perhaps the most engaging of all Mr Narayan's characters.'[126]

In fact, Balu was born after several years of marriage. To fulfil the vow the child was carried to Tirupati as a child, to present silver coins worth his weight to the God Venkateswara. He grows up a completely spoilt child. His stupidity lies in his freeing himself from the bondage of his father and running away to Madras. He comes back with much difficulty. He encashes father's attachment to lay his hands on father's money. Lakshmi Holmstrom highlights the opposing philosophy of father and son and at the same time establishes their inter-dependence over each other:

> Margayya's only ambition–apart from the goal of making money, which he sees as an end in itself–is to see his son freed from his dubious corpse–bearing ancestry, and settled in Lawley Extension among the most respected citizens of Malgudi. But for Balu, money means ease and luxury and an access to cards and prostitutes. The goals of these two are completely opposed. Yet Margayya and Balu balance and need each other. Margayya loves his son. Balu needs his father's financial support.[127]

Balu is a dullared and shatters his father's hope of becoming a doctor by obtaining 12% marks in Hygiene. His life has been painted as it is seen by Margayya or communicated to him by others. Margayya expresses his concern for his son by interviewing the astrologer about his son's horoscope that he finds essential in an orthodox Indian family. He calmly instructs the angry astrologer to ensure that his son's horoscope is compatible with the girl he wants him to marry.

Dr. Pal, the enterprising pornographer, occupies the place which Sampath has as a comic villainous disturber in *Mr. Sampath.* He enables the hero, Margayya, who has been leading an innocent, useful and happy life as the financial expert to the village peasants, with his headquarters under a banyan tree, to embark on an ambitious career in business. Dr. Pal who is at first a benefactor turns out to be a monster because he corrupts Margayya's son, both sexually and financially. Dr. Pal, who in fact is a journalist and the correspondent of *Silver Way* of Madras, lures Margayya into purchasing his book on sex and thereby making him rich.

William Walsh finds a similarity among Morco in *The Guide,* Vasu in *The Man- Eater of Malgudi,* and Dr. Pal (in *The Financial Expert).* He maintains:

> Certain characters have a kind of personality which is both hard and rigid in outline, in which there is, as it were, a massively bony structure which does not yield to the environment, which thrusts strongly into it. The conduct of such a character has about it a certain peremptory authority, which we observe in Marco, Vasu and in Dr. Pal. They lack that sensitive accommodation to the interlocutor which the Indian sensibility regards as an essential in human relationship.[128]

Dr. Pal is both the instrument of Margayya's rise and fall. He is a self-declared sociologist and psychologist. At one place he says, 'I feel I am made by God in order that I may enlighten people in these matters and guide their steps to happiness'.[129] He is the real spirit behind the schemes of Margayya. He gives him the book, finds room in Market Road for banking operations and brings depositors for financial operations. He also proves to be the evil genius for Balu and brings the final ruin of the financial wizard.

REFERENCES

1. John Haverstick, 'Sly Rascal,' *Saturday Review of Literature,* 40 (11 May, 1957), p. 20.
2. Donald Barr, 'Three Minds in Trouble,' *New York Times Book Review,* 12 May, 1957, p. 4.
3. Christine Weston, 'Odd, Entertaining Doings in Small Town in India,' *New York Herald Tribune Book Review,* 2 June, 1957, p. 6.
4. Anne Fremantle, 'Absurd and Credible Events,' *Commonwealth,* 66 (2 August, 1957), p. 52.
5. Margaret Palmer Beals, 'Light Side of India,' *Chattanooga Times (Tenn),* 13 Oct., 1957, p. 20.
6. Welford Inge, 'They Share Some Fears,' *Oklahoman* (Oklahoma city), 20 October, 1957, p. 27.
7. A. V. Krishna Rao, *The Indo-Anglian Novel and the Changing Tradition* (Mysore, 1972), p. 78.
8. H. M. Williams, *Indo-Anglian Literature* (1800-1970): *A Survey* (Bombay, 1976), p. 56.
9. Lakshmi Holmstrom, *The Novels of* R. K. *Narayan* (Calcutta, 1973), p. 57.
10. P. S. Sundaram, R. K. *Narayan* (New Delhi, 1973), p. 63.

11. V. Panduranga Rao, 'The Art of R. K. Narayan,' *The Journal of Commonwealth Literature,* 5 (July 1968), p. 33.
12. R. K. Narayan, *My Days* (Mysore, 1975), p. 154.
13. *Ibid.,* p. 160.
14. R. K. Narayan, *Mr. Sampath* (Mysore, 1983), p. 63.
15. *The Indo-Anglian Novel and the Changing Tradition*, p. 78.
16. Harish Raizada, *R. K. Narayan: A Critical Study of His works* (New Delhi, 1969), p. 89.
17. *Ibid.,* p. 97.
18. William Walsh, *R. K. Narayan: A Critical Appreciation* (New Delhi, 1983), p. 66.
19. *lbid.,* p. 66.
20. Donald Barr, *The New York Times Book Review,* May 9, 1957, p.14.
21. Nirmal Mukherji, *The World of Malgudi: A Study of the Novels of* R. K. *Narayan,* unpublished doctoral dissertation (Louisiana State University, 1960), p.70.
22. *Ibid.,* p. 109.
23. *Mr. Sampath,* p. 45.
24. *R. K. Narayan: A Critical Appreciation*, p. 67.
25. *Mr. Sampath*, p. 68.
26. *Mr. Sampath*, p. 214.
27. *Mr. Sampath*, p. 161.
28. *Mr. Sampath*, p. 179.
29. *Mr. Sampath*, p. 67.
30. *Mr. Sampath*, p. 169.
31. *R. K. Narayan: A Critical Appreciation*, p. 67.
32. *R. K. Narayan: A Critical Appreciation*, p. 67.
33. *Mr. Sampath*, p. 141.
34. *Mr. Sampath*, p. 175.
35. *Mr. Sampath*, p. 175.
36. *Mr. Sampath*, p. 179.
37. M. K. Naik, S.K. Desai and G.S. Amur (eds), *Critical Essays on Indian Writing in English* (Dharwar, 1972), p. 296.
38. *Ibid.*, p. 296.

39. *Indo-Anglian Literature* (1800-1970) (Bombay, 1976), p. 57.
40. *The World of Malgudi: A Study of the Novels of R. K. Narayan, p.* 73.
41. *Ibid.*, p. 73.
42. R. K. Dhawan (ed.), *Explorations in Modern Indo-English Fiction* (New Delhi, 1982), p. 145.
43. M. K. Naik, *The Ironic Vision* (New Delhi, 1983), p. 30.
44. *Mr. Sampath,* p. 6.
45. *Ibid.*, p. 24.
46. Anand K. Coomaraswamy, *Essays in Indian Naturalism* (Madras, 1909), p. 45.
47. *The Indo-Anglian Novelists and the Changing* Tradition, p. 80.
48. V. Panduranga Rao, 'The Art of R. K. Narayan,' p. 33.
49. K. Venkatachari, 'R. K. Narayan's Novels: Acceptance of Life,' *Osmania Journal of English Studies,* 1969, p. 75.
50. *Mr. Sampath* (Mysore, 1983), p. 9.
51. *The Novels of R. K. Narayan*, p. 55.
52. *Mr. Sampath*, p. 63.
53. *The Novels of R. K. Narayan*, p. 66.
54. *Mr. Sampath*, p. 51.
55. *Mr. Sampath*, p. 51.
56. *R. K. Narayan: A Critical Appreciation*, p. 65.
57. 'The Art of R. K. Narayan,' p. 34.
58. Shirley Chew, *Readings in Commonwealth Literature* (London, 1973), p. 65.
59. *Mr. Sampath, p.* 139.
60. *Mr. Sampath*, p. 154.
61. *R. K. Narayan: A Critical Study of His Works*, p. 97.
62. Atma Ram (ed), *Perspectives on R. K. Narayan* (Ghaziabad, 1981), p. 67.
63. O. P. Saxena, *Glimpses of Indo-English Fiction,* Vol. III (New Delhi, 1985), p. 33.
64. *Ibid.*, p. 36.
65. *Ibid.*, p. 37.
66. *Mr. Sampath*, p. 109.

67. *Mr. Sampath*, p. 7.
68. Ram Sewak Singh, *The Guide: Some Aspects*, (Delhi, 1977), p. 10.
69. *The World of Malgudi: A Study of the Novels of* R. K. *Narayan*, p. 44.
70. *The Ironic Vision: A Study of the Fiction of* R. K. *Narayan*), p. 44.
71. *Explorations in Modern Indo-English Fiction* (New Delhi, 1982), p. 132.
72. R. K. *Narayan: A Critical Appreciation,* p. 70.
73. Bhagwat S. Goyal, *R. K. Narayan: A Critical Spectrum* (Meerut, 1983), p. 20.
74. *The Guide: Some Aspects*, p. 10.
75. 'The Art of R. K. Narayan,' p. 34.
76. *The World of Malgudi: A Study of the Novels of* R. K. *Narayan,* p. 126.
77. Uma Parameswaran, *A Study of Representative Indo-English Novelists* (New Delhi, 1976), p. 59.
78. *Ibid.,* p. 59.
79. Rumer Godden, 'Under a Banyan Tree Sat One with a Knowledge of the Human Heart,' *New York Herald Tribune Book Review,* 19 April, 1953, p. 3.
80. Frank Getleen, 'The Little Life of Everyman,' *Commonwealth* 58 (8 May, 1953), p. 126.
81. Anthony West, 'Happy and Happy-Go-Luckily,' *New Yorker,* 29 (25 April, 1953), pp. 129-30.
82. Review, *Booklist,* 53 (15 July,1953), p. 57.
83. John Frederick Muehl, 'Indian Operator,' *Saturday Review of Literature,* 36 (18 April, 1953), pp. 22-23.
84. 'Under a Banyan Tree Sat One with a Knowledge of the Human Heart,' p. 3.
85. *Ibid.*
86. R. K. *Narayan,* p. 74.
87. *Readings in Commonwealth Literature,* p. 67.
88. *Ibid.,* p. 67.
89. R. K. Narayan, *The Financial Expert* (Mysore, 1984), p. 22.
90. *The Financial Expert,* p. 23.
91. *The Financial Expert,* p. 163.
92. *The Financial Expert,* p. 120.
93. *Ibid.,* p. 22.

94. *Ibid.*, p. 17.

95. *Ibid.*, p. 108.

96. R. K. Narayan, *The Financial Expert* (Mysore, 1984), p. 17.

97. *Ibid.*, p. 102.

98. *Perspectives on R. K. Narayan, p. 113.*

99. *Readings in Commonwealth Literature*, p. 67.

100. Suresh Nath in *Perspectives on R. K. Narayan,* ed. Atma Ram, p. 116.

101. *The Fnancial Expert*, p. 1.

102. R.K. Dhawan in *Perspectives on R. K. Narayan,* ed. Atma Ram, p. 122.

103. *The Indo-Anglian Novel and the Changing Tradition*, p. 82.

104. *The World of Malgudi: A Study of the Novels of R. K. Narayan,* p. 83.

105. *The Financial Expert*, p. 178.

106. A *Study of the Representative Indo-Anglian English Novelists,* p. 76.

107. *The Financial Expert*, p. 23.

108. *The Financial Expert*, p. 122.

109. *Critical Essays on Indian Writings in English,* p. 298.

110. *Ibid.*, p. 298.

111. A *Study of the Representative Indo- Anglian Novelists,* p. 78.

112. *Critical Essays on Indian Writings in English*, p. 296.

113. *Ibid.*, p. 304.

114. *The Ironic Vision, p.* 49.

115. 'The Art of R. K. Narayan,' p. 34.

116. A *Study of the Representative Indo- Anglian Novelists*, p. 79.

117. 'The Art of R. K. Narayan,' p. 34.

118. *The Financial Expert*, p. 178.

119. *The Financial Expert*, p. 20.

120. Nirmal Mukherji, 'Some Aspects of the Literary Development of R. K. Narayan,' *The Banasthali Patrika,* 5, 13 (July 1969), p. 82.

121. A *Study of the Representative Indo- Anglian Novelists*, pp. 80-81.

122. 'R. K. Narayan's Novel: Acceptance of Life,' p. 60.

123. *R. K. Narayan*, pp. 81-82.

124. *Indo-Anglian Novel and the Changing Tradition*, p. 81.

125. *Ibid.*, p. 84.

126. Introduction to *The Financial Expert*, p. viii.

127. *The Novels of* R. K. *Narayan*, p. 57.

128. R. K. *Narayan: A Critical Appreciation*, pp. 77-78.

129. *The Financial Expert*, p. 69.

5

TENSIONS AND AGONIES OF MODERN MAN: WAITING FOR THE MAHATMA AND THE GUIDE

Being human in our modern civilization is
being forced into a boxing ring with Nature.
And we're bloodied everytime.

—M. Robin D'Antan

WAITING FOR THE MAHATMA

Waiting for the Mahatma was published in 1955. Among Narayan's novels, this novel remains perhaps the most controversial. While some of the critics hail the novel, others condemn it. William Walsh praises this book highly:

> Perhaps the greatest achievement of this novel is indeed in the construction of one who is in the book a minor character, namely Gandhi himself... The triumph of this novel is to show in an ordinary story in a historical context a persuasively human figure who can have this immense spiritual significance...[1]

William Walsh finds this novel important also for 'the richness and variety of its minor characters'.[2] A. V. Krishna Rao appreciates this novel for projecting the 'archetypal image of this Universal Man [Gandhi]... with a rare perspicacity and respect for historical experience.'[3]

He further adds:

> ... Narayan's canvass is big; but the image of Gandhi is bigger still, for while the canvass is time, the image is eternity.[4]

The novel has not only pleased, but also displeased many important critics. They hurled their condemnation to the extent of declaring the novel partially or totally a failure. Dr A. N. Kaul boldly declares: 'to the extent to which it is a political novel… it 'hasn't enlarged our awareness of Gandhi or his era one bit' and that Raja Rao's *Kanthapura* and Mulk Raj Anand's *Untouchable* are incomparably superior Gandhi-Novels."[5] Prof. Kaul goes on to assert that the novel seems to be "pointless."[6] Dr. C. D. Narasimhaiah also indicts the novelist:

> An excellent exploitation of the Gandhian principle of which, by the way, Narayan has made a muddle in his *Waiting for the Mahatma*, a novel which he would do well to withdraw.[7]

Metro, Narayan's American friend and himself a novelist also impeaches the novel:

> I think the book is weak in motivation, we don't learn anything about Mahatma Gandhi, and the narrative lacks punch. [8]

Uma Parameswaran condemns it as the 'weakest novel."[9]While making a comparison with *The Guide,* she charges it as an inferior novel:

> *Waiting for the Mahatma* shows all his weaknesses. Unlike *The Guide* which reveals his strength as well as shortcomings, *Waiting for the Mahatma* has very little in its favour.[10]

She rationalizes its failure by saying that 'not only is the portrait of Gandhi weak and uninspiring, but the novel is lacking in characterization, development, meaning, technique and language.'[11] She adds some more convincing reasons for its failures: .... he (Narayan) is uninteresting when moulding good men, and positively out of his depth with supermen.... Lakshmi Holmstrom also does not feel enthusiastic about declaring the novel "wholly a success"[13] because of Narayan's limited capacity to explore the relationship between his two main chracters–Bharati and Sriram.

The most important point about the novel raised repeatedly is whether this is a political novel. Further, if this is a political novel, does it succeed as a political novel? Here R. K. Narayan's own observation deserves mention:

> Politics is the least interesting aspect of life, in my view. I don't attach too much importance to it as literary material. Because most politically inspired novels die in good time. They don't last.

> It's only the human elements which last, not the political concepts or the pressures. They become just insignificant.[14]

Thus, it is quite clear that Narayan does not take pains to make it a political novel. In an interview with *The Deccan Herald* too, he makes a clear breast of his intention:

> When I wrote *Waiting for the Mahatma* I did not want it to be a political chronicle. I wrote it because he was a great personality.[15]

We do not share either Narayan's above comment or William Walsh's view that *Waiting for the Mahatma* is not a political novel. Actually to settle the question about its real identity, a meditation on some of the definitions of the term 'political novel' is necessary. H. A. L. Fisher thinks that it 'concerns itself with men and women engaged in contemporary political ideas.'[16] In the opinion of Joseph L. Blotner, it is 'a book which directly describes, interprets or analyses political phenomena.'[17] Irving Howe thinks it to be 'a novel in which political ideas play a dominant role or in which the political milieu is the dominant setting.'[18] The above viewpoints suggest that the novel is concerned with at least one man and one woman 'engaged in contemporary political life' and the dominant setting in it is the political milieu itself. Thus, it is clear that however hard he tries not to make it a political novel, the novel falls into this category by its own intrinsic merit, though Narayan's experiment fails. M. K. Naik attributes two reasons for its failure:

> First, his treatment of the political theme is superficial, sketchy and uninformed by a meaningful vision; and secondly, he cheapens the theme still further by making it a peg on which to hang a conventional love-story.[19]

We may divide *Waiting for the Mahatma* into five parts. Part I constitutes a little over one third of the novel. It introduces Sriram, an orphan, brought up by his Granny, celebrating his twentieth birthday alone with his Granny. Sriram falls in love with Bharati, one of Gandhi's followers, and decides to join Gandhi's camp also. Part II takes Sriram and Bharati to various villages with Gandhi. Sriram makes his new home in a deserted shrine on a slope of the Mempi Hill. By dint of hard work he learns to spin and feels exulted when he wears clothes made of the yarn spun by him. He also spreads Gandhi's messages in the various villages by painting it on the walls and other places. He exchanges letters with Gandhi when he feels disheartened by people's behaviour.

Part III describes his close association with Jagdish, a terrorist and a supporter of I.N.A. He learns from Jagdish that Bharati is imprisoned in the old Slaughter House. He has a very short meeting with her and starts for his home at Kabir Lane when he gets news of the critical illness of his Granny. Unfortunately, he arrives too late to see her. She is already dead though to the people's surprise she regains consciousness at the pyre. This part of the novel ends with Sriram's arrest from the funeral ground. Part IV recounts Sriram's experiences in the Central Jail. He is released with the departure of the British from India. Part V leads the novel to the conclusion. Sriram learns of Gandhi's mission of peace in Noakhali torn by communal riots and of Bharati's presence in that mission. He is advised to meet Bharati at the Birla House in New Delhi where Mahatma blesses them and grants them permission to marry. The next morning Gandhi is shot dead.

Sriram, the hero of the novel, is brought up by his Granny in the manner of a minor zamindar. In the beginning, every fact about Sriram derives from the concrete. The remote and misty quality of his parents is made familiar to us first by means of the mother's picture, which is placed too high for him to see when young and too dim to be pleasing when he grows. The brown envelope is the only message that he now receives from his father at regular intervals. He is the only receiver of Granny's tenderness. In the beginning, he lives a lonely life as a child. The lonely life of the boy is conveyed to us in his habit of reclining on the cold cement windowsill contemplating the things he had done since he was an infant. The intensity of this solitariness surfaces when he celebrates his twentieth birthday alone with his Granny:

> So all alone next day he celebrated his twentieth birthday. His guest as well as hostess was his grandmother. No one outside could have guessed what an important occasion was being celebrated in that house in Kabir Street numbered '14'. [20]

In the remaining four parts of the novel, Sriram finds himself in the midst of a vast crowd. William Walsh is aware of this duality of his personality:

> The opposition of shuffling multitude and solitary individual, of babble and silence, is one of the deep constitutive intuitions of Narayan's fiction, and is part of that inner dialectic which supports the universe of the novel. [21]

Sriram, like other Narayan's characters, has been a poor student and has anyhow plodded his way through high school. On his 20th birthday, Granny hands over to him the accumulated military pension and he finds himself a lord of 38,500 rupees, 7 annas and 6 pies.

One April evening, at the market, he encounters a young woman collecting money for Gandhi's visit. 'But Sriram, unlike some other Narayan heroes–Chandran in *The Bachelor of Arts* or Ravi in *Mr. Sampath* or Narayan himself–is not a romantic lover who falls in love at first sight and for ever.'[22] However, she leaves a lasting impression on him and he starts speculating about the woman who fits in the role of his wife.

He gains access to Gandhi's hut and makes acquaintance with Bharati and decides to be a Gandhian in order to win her. He joins Gandhi's movement for the freedom of the nation and thus we find Sriram, the lazy, goodhearted, average young man turning into a purposeful adult, an obedient disciple and a devoted lover. Sriram succeeds in meeting Bharati at Congress Camp. There, he expresses his deep longing to be her friend and if possible, her life-partner too. Bharati behaves decently with Sriram and promises to arrange an interview if he adheres to truth. Sriram accepts her suggestion though he is courageous enough to say 'I like you and I like to be with you.' Next morning, as per Bharati's instruction, he meets Gandhi. The meeting is symbolic of their respective roles:

> The door of Mahatma's hut was half-open. Light streamed out through the gap. Sriram went towards it like a charmed moth.[23]

Sriram does not understand the meaning of Gandhi's utterances like these:

> When someone has wronged you or has done something which appears to you to be evil, just pray for the destruction of that evil.[24]

> I want you really to make sure of a change in your hearts before you ever think of asking the British to leave the shores of India.... 'If I have the slightest suspicion that your heart is not pure or that there is bitterness there, I'd rather have the British stay on. It's the lesser of the two evils.' [25]

For Sriram all these words sound mysterious. He does not believe that evil can really be destroyed by prayer. He also gets confused over

Gandhi's intention because his primary task is to bring a change in Indians' hearts and not to bring freedom to the country. Still he decides to follow him in order to enjoy the company of Bharati who is presented to us as sharptongued, witty, and a real termagant.

When Sriram and Bharati are surveying various villages with Gandhi, they seem to remain unaffected by the horrible condition of villagers worsened by famine:

> However grim the surroundings might be, Sriram and Bharati seemed to notice nothing. They had a delight in each other's company which mitigated the gloom of the surroundings. [26]

Here we find the novelist making a contradictory statement soon:

> The thought of having to live a mundane existence without Mahatmaji appalled him. Not even the proximity of Bharati seemed to mitigate his misery.[27]

Supposedly, by making such a contradictory statement the novelist only adds some sort of unconvincingness to Sriram's character. Sriram sounds unconvincing many times. Once when being advised by Bharati on doing a serious business of writing 'Quit India' all over the district, he, instead of being serious, shows his detachment to the noble work: 'He lost count of time. He went on doing things in a sort of machine-like manner.'[28] Further, on being asked about the reason behind writing these words, he replies that he is merely carrying out an order. Uma Parameswaran rightly comments: 'it becomes more and more obvious that Sriram has not understood what the whole non-violent, non-co-operation movement is about; his is an inferior path altogether–the path of blind obedience. Gandhi is a Mahatma. Mahatma must be obeyed. Therefore, do what Gandhi says without questioning or comprehending. Because he does not understand the ABC of Gandhism, he is its worst advocate'.[29] Therefore, when Matheson reports him that the Cripps' offer has been rejected, Sriram keeps silent because such intricate academic technicalities does not enter his head. He only remarks: "It is just an eyewash.".[30]

The strong proof of Sriram's incomprehension is the way he is taken in by Jagdish, a prosperous photographer and supporter of Indian National Army. He exploits Sriram. He is presented a radio-set that receives Netaji Subhas Chandra Bose's broadcast to the underground workers of Indian National Army. Sriram faithfully transcribes the messages even without questioning whether the resort to violent means in their fight for freedom conforms to Gandhian ideology.

Bharati remains throughout the centre of Sriram's life. Even when he faces public apathy while propogating the mantra of 'Quit India' and feels broken, he spares time to come closer, rather dangerously close to Bharati to 'violently' possess her. His indulgence in terrorist activities gives him a satisfaction since 'his whole being acquired a meaning only when he was doing something in relation to Bharati'.[31] On a closer analysis, nonetheless, we conclude that even his love-affair shows his immaturity. Uma Parameswaran has a deep insight into their relationship:

> With Bharati he is always a child, sometimes petulant, sometimes wilful, sometimes pathetic, but always childish. His first meeting sets the tone for the entire relationship. At first, he is a braggart, a little boy on an adventure, immensely proud and vaulting. Then he is a pathetic little boy, feeling lost and scared on alien ground. His speech and manners are not those of a man of twenty-four but a boy of ten. His love, too, smacks of a small boy's intense calf-love.[32]

Sriram's personality lacks seriousness and depth. When informed of his Granny's death, he, instead of being grief-stricken, checks his whole trunk to find out whether everything is in order. He sobs for a while and then tells Kanni that he is hungry. Assumedly, Sriram's portrayal instead of evoking sympathy evokes repulsion. Readers develop a hatred for such a character who enquires about his Granny's last days only after satisfying his hunger.

The novel moves to an end with Gandhi's permission and blessings wishing Sriram and Bharati a happy married life. However, Gandhi cannot present himself to witness their wedding the next morning as he is shot dead by an assassin.

William Walsh notices many stages in the transformation of Sriram. We witness first his lyrical love for Bharati, then his initiation into Gandhian ideology and finally his engagement in many sorts of strenuous terrorist activities, perhaps, goaded by a strong sense of patriotic feelings. Here any sensitive reader may discover that he changes but does not grow. When we last meet him, he is well over thirty and yet he is helpless and childish as he was on our first meeting. Nothing–

Gandhi or a decade of experience or his love for a mature idealistic woman–has made him mature. He appears emotional at the very thought of going without Bharati towards the end of the novel: 'Bharati went away to jail, and there was no one who could tell me what to do'. [33] Lakshmi Holmstrom provides possible reason behind his immature presentation: 'Sriram is constantly shown in terms of other people's ideologies rather than in terms of his own self-deception and self-awareness'.[34] Rajeev Taranath's view that averageness is the positive quality of Narayan's characters also holds good for Sriram's character:

> He moves from Gandhian non-violence to terrorism under the influence of the revolutionary Jagdish, is jailed, comes out chastised and subdued and is about to marry Bharati as the novel ends. What is natural to him is a young man's love for an attractive girl. That is where he starts from and to which he returns, his other states are temporary deviations from the ordinary. [35]

Among his fifteen novels and over one hundred short stories, R. K. Narayan presents Gandhi predominantly only in his novel, *Waiting for the Mahatma.* In this novel, Gandhi actually appears in person, addresses huge gatherings and inspires people for the Quit-India movement. In *The Man-Eater of Malgudi,* we find only the echo of Gandhi's belief in non-violence. In *The Vendor of Sweets,* too we only witness this echo and miss a Gandhian canvas. In the present novel, he appears only twice–once at the beginning and again at the end of the novel. Still his extraordinary influence seems to dwarf all his associates. He instills in Harijans a sense of equality and initiates the 'Quit-India movement.' Not only this, he also inspires the picketing of foreign goods shops. Nonetheless, almost all the characters of this novel are involved in and react to Gandhi. Therefore, this novel may also be labelled as a 'Gandhian novel'. Gandhi appears both as man and God in the novel.

Gandhi was a great monumental figure all his real life, but his characterization in this novel is weak and faulty. Uma Parameswaran's analysis of Gandhi's character sounds convincing:

> It is well-known that Gandhi always used simple and lucid language that he started most public meetings with bhajan... But the way Narayan inserts them within minutes of bringing Gandhi on the scene is inartistic. Neither his language nor his organization helps to mend matters.[36]

Here is what happens at the first public meeting addressed by Gandhi:

> Then he raised his arm, and instantly a silence fell on the gathering. He clapped his hands rhythmically and said: '1 want you all to keep this up, this beating for a while.' [37]

Here the weakness of language is noticeable besides several Bourgeois Indian English phrases, for example, 'you all' and 'this beating' that Gandhi in flesh and blood always tried to avoid. Subjective responses handled by Gandhi's presence are even more poorly handled.

Contrary to Mahatma's effect on people, we may consider Raja Rao's handling of Moorthy's conversion in *Kanthapura.* In the identical circumstances, Moorthy, a university student pushes his way through the crowd, and gets a vision of Gandhi and listens to certain messages in simple monosyllabic language, having a taste of sublime music:

> Then came a dulled silence of his blood and he said to himself 'Let me listen' and he listened, and in listening heard, 'There is but one force in life and that is Truth, and there is but one love in life and that is the love of mankind, and there is but one God in life and that is the God of all,' and then came a shiver and he turned to the one behind him and said, 'Brother,' and the man took the fan from Moorthy and Moorthy trembled back... And he sat beside the platform, his head in his hands, and tears came to his eyes, and he wept softly and with weeping came peace. He stood up, and he saw there, by the legs of the chair, the sandal and the foot of Mahatma, and he said to himself, 'That is my place...'[38]

If we compare the two extracts quoted above from the two novels, we feel that 'everything that Narayan has tried and failed to convey in the novel *Wating for the Mahatma* is present in this single passage [from Kanthapura], so rich in objective.'[39] A. V. Krishna Rao is also aware of the spiritual bankruptcy of Gandhi's character:

> The historicity of the Gandhian image in Narayan's *Waiting for the Mahatma* is certainly unimpeachable, but lacks the religiosity of a literary myth like *Kanthapura.*[40]

P. S. Sundaram too visualizes Narayan's limitation in portraying Gandhi: 'He certainly has not "enlarged" that awareness in the sense of painting a picture larger than life.'[41]

Bharati is an orphan brought up by the Sevak Sangh. She herself makes a confession to this effect:

> I do whatever I am asked to do by the Sevak Sangh. Sometimes they ask me to go and teach people spinning and tell them about Mahatmaji's ideas. Sometimes they send me to villages and poor quarters. I meet them and talk to them and do a few things. I attend to Mahatmaji's needs.[42]

'This deliberate impersonality makes Bharati unreal compared to even minor characters in the novel such as Kanni, the shopkeeper or Sriram's grandmother.'[43] It is really surprising that the novelist inverts the roles of Bharati (a girl without roots and consequently, appearing unreal) and Sriram. Bharati is the guru, whereas Sriram, the unwilling disciple. We do not notice any real meeting point between them because she is totally committed to the Gandhian way of life, which does not have any place for personal emotions. Actually personal emotions matter less than her commitment to non-violence, truth and self-discipline. Her utterances are testimony to her commitment:

> I won't marry if he doesn't sanction it. I can't do it.[44]
>
> How can we do anything other than what Bapuji asked us to do?[45]
>
> You now understand why I could not talk to Mahatmaji of our own affairs. It would have been sacrilegious.[46]

Naturally, there is no communication between Sriram and Bharati. Sriram who is lovesick comes up against a rigid set of rules at every point: 'Everything that she thought or said or expected was set in grooves and hard to practise.'[47]

The novel is rich with a variety of its minor characters. There is Granny, an extrermely sensitive and orthodox woman, who is always tender and soft to Sriram. We meet Kanni, the shopkeeper and a good neighbour in the time of need. We also feel amused at the 'living portrait of the half sinister, half clownish revolutionary photographer, Jagdish, who sees himself as the chief architect of independent India, and who has assembled numerous albums of photographs to prove it.'[48] We also witness the ironic account of the doings of Mr. Natesh, the Municipal Chairman who insists on playing host to Gandhiji at his palatial house, Neel Bagh and tries hard to prove that he lives a life of a simple man and has never enjoyed the luxuries of a life. In fact, 'these are the people who are given animate and eloquent identity by Narayan,'[49] observes Uma Parameswaran.

The Guide

The Guide (first published in 1958) is the most popular of Narayan's novels in India. This novel won the Sahitya Academy award for the year 1961. The novel is unique in many ways. It has 'unity of vision and tranquility of temperament. The language is correspondingly temperate, mild in metaphor and simple in syntax and its easy action and unemphatic delivery are exactly suited to express the special quality of the feeling, an observant and unrelaxed gentleness, which Narayan displays towards his characters.'[50] Further, this novel is a special example of the clarity with which even the most difficult experiences are communicated to the Western reader.

The Guide has received appreciation from several reviewers and critics. Edgar L. Jones discovers that it 'is full of human qualities that hold true from Baltimore to Bombay, bringing India to life with rare jest and insight.'[51]Margaret Parton observes that Narayan's all other novels were 'brilliant reflections of one colour of the Indian prism. *The Guide* is the whole range.'[52]

Time holds this novel in high esteem: '*The Guide* floats as gently as a lily pad on the surface of Indian life and yet suggests the depth beneath.'[53] Robert Hoover hails the novel for its characteristic 'subtlety, humour, understatement and tacit understanding of the relationship of God and man that is associated with the people of India.'[54] He further eulogises this novel: 'It is at this point that the real quality of Mr. Narayan's writing crystalizes; humour, with pathos are all transcended to show a glimpse of the sublime.'[55] Carol Willis gives a big hand to Narayan for his 'depth of perception.'[56] John L. Mish commends it for presenting 'a delightful picture of human frailities, described with a sympathetic twinkle of the eye.'[57] Anthony West considers it 'a profound statement of Indian realities.'[58] Santha Rama Rau endorses Narayan as 'a writer with courage and mastery – enough to cope with comedy, tragedy, satire, all in the same book, and very often in the same scene...'[59] William Habich grants Narayan the status of an 'Oriental Voltaire.' [60]

Not only reviewers but also critics enjoy this novel. C. D. Narasimhaiah speaks highly of his use of comic mode in the novel:

> ...it is a rare privilege of Narayan to use the comic mode to prove the highest kind of reality in *The Guide*–it is a strength which is his and that of his own tradition. [61]

William Walsh appreciates this novel as 'the greatest of Narayan's novels.'[62] Lakshmi Holmstrom views this novel as 'a carefully worked examination of motives, explanations and performances against existing ideals.' [63]

In spite of its several merits, the novel has some weaknesses. *Los Angeles Times* strongly recommends Naravan because he is 'enjoyable to read.'[64] Nevertheless, it disapproves of the novel because 'sometimes it appears 'uneven'.[65] Arthur MacGilliuray also has reasons to dislike it:

> ...The book is a waste of time for any adult reader. Cross your finger when you hear of the charm and the delight of this author. His yawn may not be barbaric, but it is contagious. Let no plague spread.[66]

However, overall, we believe this novel is interesting and enlightening.

The Guide is the story of Raju's growth from the ordinary to the extraordinary–from a petty Railway guide to a spiritual guide. The story may be divided into two parts. Part one describes the growth of Raju as a child and a young man madly in love with an unhappy dancing girl whose interest has been ignored by her husband. This part ends with Raju's arrest. The second part records his emergence into a swami.

Raju's story is the story of his search for a meaning in life. He stumbles at times, but he is always on a pilgrimage. Raju gets a very elementary education in a school, but he gets an opportunity to increase his knowledge while dealing in old books and magazines. In due course, he starts taking interest in guiding passengers and is affectionately called 'Railway Raju'. His profession of a Railway guide changes the entire course of his life. Once while guiding passengers he comes across Marco, an archaeologist and his wife Rosie, a talented dancer. Rosie becomes his dream-girl. Raju finds excuses to be in the company of Rosie. In addition, as soon as Raju knows that Rosie's only passion for dancing has been thwarted by her husband, he takes steps to sharpen her talent. Thus, he wins her over. The intimacy grows into love. Marco deserts her because of her disloyalty. She comes back to Raju with a greater sense of freedom and in due course gains a great expertise in dancing. She gets shocked at Raju's forging of her signature. He is put behind the bars. She tries her best to help him. After his release from the jail, he is misunderstood as a holy man by the villagers and is forced to undertake the fast to bring rains. He undertakes fast with all his earnestness and finally, dies on the twelfth day of his fast. Finally, it rains after his death.

Raju's character can only be understood fully in relation to the narrative employed in the novel. We come to know him in two different ways–'one told in the third person by an unnamed and impersonal narrator in the historic present and the other in the first person, past tense, by the chief protagonist Raju himself.'[67] While Raju describes his life from his childhood to the time of his imprisonment for two years, the author describes his life after his release from the jail till the time he turns a saint and fasts unto death. The author's description uses 'flash on' and 'flash back' technique in juxtaposition. Actually, we encounter Raju in different styles in various sections. Harish Raizada rightly observes:

> In the former section we see Raju as he wishes to be seen, while in the latter as the 'uninvolved' and impersonal narrator wishes us to see him. We thus get a real and complete picture of Raju's personality.[68]

Narayan's use of this dual mode in describing Raju's character has been justified by Harish Raizada in a very convincing way:

> ...Had the author told the story in a single narrative, he would have found it difficult either to account for or to skip over the period of two years which Raju passes in the jail... Similarly, since the earlier career of Raju revolves mostly round his passion for Rosie and is thus related to his emotional life, it can be narrated more effectively by Raju himself as a protagonist-narrator. [69]

Raju gives an affectionate and unsentimental story of his childhood. He is controlled, influenced and guided by 'the gruff, gossipy father, the wary and practical mother, the irritable school master and his ferociously antiquated methods.'[70] Raju's education begins with his father's instruction:

> What a mess! You will never prosper in life if you disfigure the sacred letters of the alphabet. [71]

> If you spoil this, you will make me wild. Trace them exactly as I have written. Don't try any of your tricks on them.[72]

Raju gets his early schooling from an old schoolmaster holding class on the pyol in front of his narrow old house in Kabir Lane. Though the master's interest in the students is confined to one rupee a month and the articles they offer him, he learns to read and write before he goes Board High School.

He helps his father in selling peppermints, fruits, sweets, tobacco and betel-leaf. Later on, he is made in-charge of a newly-opened shop with more space and articles at the railway-station. It is here that the mechanization introduced in the tiny sleepy village thrills him. He leaves his school so that he can be one with the railway. He asserts:

> Don't laugh at my railway associations.The railways got into my blood very early in life... I felt at home on the railway platform, and considered the station-master and porter the best company for man, and their railway talk the most enlightened. I grew up in their midst.[73]

As a railway guide he is 'an institutional figure' [74] and, therefore, he is always ready to extend help to the needy, ignoring his own needs. He confesses: 'Anything that interested my tourists was also my interest. The question of my own preferences was secondary.'[75] We may discover an underlying connection between Raju, the guide, and Raju, the prophet. Both live for others and are 'reflections of otherness.'[76]

Raju's life takes a turn when he encounters Rosie. He sizes up the whole situation–Marco's serious preoccupation with his archaeological feat and Rosie's dissatisfaction with the way she has been made to live. He tries to seduce the love-starved Rosie who is 'the only reality in life and consciousness.'[77] He takes advantage of the emotional shock that she gets from her husband: 'You are not my wife. You are a woman who will go to bed with anyone that flatters your antics.' [78] He accommodates her in his house, trains her as a dancer and flirts with her. His involvement with Rosie makes him suffer losses in business. Consequently, he gets entangled in litigation. Even at this moment of crisis, he goes on selling her art. Her Bharat Natyam fetches him phenomenal wealth. When she feels that she is being exploited, she turns into a rebel. In the Raju-Rosie relationship, Rosie appears more sincere than Raju. Rosie does not forsake Raju even in his rainy days whereas Raju stoops very low to tell Mani: 'Be careful... Beware of the snake-woman.'[79] Further, he does not feel comfortable with her giving programme without his help.

On his release from jail, he is seriously concerned about his future. His previous habit of involving himself in other people's affair works wonders. He is elevated to the stature of the saint. He talks only wisdom:

> If you show me a person without a problem, then I'll show you the perfect world ...[80]
>
> What must happen must happen; no power on earth or in heaven can change its course ...[81]

Raju's choice of playing the role of a swami is persuaded by his immediate needs. As a swami, he may earn not only bread and shelter but also people's respect. To fit in the changed role he grows his hair and long beard and wears a necklace of prayer beads. He befools the villagers with the help of the knowledge gained in his second hand bookshop. He deceives them even when the rain fails: 'It must have been bitten by a poisonous insect.'[82] However, his trick does not mitigate people's miseries. Cattle die; prices go up; loot and violence increase and the village turns into a battlefield. He anticipates the interference of police. He, therefore, tells a cattle grazer: 'Tell your brother immediately, wherever he may, that unless they are good I'll never eat.' [83] The fellow passes on the distorted version to the Mangal folk: 'The Swami, the Swami, does not want food any more... because... it does not rain.'[84] People feel delighted and grateful to the Swami. When asked to fast he confesses his whole past to Velan to escape the fast, but even his confession does not bear any fruit. Finally, he resolves, 'If by avoiding food I should help the trees bloom, and the grass grow, why not do it thoroughly?'[85] Here on the surface we may notice Raju's transformation could be considered valid only if Raju's decision had been prompted by compassionate understanding or grateful benevolence.'[86] Raju's interview with Malone also exposes his true character. He confides in Malone that he will break his fast on the 'twelfth day.'[87] In case of a genuine fast he might have said that he would continue till this village is blessed with rain.

A proper evaluation of Raju's personality is not possible without making an accurate analysis of his relationship with different persons, especially with Rosie. To William Walsh, Raju-Rosie relationship 'appears to be... one of feelings than sensuality, a temperamental rather than a passionate union.'[88] Here Walsh does not sound just because their relationship is sensual and passionate one. They share a rich repast of hugging, embracing and lovemaking. O. P. Saxena disagrees with William Walsh:

> There is nothing genuinely inspiring or ennobling in their love relationship. It is an affair of illicit relationship between the two. The relationship is carried on with the ever present consciousness of guilt on Rosie's part.[89]

Really, she has always a feeling of betraying her husband, but her betrayal stems from her helplessness. She gets the warmth of companionship from Raju. At the very beginning, he notices the difference between Rosie and Marco. 'Anything that interested her seemed to irritate him.'[90] Moreover Marco's excessive engagement with his research and his indifference to her needs and taste make him courageous enough to make amorous advances towards Rosie. Repeatedly he makes a loving and eulogistic speech just to cheer her up:

> The way you danced, your form and figure haunted me all night.[91]
> You may come out as you are and no one will mind it... who would decorate a rainbow? [92]
> ...Life is so blank without your presence.[93]

She gets all the essentials of life from Raju–love, attention, freedom and guidance. The relationship soon develops into touches and whispers and it finally leads to lovemaking. O. P. Saxena rightly evaluates their relationship: 'Here is a union of two self-seekers and no genuine devotion is possible between them.'[94] However, the moment her physical passion loses its charm, she becomes conscious of sinning against her husband.

When Raju's all efforts fails to draw her attention, he instils in her a deep interest in dance to drive away the husband from her thoughts. He talks of the success of his plan: ... It gave us a fresh intimacy. This common interest brought us 'close together.'[95] Her love for Raju is restored. For the first time she gets a freedom to dance in an esstatic mood. On being disowned by her husband, she gets more opportunities to enjoy Raju's company. Raju also goes on squeezing maximum money out of her programme. He does so because earning more and more money is part of his philosophy. He asserts, 'If I were less prosperous, who would care for me?' [96] On the other hand, Rosie grows tired of this robotlike existence. She stops giving stage performances.

It sounds ironical that Raju misconceives her even after such a long association. Perhaps he is guided by his own urgencies. He hides

The Cultural History of South India from Rosie just to keep her ignorant of Marco's merit. He forges Rosie's signature to grab her ornaments. Naturally, Rosie is shocked at Raju's steps and defends Marco. In fact, 'Raju's unworthiness and Rosie's adventure cannot be welded into harmony or unity by force of argument. They both vascillate, in different ways, from their indulgence in love: money and social status are what Raju is after, and for Rosie, the perfection in her art... above all other things.'[97] O. P. Saxena, however, explores certain points of contact between the two:

> Both Raju and Rosie discard the traditional etiquette and moral values. Both disturb family life due to foolish physical passion...Their relationship comes to a tragic end: Raju goes to jail and Rosie has uncertain days ahead. They are ultimately redeemed in different ways. For a man like Raju sacrifice resulting in death is the only possible redemption, and although he "reluctantly assumes the role of a martyr," yet he does it rightly and with full application, Rosie's achievement of perfection in Bharat-Natyam is the redeeming factor in her case. [98]

Raju as a prisoner is perfectly happy in jail. He responds enthusiastically to the various demands made by his fellow prisoners. He turns into a guide of the prisoners and a friend of the Warden. On being released from the jail, he lands himself in a neglected temple and slowly picks up the style of a saint. It is interesting to note 'how the outer fit becomes an inner one, how the manner turns into the identity.'[99] (Whatever he utters becomes profound and important. Wisdom wells out from the depth of his being. Slowly, he goes deeper into the lives and problems of villagers. 'He counsels on marriages, arranges schooling for the children, resolves feuds, gives spiritual guidance, medical treatment and practical advice.'[100] His habit of counselling makes him suffer too. William Walsh finds his own nature responsible for his suffering:

> ...His own nature is the most positive of the several influences – the drought, the plight of the people, the context of tradition and religion which force him into his predicaments.[101]
>
> He acts too fast, but surprisingly after some time his acting becomes his deed; 'the inner pattern and the outer events flow together.'[102]

Raju associates himself so much with the dreams and aspirations of the common folk that he considers his death a triumph of what the commoners expect from one who is uncommon. Really, he dies 'to preserve the cherished hopes of the ordinary man in the extraordinary myth that he was to them.'[103]

Thus, Raju passes through different phases of his life–from a stall keeper to a guide and from a guide to Mr. Know-It-All. Sundaram finds 'a curious evolution–stall keeper, guide, lover, dance manager, convict, Mahatma–but one thing naturally out of another, and there is not a single false note anywhere.'[104] Rajeev Taranath goes deeper and he rightly asserts that Raju's career 'follows the familiar pattern of anonymity to glory followed by deflation.'[105] Really, he begins his career as a railway guide, moves on to become Rosie's guide, but suddenly he is reduced to the level of a prisoner. In fact, the average and the extraordinary are 'diametrically co-existent'[106] in Raju, observes Rajeev Taranath. Taranath's point may be illustrated by Raju's different reactions to his undertaking the fast. His one self revolts against the proposal whereas his other self accepts it because of the people's immense faith in him. C. N. Srinath also notices Raju's paradoxical character:

> As a guide, he can speak eloquently about a water fall or a temple or a hill top, though is not really interested in it; he speaks like a connoisseur of dancing, shows a sensitive appreciation of Rosie's art and does everything to promote her, but turns out to be a mercenary manager who craves only for fame.[107]

Raju has been compared to and contrasted with several other characters drawn by R. K. Narayan and other creative writers. C.N. Srinath finds a great resemblance between Raju and Ramaswamy in *The Serpent and the Rope:*

> The growth of self-knowledge in Raju, interestingly enough comes mainly through Rosie... Similarly, though on a different plane, Ramaswami... needs Savitri for his self-knowledge for she represents essential Indian womanhood. [108]

D. V. K. Raghavacharyulu discovers a striking difference between Raju and V. S. Naipaul's Biswas. According to him, Raju 'fulfills his will to live even if that should involve self-mortification, and eventually death,'[109] but the tale of Mr. Biswas is a 'suffocating tale of an unfinished man, whose history is one of might have beens.'[110] A deeper analysis reveals that the difference between these two characters lies in the attitudinal and artistic differences between the two writers:

> Narayan proceeds from the assurance of a stable society... Naipaul, on the contrary, is dealing with an unstable, mutable and unframed society, which is more a process in the making than a settled system of values and traditions. [111]

We cannot do justice to Raju unless we make a thorough analysis of Rosie's character. Rosie introduces herself:

> I belong to a family traditionally dedicated to the temples as dancers; my mother, grandmother, and before her, her mother. Even as a young girl, I danced in our village temple.[112]

Naturally, she is viewed as a 'public woman,' though she holds a master degree holder in Economics. By chance she is wedded to Marco, a rich and scholarly person, Marco does not approve of her traditional merit in art. So she sacrifices it for the stability and prosperity of the family, but her artistic urge continues. Raju exploits her passion for art and develops good terms with her. Consequently, Macro deserts her. She is driven into the company of Raju. Now she enjoys more freedom and greater opportunity to sharpen her artistic talent. Later on when she is fed-up with stage performances and Raju's insatiable lust for money, she grows indifferent toward Raju. Raju's criminal forgery shocks her, but she tries her best to save him from imprisonment.

A. V. Krishna Rao has successfully presented her character as a lover of art in relation to some other characters:

> Narayan's delineation of Rosie's character can probably be compared with Vimla Raina's portrayal of 'Raj Nartaki' or the Court Dancer in Ambapali..., who finally embraces Buddhism, ordained by the great Buddha Himself. This is more than a mere parallel because Rosie belongs to the same tradition of Devadasis, dedicated to the worship of God. Ambpali's renunciation of the palatial aristocracy by following the Buddhistic path of virtue, and Rosie's final retirement to Madras in order to rededicate herself to the practice and propagation of the Art of Bharat Natya, the traditional classical dance form are born out of the same spiritual motivation,...[113]

Throughout her appearance in the novel 'there is a continual polarity and conflict within Rosie/Nalini: the tension between the life of passion and the need for respectability represented by her own family of dancers and her husband Marco.'[114] Her liking for snake dance is also a reflection of her psyche. As a 'snake' is characterized by passion and dance, Rosie has been described as an embodiment of passion and an admirer of art.

A uniqueness with Rosie is that she has been spared from ironic handling. Probably the reason is that she is an educated woman and Narayan sticks to the traditional Hindu Code of Conduct. She deviates, but always with a sense of guilt. C. D. Narasimhaiah seems to err while commenting on her character:

> ...She has always been dignified, noble and the wary picture of ideal womanhood in spite of her loss of chastity.[115]

The above statement about Rosie is self-contradictory. Can a woman claim to maintain her nobility and dignity even after her loss of chastity, especially in the Indian context?

Our knowledge of Rosie is limited. We know about her through Raju. Rosie's feelings and sentiments have not been given free expression. Thus, the total impression of her character remains vague. At best, she remains 'a shadow of shadow.' Nirmal Mukherji also asserts that she should be drawn in a more lively way: 'The circumstances under which Raju's mother has to leave her own ancestral house have hardly any effect on Rosie. She acts like a machine, a dancing machine.'[116] Really, she appears pale and weak when compared with Sushila and Bharati. 'She is tender, beautiful and artistic, but still she hardly comes to life.'[117]

Marco, the research scholar, has been constructed around a single idea–his engagement with writing a book on the ancient culture of South India. His marriage with Rosie is on the rocks. 'Perhaps he married out of a desire to have someone care for his practical life, but unfortunately his choice was wrong–this girl herself was a dreamer if ever there was one.'[118] As Marco neglects his wife, she gets drawn towards Raju, and the relationship matures. Marco gets suspicious of their relationship and, therefore, forsakes her. His treatment of Rosie convinces us that he is heartless, inhuman, selfish and devoid of any sympathy and good feelings. However, he is inconsistent in his behaviour. Marco who forsakes Rosie, is also highly concerned about the delivery of ornaments to her. Nirmal Mukherji has thought about Marco's contradictory behaviour patterns:

> The technique of the novel is such that he is directly controlled by Raju, the narrator of the story. The facts are likely to be distorted in such a narration. It is... possible that Raju is bringing out only those facts which are favourable to him and concealing others.[119]

Thus, Narayan's characters may have some limitations, but the portrayal of those characters in different life-roles produces various patterns of human relationships.

REFERENCES

Waiting for the Mahatma

1. William Walsh, *R. K. Narayan: A Critical Appreciation,* pp. 91-92.
2. *Ibid.*
3. A. V. Krishna Rao, *The Indo-Anglian Novel and the Changing Tradition, p.* 88.
4. *Ibid.*
5. 'R. K. Narayan and the East-West Theme,' p. 227.
6. *Ibid.,* p. 223.
7. C. D. Narasimhiah, *The Swan and the Eagle* (Simla, 1969), p. 123.
8. *My Dateless Diary,* p. 123.
9. Uma Parameswaran, *A Study of Representative Indo-English Novelists,* p. 45.
10. *Ibid.,* p. 65.
11. *A Study of Representative Indo-English Novelists,* p. 63.
12. *Ibid.,* p. 66.
13. Lakshmi Holmstrom, *The Novels of R. K. Narayan,* p. 59.
14. Susan Ram, '50 Years of Story Telling,' *The Telegraph,* 11 May 1986, p. 7.
15. Krishna Uttam, 'Interview with R. K. Narayan,' *The Deccan Herald,* 29 June 1980, p. 6.
16. H.A.L. Fisher, *The Political Novel* (Norman, 1966), p. 4.
17. Joseph L. Blotner, *The Political Novel* (New York, 1955), p. 19.
18. Irving Howe, *Politics and the Novel* (New York, 1957), p. 19.
19. M. K. Naik, *The Ironic Vision,* p. 38.
20. *Waiting for the Mahatma* (Mysore, 1971), p. 4.
21. William Walsh, *R. K. Narayan: A Critical Spectrum* (New Delhi, 1983). p. 88.

22. *A Study of Representative Indo-English Novelists,* p. 69.
23. *Waiting for the Mahatma,* p. 43.
24. *Waiting for the Mahatma,* p. 18.
25. *Waiting for the Mahatma,* p. 19-20.
26. *Waiting for the Mahatma,* p. 59.
27. *Waiting for the Mahatma,* p. 62.
28. *Waiting for the Mahatma,* p. 73.
29. *A Study of Representative Indo-English Novelists,* p. 69.
30. *Waiting for the Mahatma,* p.76.
31. *Waiting for the Mahatma,* p. 109.
32. *A Study of Representative Indo-English Novelists,* p. 71.
33. *Waiting for the Mahatma,* p. 171.
34. *The Novels of R. K. Narayan,* p. 61.
35. M. K. Naik, S. K. Desai and G. S. Amur (eds.), *Critical Essays on Indian Writings in English* (Dharwar, 1972), p. 297.
36. *A Study of Representative Indo-English Novelists,* p. 66.
37. *Waiting for the Mahatma,* p. 16.
38. Raja Rao, *Kanthapura* (New York, 1963), p. 33.
39. *A Study of the Representative Indo-English Novelist,* p. 68.
40. *The Indo-Anglian Novel and the Changing Tradition,* p. 88.
41. R. K. *Narayan,* p. 88.
42. *Waiting for the Mahatma,* p. 39.
43. *The Novels of R. K. Narayan,* p. 59.
44. *Waiting for the Mahatma,* p. 91.
45. *Waiting for the Mahatma,* p. 93.
46. *Waiting for the Mahatma,* p. 167.
47. *Waiting for the Mahatma,* p. 136.
48. R. K. *Narayan,* p. 91.
49. *A Study of Representative Indo-English Novelists,* p. 74.

The Guide

50. R. K. *Narayan: A Critical Spectrum,* p. 114. .

51. Edgar L. Jones, 'Delightful Humbug,' *Baltimore Sun,* 16 March, 1958, Sec. A, p. 6.
52. Margaret Parton, 'Rare, Fine Tales from India,' *New York Herald Tribune Book Review,* 16 March, 1958, p. 5.
53. 'The Reluctant Swami,' *Time,* 24 March, 1958, p. 116.
54. Robert Hoover, 'Humour and Substance in a Novel,' *Columbus Despatch,* 6 April, 1958, p. 12.
55. *Ibid.*
56. Carol Willis, 'Glimpse of Life in India Proves Odd, Fascinating.' *Buffalo Evening News,* 12 April, 1958, Sec. II, p. 10.
57. John L. Mish, 'Review' *Library Journal,* 83, 15 April, 1958, p. 1230.
58. Anthony West, 'Books,' *New Yorker,* 34 (19 April, 1958), p. 145.
59. Santha Rama Rau, 'Man with Answers,' *Saturday Review of Literature,* 41 (3 May, 1958), p. 21.
60. William Habich, 'A Comic Novel from India,' *Louisville Courier.*
61. C. D. Narasimhaiah, *The Swan and the Eagle,* (Simla, 1969), p. 148.
62. R. K. *Narayan: A Critical Spectrum*, p. 21.
63. Lakshmi Holmstrom, *The Novels of* R. K. *Narayan* (Calcutta, 1973), p. 68.
64. 'Hero of Indian Novel "Reluctant" Holy Man,' *Los Angeles Times,* 10 August, 1958.
65. *Ibid.*
66. Arthur Mac Gilliuray, 'Review,' *Best Sellers,* 18 (1 April 1958), p. 6.
67. Harish Raizada in *Perspectives on* R. K. *Narayan,* ed. Atma Ram (Ghaziabad, 1981), p. 83.
68. *Ibid.*
69. *Ibid.*
70. R. K. *Narayan: A Critical Spectrum*, p. 113.
71. R. K. Narayan, *The Guide* (Mysore, 1983), p. 12.
72. *Ibid.*
73. *The Guide*, p. 10.
74. R. K, *Narayan: A Critical Appreciation,* p, 121.
75. *The Guide*, p. 57.
76. R. K. *Narayan: A Critical Appreciation,* p. 121.

77. *The Guide,* p. 104.
78. *The Guide,* p. 134,
79. *The Guide,* p. 199.
80. *The Guide,* p. 14.
81. *The Guide,* p. 20.
82. *The Guide,* p. 83.
83. *The Guide,* p. 87.
84. *The Guide,* p. 89.
85. *The Guide,* p. 213.
86. *Perspectives on* R. K. *Narayan,* p. 134.
87. *The Guide,* p. 218.
88. R. K. *Narayan: A Critical Appreciation,* p. 123.
89. O. P. Saxena, *Glimpses of Indo-English Fiction,* Vol. III (New Delhi, 1985), p. 46.
90. *Ibid.,* p. 49.
91. *The Guide,* p. 64.
92. *Ibid.*
93. *The Guide,* p. 65.
94. *Glimpses of Indo-English Fiction,* p. 47.
95. *The Guide,* p. 109.
96. *The Guide,* p. 174.
97. *Glimpses of Indo-English Fiction,* p. 47.
98. *Ibid.,* pp. 54-55.
99. R. K. *Narayan: A Critical Appreciation,* p. 127.
100. *Ibid.,* p. 128.
101. *Ibid.*
102. *Ibid.,* p. 129.
103. Rajeev Taranath in *Critical Essays on Indian Writings in English,* eds. M. K. Naik, G. S. Amur and S. K. Desai (Dharwar, 1972), p. 303.
104. P. S. Sundaram, R. K. *Narayan* (New Delhi, 1973), p. 91.
105. *Critical Essays on Indian Writings in English,* p. 298.
106. *Ibid.,* p 299.

107. C. N. Srinath, *The Interior Landscape: Essays on Indian Fiction and Poetry*, A Dhyanaloka Publication, 1982, p. 6.

108. *Ibid.*

109. D. V. K. Raghavacharyulu, *The Critical Response* (New Delhi, 1980), p. 122.

110. *Ibid.*

111. *Ibid*, p. *123*.

112. *The Guide*, p. *75*.

113. A. V. Krishna Rao, *The Indo-Anglian Novel and the Changing Tradition* (Mysore, 1972) pp. *89-90*.

114. *Perspectives on* R. K. *Narayan*, p. 69.

115. *The Swan and the Eagle*, p. 148.

116. Nirmal Mukherji, *The World of Malgudi: A Study of the Novels of* R. K. *Narayan*, an unpublished doctoral dissertation (Louisiana State Univ., 1960), p. 95.

117. *Ibid.*

118. *The Guide*, p. 100.

119. *The World of Malgudi: A Study of the Novels of* R. K. *Narayan*, p. 90.

6

ETERNAL STRUGGLE BETWEEN THE GOOD AND THE EVIL: THE MAN-EATER OF MALGUDI AND THE VENDOR OF SWEETS

> It's not that good does not triumph over
> eveil; it's that the point spread is too narrow.
>
> —Bob Thaves

THE MAN-EATER OF MALGUDI

The Man-Eater of Malgudi belongs to that group of Narayan's novels which shows the expanding horizon of his objective experience. It was published in 1961. The theme of the novel is based on a Hindu mythology. Regarding the choice of theme Narayan remarks:

> ...Some years ago I suddenly came across a theme which struck me as an excellent piece of mythology in modern dress. It was published under the title *The Man-Eater of Malgudi*... I based this story on a well-known mythological episode, the story of Mohini and Bhasmasura.[1]

In this novel Vasu, the embodiment of Bhasmasura, dies in the same manner in which Bhasmasura dies.

Most of the critics and reviewers accorded appreciation to the novel. Only some scholars have condemned it. According to P. S. Sundaram this novel is 'Narayan's greatest work.'[2] M. K. Naik considers it 'one of the masterpieces of Narayan's novels.'[3] He also appreciates the novel on ethical grounds:

> *The Man-Eater of Malgudi* is the impressive fictional statement dealing with ethical issues such as the fate of evil and the question of human relationships, and the precepts and practice of the entire business of living.[4]

K. R. S. Iyengar confirms that the novel 'jumbles the ingredients of comedy to excellent purposes and provides ample entertainment.'[5] Harish Raizada finds Narayan's comic vision 'unmingled with pathos or tragedy.'[6] A. V. Krishna Rao observes that the novel is 'an apocalyptic vision of India.'[7] and 'an allegorical representation of the problem of evil, self consuming when confronted with the divinity immanent in Man and Nature.'[8] V. Panduranga Rao finds it an indicator of 'a fair measure of the maturity of Narayan's art.'[9] He also endorses it because of its relevance to our time:

> The novel is a myth. It is the fight against all the laws of nature. But the end of the novel demonstrates the triumph of Nature. The fight is typically modern, hence the relevance of the novel to the modern times.[10]

Reviewers also give credit to the book. Maurice Dolbier eulogizes Narayan for his 'swift, artful, ingratiatingly individual manner of telling it.'[11] In the opinion of Rosanne Archer it is 'an occasion of rejoicing.'[12] L. Wheildon hails it as 'the best in a wonderful series.'[13] Alan Price-Jones finds the book to be showing India 'through sharp but affectionate eyes.'[14] Ved Mehta prizes this novel for imbibing Indian spirit to the core:

> The India Mr. Narayan deals with is of ages and sages. It overflows until all her people in whatever occupation, are engulfed in the novelist's ink.[15]

Narayan's sense of humour is highly appreciated by critics and reviewers. Charles Poore considers *The Man-Eater of Malgudi* 'a splendid humorous novel.'[16] Charles W. Mann calls him 'Kafka with humour.'[17] Collier Ford finds the novel 'rich with a story of quiet humour and soft laughter.'[18]

The novel has not only earned laurels from several quarters, but has also received condemnation from a selected few. For instance, Mary McGregory feels that in the last analysis the novel seems 'merely trifling.'[19] Leon Bell Bagai finds it ' a whimsical Hindu Whodunit.'[20] Lakshmi Holmstrom places it ' closer to fantasy.'[21]

N. Mukherji observes the author 'merely repeating himself particularly in drawing Nataraj's character.'[22] Of course, these depreciations throw some light on the grey aspects of the novel. Besides, sometimes the critics take the extreme view while making judgement on a book, Alfred P. Klouder seems to be balanced in his judgement:

> ...*The Man-Eater of Malgudi* is to be recommended to all who are not yet acquainted with this sparkling, truly gifted Indian novelist. Herein is humour, even uproarious fun... chances are, once you start the novel you won't want to lay it down, and once you have laid it down you will want to find some more Narayan novels.[23]

This novel has some specialities. First, this novel indicates 'a fair measure of the maturity of Narayan's art' [24] because with the publication of this novel Narayan completed more than twenty five years of creative work. Secondly, here 'a character controls action with an emphasis more pressing than before.'[25] Thirdly, it has a well-knit plot and is very compact in form. It makes little allowance for digression. And finally, in this novel, the cycle of events is caused, not by the main character's attachment to love or money, but because Vasu attaches himself to Malgudi.[26]

The novel tells the story of Vasu's demonic feats. His one such feat is the appropriation of the attic above the press. He remains busy with shooting of wild animals and stuffs them in his room. *Radhakalyan,* a masterpiece written by Nataraj's friend, is to be dedicated during the annual festival at the Krishna temple in Malgudi. An elephant is also hired for this occasion. Vasu plans to shoot this elephant. Nataraj and his friends request Vasu not to do it, but Vasu turns down their request. However, the procession passes by safely. The next morning Vasu is found dead. Later on, we come to know that he dies at his own hands while trapping a mosquito on his forhead.

The novel has two important characters–Nataraj and Vasu. Vasu, a taxidermist, is the incarnation of evil while Nataraj, the printer, upholds the values of a cherished tradition and culture. We find a perpetual fight between good and evil. Finally, evil is defeated. Thus, the herohood goes to Nataraj. Further, all the events of the novel have been seen through the eyes of Nataraj. Moreover, the novel is not so much the story of Vasu as of Nataraj.

Nataraj, like Srinivas in *Mr. Sampath,* is the narrator agent in the novel. As he is out and out a traditionalist, he continues the tradition of his ancient house in the Kabir Street in Malgudi. His printing press on the Market Road is a paradise for his well-meaning friends like Sen, a journalist and a fiery critic of Nehru, and a poet, a modest and inoffensive man, at present engaged in writing a biography of Lord Krishna in monosyllables. He is privileged to have Shastri as his assistant who is a semi-scholar in Sanskrit and has an encyclopaedic knowledge of mythology and legends. Nataraj totally depends on Shastri for the printing work. However, in the presence of a customer he shouts for his foreman, his compositor, his office boy or his binder, but in fact, he has only one staff–the respectable old man, Mr. Shastri. Mr. Shastri helps him to set up the type, print the forms, sew the sheets and carry them away for binding. In the hours of crisis, he proves to be a very good counsellor. It is Mr. Shastri who first informs him of Vasu's demonic qualities and exposes him as a womanizer. Later on, Shastri also solves the mystery of his death.

Nataraj lives at home with his wife and little son. His house reminds us of a traditional extended family. Even the description of his family estate renders it into 'a comic geneology implying the continuity rather than the abrogation of tradition and inheritance, beyond the perquisites'[27]:

> A rotten easy chair on which my grandfather used to lie in the courtyard, watching the sky, was claimed by my second uncle whose wife had started all the furore over the property. She also claimed a pair of rosewood benches which shone with a natural polish, and a timber wooden chair that used to be known as the bug-proof chair. My father's third brother, as a compensation for letting these items go, claimed a wooden almirah as his own and a 'leg' harmonium operated by a pedal…[28]

Here the bizarre history of the furniture may appear a lively comedy, but there is a historical sense underlying it. The whole picture refers to the dynastic continuity. D. V. K. Raghavacharyulu effectively contrasts Nataraj's family estate with Biswas (a character in *A House for Mr. Biswas* by V. S. Naipaul):

> Naipaul's household affects spell out dissolution, displacement and the withering away of personality. Hence, the Biswas children have no identification with them; they recall no usable, living past which can be meaningfully integrated into their present. Their inheritance hurts them with a sense of lethal dispossessions and disinheritance.[29]

Nataraj's wife also keeps the old family tradition by keeping a well stocked pantry and the kitchen fire aglow. Young Babu attends to the school and is adequately supplied with toys, sweets and books. Nataraj has enough money to buy his wife a glittering sari on some special occasion. He owes all this to Goddess Laxmi. Therefore, he has hung a framed picture of the goddess in the little room in front of his press. There is a big Star Press adjacent to his press. Naturally, customers doubt whether Nataraj himself owns it or the Star Press owns his establishments. The room in front of his press is used as a club where all sorts of people are received warmly. Even the sanitary inspector drops in for rest when he is tired of too much supervision of the Market Road.

William Walsh makes a conclusive remark about Narayan's character: 'Character is action and action is plot, and it is by means of the action of his character that Narayan summons up the world in which he lives.'[30] Nataraj is not an exception to the above view. His friendliness is confirmed by his meetings with the milkman, the old asthma patient at the end of the street, the watchman at the Taluk office. Further, Nataraj's meeting with the Adjournment Lawyer and the talking septuagenarian creates the background of the novel. Nataraj is unambitious and peaceloving. He does not dream of becoming a rich man. He is happy in his own world–'the world composed of shades and subtleties, of relationships, of tradition, of feeling, of ancient hollowed objects transmitted to the generations, of modes, of conduct and habit of thought which were both realistic and homely... .'[31]

Nataraj's daily life consists of a quiet and ordinary personal routine, mild business activity and some exchanges on poetry and politics with his friends. This very physical limit reveals 'his culled and finicky task.'[32] He establishes a little sitting room opposite his shop where friends, possible customers and weary passers-by are most welcome. Here Nataraj appears as an urbane social being, and an obliging but astute businessperson. His printing press lies beyond this parlour cut off by a blue curtain. This blue curtain reminds one of his right to privacy and also brings a certain amount of desirable ambiguity in connection with the operation of the press. Nataraj's society has such observable norms that none has dared to pierce the curtain so far, but his cool pattern of living is disturbed by the intrusion of Vasu in his life-scheme. It is Vasu who first sweeps his curtain aside only to state his purpose.

Slowly he thrusts his intimacy upon Nataraj to such an extent that he unconditionally occupies his attic. He uses this place to clean and stuff the animals killed in the Mempi forest. He exports his handiwork all over the world. Nataraj's orthodox Hindu soul is simply outraged to witness all this. However, he greatly admires Vasu's physical strength and his uncompromising scientific-mind in the face of which any appeal to sentiment and taste is useless.[33]

Nataraj continues to feel restless because of Vasu's bloodthirsty habits of killing innocent animals. He cannot swallow his philosophy of killing inadvertently because of his different type of upbringing: 'I had been brought up in a house where we were taught never to kill.' [34] Thus, a person like Nataraj simply gets appalled at the idea of giving such a monster shelter under his room, but he does not dare to oust him. He fears 'he might do anything–bellow at me, or laugh scornfully, or rattle my bones. I felt dwarfed and tongue-tied before him.'[35] Supposedly, it appears incredible that Nataraj gives so long a rope to Vasu. How is it that he simply does not get him out when he proves such a nuisance not only to Nataraj but also to the entire neighbourhood? P. S. Sundaram tries to satisfy this doubt:

> ...I can think of dozens of people like Nataraj who... hope that somehow someone will come to their rescue, "what can we do against a rakshasa?" they say, "God will have to deal with him..." [36]

Really, God deals with Vasu. He causes the death of that very Vasu, the *pahelwan* who can splinter a wooden panel three inches thick with his bare hand. Vasu driven to madness by a mosquito hits out against it bringing down his enormous strength on his head and thus, he dies of the impact.

Nataraj does not fight against Vasu because he believes that violence only begets violence. Even an angry word, an authoritarian manner leads to counter-attack and conflict. Nataraj himself proclaims: 'Aggressive words only generate more aggressive words.'[37] Though Nataraj believes in the philosophy of non-violence, he gets fed up with the neighbours' complaints about the stench coming out of his attic. He, thereupon, proposes him to take another shelter. This leads to a fresh trouble with Vasu. The latter files a suit to the rent controller. Nataraj simply shivers at the names of courts and lawyers. This fear crosses its limit after he receives summons from the rent controller:

> ...even the sound of his [Vasu's] footstep seemed to me aggressively tenant-like, strengthened by the laws of the rent-control court. He pretended that I did not exist. He seemed to arrive and depart with a swagger as if to say, 'you may have got an adjournment now, but the noose is being ready for you.' [38]

Nataraj may be timid but he has several humane qualities. For instance, he is so 'self-effacing and altruistic that he must always volunteer to do things for others with considerable inconvenience to himself, and make promises in good faith that he is sometimes unable to fulfil.'[39] He bleeds and cries at others' suffering. When the septuagenarian complains that his grandson's dog has been shot dead by someone, he at once promises to bring him a beautiful black dog. Though finally he comes to realize that he 'had promised in a moment of emotional stress, and now in the cold light of day it appeared to me an unreal impossible task.'[40] Again on the crucial day of procession, he undertakes to do all kinds of job undermining his limitations. M. K. Naik discovers the similar self-effacement in the heroine in Chekov's well-known story *The Darling:*

> She gets completely absorbed in the life and ways of the man she marries, and when she dies, her absorption in those of the next important persons in her life is equally complete.[41]

In the opinion of M. K. Naik, Nataraj's 'excessive altruism is perhaps the result of an extreme congenital timidity and weakness in Nataraj.'[42] He himself admits frankly: 'The trouble with me was that I was not able to say 'no' to anyone and that got me into complications with everyone.'[43] Had he denied Vasu's proposal to stay in the attic, he would not have fallen into endless troubles. Moreover, his timidity also makes him conjure up visions of possible dangers. For instance, when he receives the court summons he feels: 'Tomorrow, I shall probably be led off straight from the court to the jail.'[44] He also visualizes that his wife and child must visit him on permissible days in the jail. His habit of daydreaming can also be associated with his timidity. Perhaps it gives him an escape from the humdrum and ignoble reality of the daily life and it also compensates for his inborn timidity. His very first meeting with Rangi lets his 'mind slide into a wild fantasy of seduction and passion.'[45] He feels:

> I was no longer a married man with a child and home. I was an adolescent lost in dreams over a nude photograph.[46]

His quality of daydreaming is also unique after he faints in the crowd: 'There was not a single person in that whole throng who could organise and guide a procession as I could. I swelled with pride. I was the one man who could still achieve results.'[47] B. Parvathi is also convinced that 'an important feature about his [Narayan's] major characters is their free flight into the past and future as well, in times of stress.'[48] She further elaborates:

> Nataraj under tension and stress escapes from the harsh reality of the present through fantasising over the grim possibilities.[49]

Nataraj is not only a daydreamer but also a fickle-minded person. He is at once attracted and repulsed by Vasu:

> ...He was a terrible specimen of human being no doubt, but I wanted to be on talking terms with him.[50]

He also admits:

> I couldn't say that I liked him or approved of anything he said or did, but I didn't want to be repulsed by him ...[51]
> I admired him for his capacity for work, for all the dreadful things he was able to accomplish single-handed.[52]

The novel is full of such dialectics. Nataraj is, no doubt, timid and fickle, but he survives all the trials and tribulations because of his complete faith in tradition and values. He gets inspiration from a Puranic story about the gifted elephant who survives the greatest trouble:

> ...the elephant Gajendra... who stepped into a lake and had his leg caught in the jaw of a mighty crocodile; and the elephant trumpeted helplessly, struggled, and in the end desperately called on Vishnu, who immediately appeared and gave him the strength to come ashore out of the jaws of the crocodile.[53]

Here we definitely find a parallelism between the elephant and Nataraj. As the elephant has been saved by Lord Vishnu, Nataraj regains his lost peace by the grace of the values he cherishes.

In the considered opinion of Rajeev Taranath, Nataraj confirms the usual pattern of the main character–'from the average to the extraordinary and back again to a more poignant state of the average.'[54] Really Nataraj's usual tranquil life undergoes shocking experiences but finally regains normalcy. K. R. S. Iyengar shares Taranath's view: 'In novels, there is generally a flight, an uprooting, a disturbance of order– followed by a return, a renewal, a restoration of normalcy.'[55] Certainly, the novel begins where it ends. In the beginning, we witness Nataraj printing coloured labels for K. J. and it closes with Nataraj's again concentrating on K. J.'s work.

Nataraj may be contrasted with Vasu for having two diametrically opposed attitudes to life. 'It is a contrast between the demonical, self-centred egotism of Vasu and the ineffectual altruism of Nataraj, between the temerity of Vasu and the timidity of Nataraj.'[56] M. K. Naik rightly elaborates: 'For Vasu everything in the external world must subserve his own interests. Nataraj's altruism is as extreme as Vasu's egotism. It makes him most unworldly and unbusiness-like in his own profession.'[57] The second difference between them lies in their different relationships to animal kingdom. While Nataraj had been brought up in the family where killing even a fly or an ant was considered a sin, Vasu takes delight in killing birds and animals. H. M. Williams establishes an enlightening contrast between Mr. Sampath, the printer and Mr. Nataraj:

> Lacking Sampath's furious energy, greed, ambition, amorousness and inordinate vanity, he [Nataraj] is content to be the unofficial chairman and host of the Malgudi literary and political bohemia. A quiet man and dreamer, steeped in the life of Malgudi, shaped and stamped by his family and ancestry, totally unlike the rootless cosmopolitan Sampath, he is inclined strongly to non-violence...[58]

Vasu is the polar opposite counterpart of Nataraj. He is the most alarming and violent of all Narayan's characters. His character has been brilliantly created. He bursts upon the peaceful little world of the printer and his friends–with all the sudden fury of a man-eating tiger. He first appears in the second chapter. He bursts into Nataraj's press while Nataraj is busy preparing soft-drink labels. His visit has been first noticed by the poet. He first sees his head as if detached from his body and describes it pictorially giving a symbolic presence of ogre: 'a tanned face, large powerful eyes under thick eyebrows, a large forehead and stock of unkempt hair, like a black halo.'[59] The 'tanned face' and 'black halo' of hair are characteristic of a rakshasa. His picture is later completed by his six feet tall stature and enormous strength. He takes over the spare room above the press, monopolizes his parlour, silences with scorn and threatens the poet and the journalist. In short, 'his words and actions violate accepted manners and every tradition implicit in them.'[60] He is evil personified and naturally ' he is of blackness all compact, he glows with evil, he is the prince of darkness.'[61] K. R. Srinivasa Iyengar goes on to the extent of saying: 'In *The Man-Eater of Malgudi* evil is as it were anti-Life, anti-Nature, anti-Faith.'[62]

Vasu is a post-graduate of Presidency College, Madras. After doing his M. A., he joins the civil disobedience movement against the British rule. He spends a great deal of time in prison. Thereafter he turns into a *pahelwan*. He can splinter solid teak doors with his flat, snap chains, twist bars and pulverize granite. Later on he develops interest in taxidermy, probably because it provides him an excuse of indiscriminate killings of animals and thus finds an outlet for his barbaric nature.

Vasu is 'a menace to all decent people.'[63] He befouls the atmosphere with the carcasses of animals he kills without any licence to do it. Nataraj is very sore at the thought that he is harbouring a destroyer, the murderer of innocent creatures. He is more pained because he has been brought in a different tradition altogether where non-violence is the be-all and end-all of life, and the wonder of all wonders is that when he is asked to vacate the attic, he files a suit to the Rent Controller. Vasu charges Nataraj for over-payment of rent, though in fact he is living without paying any rent.

Vasu is dangerous and fearless. The 'blue curtain' in the office of Nataraj that all the people respect is torn open by Vasu. Thus he exposes the 'traditional society to the modern monstrosity of materialism.'[64] He does not even spare his *pahelwan* guru who has fed him tons of milk, eggs, almonds and chickens while training him (Vasu). He 'turns on his guru in the end and half-kills him before leaving to take up taxidermy...' [65] He is 'indeed the perfect embodiment of the typical *rakshasa* of ancient Hindu mythology.'[66] M. K. Naik discovers in him all qualities of a demon described in the 16th chapter of *The Bhagwat Gita*– 'overweening pride, wealth, harshness of speech, insatiable desire and cruelty.'[67]

Really, Vasu does not simply look like a rakshasa but also behaves like a rakshasa. He is rude, aggressive and sadist. His ingratitude also adds to his demonic quality. He shows his ingratitude also to his guru. He is so proud of his merit and skill that he always wants to tame and win over nature. He himself announces: '... it is up to us to prove our superiority to nature.'[68] His 'moral nihilism also is infra-human.'[69] One gets simply shocked at his 'voracious sexual appetite.'[70]

He is a staunch critic of the conventional marriage. He asserts: 'Only fools marry, and they deserve all the trouble they get...You don't have to own a coffee estate because you like to have a cup of coffee now 'and then.'[71] Thus he makes a mockery of love and is always after the satisfaction of his carnal desires. Nonetheless, he excels in breaking laws and is a law unto himself. He does not only stuff dead animals but also kills animals indiscriminately. He even decides to kill the temple elephant, but he dies before shooting the elephant.

Vasu is troublesome even in his death. Nataraj is held guilty in people's eyes. Shastri unfolds the mystery of his death. On the temple festival day, he waits to shoot the elephant. In the meanwhile, a mosquito sits on his forehead. He tries to crush it and in the process of killing the mosquito, he kills himself. Shastri draws a moral from his death:

> Every demon carries within him, unknown to himself, a tiny seed of self-destruction, and goes up in thin air at the most unexpected moment.[72]

P. S. Sundaram also observes rightly that Vasu erupts 'like colossus'[73] causing 'a huge eclipse,'[74] but this is a temporary phenomenon. He adds:

> '...what is unnatural carries within itself its destruction. The darkness lifts, and the sun shines again.'[75]

Apparently, readers are full of hatred for Vasu because of his evil design, but on a closer study, he emerges a 'pathetic figure'[76] who dies, a spiritual death long before his physical death.

Vasu, like Shylock, is more sinned against than sinning. Perhaps full justice has not been done to his character. The reason for this may be attributed to the narrative technique of the novel. M. K. Naik illustrates that the first person narration by Nataraj makes us see:

> Vasu through the frightened eyes of an abnormally timid man ...make the 'demon' appear even more menacing than what an omniscient observer could have made him.[77]

The novel is crowded with a large number of minor characters. Though they have not been drawn in a detail, they are equally fascinating and amusing. One speciality of these characters is that 'they do not just make their appearance at one or two points of the narrative and vanish. They are Nataraj's "constant companions" throughout the novel.'[78] The other special point about them is that most of them are identified through their profession. The adjournment lawyer, the poet, K. J., the septuagenarian, the bus driver, the conductor, the tailor, the sanitary inspector and the police inspector, the municipal chairperson, the forest officer and the rent controller really do not need names in the context of the novel.

The Man-Eater of Malgudi is 'the largest single concentration of eccentrics in Narayan's single fiction.'[79] The poet is always busy writing the life of Krishna in monosyllabic verse. The Adjournment lawyer is a 'sparse hungry-looking man who shaved his chin once a fortnight.'[80] He owes money for the printing of invitation cards but refuses to mix up accounts. He wants Nataraj to send him cash every time so that he can move the court for adjournment on his behalf. Sen, the journalist is 'an arm-chair politician.'[81] He blames Nehru for everything that goes wrong. In fact, 'through characters like Sen and Dr. Joshi, Narayan shows the lingering hope and also the impossibility of achievement of human ambitions.'[82] Sen is ever ready to start his own paper. Dr. Joshi 'clings to his unborn hospital'[83] out of sheer hope. He believes that 'most animals and men are alike, only the dosage of a medicine differs.'[84] The urchin understands a peculiar way to make an elephant get up: 'When a frog is put under an elephant, it'll jump, and the elephant will jump with it.'[85] The Forest Officer has been attacked by wild elephants eighteen times in his service of thirty years. He believes in moving on foot normally and has compiled an anthology of 'Golden Thoughts' for distribution among the school children. The septuagenarian keeps himself busy repairing his dozen houses on the complaints of his tenants.

M. K. Naik rightly discovers that 'the eccentrics in *The Man-Eater of Malgudi* are obviously abnormal, but their abnormality presents a revealing thematic contrast with the abnormality of Vasu.'[86] These characters may be eccentric but they are so much alive and full of dynamism that they add to the beauty and glory of the novel.

THE VENDOR OF SWEETS

The Vendor of Sweets was first published in 1967. Its foreign edition came out with the title of *The Sweet Vendor.* In this novel, R. K. Narayan comes 'closest to a union of the perfection of art and the imperfection of man.'[87] Like other novels it has also received the attentions of critics and reviewers. For instance, Som P. Sharma finds it 'a quest novel.'[88] Lakshmi Holmstrom finds this novel in line with Narayan's other novels. She states that this novel has also a theme of 'the renunciation of worldly goods and attachment for the sake of spiritual pursuits.'[89] Shiv K. Gilra too finds a sense of continuity in the novel because 'the theme of juxtaposition of tradition and modernity'[90] recurs here. H.M. Williams appreciates it because of the comedy arising from 'contrast between the deviant characters and the fixed classical background of India with its complex rules, institutions and customs.'[91] G. S. Amur likes it for it 'derives its inner form from the transformation which the hero, Jagan, undergoes in the course of the action.'[92] Kirpal Singh finds the novel 'flawless.'[93]

The reviewers' responses to this novel are also enthusiastic and positive. Warren French conceptualizes this novel as both 'concise and incisive.'[94] John Gale approves of it because 'every page is human and forgiving....'[95] Ronald White hails it as 'the novel of the century from the sub-continent.'[96] Mary H. Freeman considers it 'warm and beguiling comedy of the universal problems of the old against the young, the past against the present.'[97] Lois Hartley likes it because 'it is a humorous but serious, a satiric but jubilant comment on life .'[98] Anthony West acclaims it as 'a beautifully written and entirely successful short novel.'[99]

Some scholars and critics point out its flaws. Lakshmi Holmstrom denounces this novel because it 'lacks the abundance of background and comic situation of, for example, Narayan's previous novel, *The Man-Eater of Malgudi....*'[100] *John* Gale is unhappy with the ending of the novel: 'the ending is abrupt and open-ended; almost hurried.'[101] No doubt, the novel has some flaws but it offers valuable insights into the working of Indian mind and provides a pleasant reading experience.

The novel deals with the theme of man's quest of identity and self-renewal. This is portrayed through its protagonist, Jagan. Jagan is a sweet-vendor by profession. He is out and out a Gandhian and follower of *The Gita* in his thought and action. He has a son, Mali. He sends his son to a special pilgrimage to Badri Hill. Jagan's wife, Ambika, dies of a brain tumor leaving behind her minor child. Though Jagan has earned a lot of money, he lives a very simple life based on Gandhian principles. One day suddenly Mali decides to leave college. He arranges to go to the U.S.A. to learn the art of novel writing. He comes back after three years accompanied by a half-American and half-Korean girl, Grace whom he claims to be his wife. He has a plan to market a novel-writing machine. He thinks that Jagan will definitely contribute a large sum of money for it. Jagan, in a bid to non-co-operate with his scheme, avoids his son's company. Jagan has been persuaded to buy a ruined garden and shrine to which a sculptor hopes to complete and install a figure of the goddess Gayatri. Before he leaves Malgudi, Jagan learns of Mali's arrest under the prohibition laws. He refuses to become involved in Mali's cases. Therefore, he takes shelter in the forest leaving behind his business in good order for Mali to take over.

Narayan draws his character from life. Naturally, each character has its real-life counterpart. Narayan for example, tries to immortalise the father and the unruly son who were in the midst of a lawsuit. Ved Mehta shares this genesis of the novel:

> The story had begun to form in his head when one of his friends, a lawyer, was handling a lawsuit that a wasteful son had brought against his indulgent father, a prosperous sweet-meat dealer, to get more money from him.[102]

As nearly all his novels designate the "hero" in the title, Jagan stands out to be the central character of *The Vendor of Sweets*. Jagan is a fifty-five year old eccentric sweet vendor who calls Gandhi his master. His Gandhian outlook is reflected in his dress and behaviour:

> ...every day he spun for an hour, and produced enough yarn for his sartorial requirements. He never possessed more than two sets of clothes at any one time and he delivered all the excess yarn in neat bundles to the local handloom committee in exchange for cash.[103]

His loyality to Gandhi makes him wear a special kind of footwear:

> ...he shod his feet with thick sandals made out of the leather of an animal which had died of old age.[104]

M. K. Naik raises a question about his real identity: 'Is Jagan a fake Gandhian or the authentic atricle? He cann't obviously be both and remain credible, but evidence to support both the theories can be found in the novel.'[105] Later, he makes it clear that young Jagan is a true Gandhian whereas 'traces of irony, however, begin to appear unmistakably in the picture of Jagan, the old man.'[106] His spirit of true Gandhian can be well established by citing his response to the word 'service' first uttered by Gandhi:

> ...every human action acquired a meaning when it was performed as a service. Inspired by this definition, Jagan joined the movement for freeing India from foreign rule, gave up his studies, home and normal life and violated the British laws of the time. Neither the beatings nor the successive periods of prison life ever touched him when he remembered that he was performing a 'service'.[107]

Jagan recollects the glorious past and muses how, 'when he was chosen to take part in the National Struggle, he took elaborate leave of everyone before volunteering for arrest... The entire family were moved by his self-abnegation.'[108] As a true freedom fighter his courage, adventure, and indomitable spirit deserve appreciation. 'He remembered how as a volunteer over twenty years ago he had rushed into the British Collector's bungalow and climbed the roof in order to bring down the Union Jack and plant the Indian flag in its place... They had to beat him and crack open his skull in order to make him let go his hold.' [109]

Whereas the young Jagan is a true Gandhian, the old Jagan is a fake Gandhian. The old Jagan is a fanatic preserver of all the externals of Gandhism. He sticks to Gandhian dietary restrictions:

> Twenty drops of honey in hot water... is the natural way of taking in the sugar we need.[110]
>
> I don't drink more than four ounces of water a day, and that must be boiled at night and cooled in a mud jug open to the sky.[111]

Jagan's identity becomes public when his business dealings are described. It sounds highly ironical that while reading *The Gita*, he has one ear perpetually cocked to the frying noises in the kitchen, and one eye glued to the front stall where customers and beggars throng. He philosophically rationalizes the use of stale food: 'After all, everything consists of flour, sugar and flavours.'[112] He maintains double account books. Out of the two, one account book is meant only for 'free cash... a sort of immaculate conception, self-generated, arising out of itself and entitled to survive without reference to any tax.'[113] He forwards logic too behind ignoring taxes: 'If Gandhi had said somewhere, "pay your sales tax uncomplainingly," he would have followed his advice, but Gandhi had made no reference to the sales tax anywhere to Jagan's knowledge.'[114]

As the novel begins, Jagan is found living in his ancestral house built by his father. Once upon a time, his ancestral house used to bustle with activities typical to an Indian family. At that time, Jagan lived in his house with his father, mother, elder brother, and sister. Later after his marriage, he started living along with his wife, son and parents. This life was free of tension and anxiety though he was emotionally split in his loyalties to his parents and his wife. Now as his wife is no more, he lives with his twenty years old son, Jagan. His existence may be, at present, roughly divided into two parts. One part of his existence runs a sweet shop and the other part is 'passionately involved with his son, Mali.'[115]

As a shopkeeper, he is very successful. 'He handles the Bombay Anand Bhavan *sait* and the delegation with seeming naivete, but it is actually suavity par excellence that makes him repeat many banalities and trivia without committing himself an iota.'[116] And there comes a time when he revises the price downward. He does it not because of a sense of competition but because of his new awareness that peace of mind matters most in the life. This very awareness makes him philosophise–let each man work for his own salvation, nobody else's.

Apart from the shop, Jagan's other involvement is his great concern for his son, Mali. He is always worrying about Mali, a helpless motherless boy:

> Poor boy, poor boy, let him be... I wonder what God has in store for him… must give him more time.[117]

All right, I'll come to your college and speak to those people.[118] He is very liberal with his lunch allowance. He also does not feel robbed when Mali steals his ten thousand rupees from the loft. Even when Mali asks for fifty thousand dollars, Jagan thinks more of his rashness than about the money. Jagan, like Margayya, is naive to the point of stupidity. Both of them always try to cover their son's failings when they abandon their studies. Both use almost the same words that he wants to educate himself in the school of life. He lies to Grace also regarding Mali's correspondence with him.

It seems an irony of fate that Mali does not respond to his father's love. We hardly find him communicating with Jagan. He spends his time with his friends. He does not even allow his father 'to have the luxury of cooking for him and expressing his love through that primitive maternal mode.'[119] There is so little contact between father and son that Jagan does not know his son's future plan. He has to ask Cousin to find out. Is it not surprising that even after living with his son for twenty years he does not know his likes and dislikes and his mental make-up? Nonetheless, he determines to go to the States in spite of Jagan's wish that he should succeed him in his business. The absence of a cordial relationship between the father and the son is obvious in their living arrangement in their house too. Jagan lives in the back quarter of the house while the son puts up in the middle front portion of the large hall-like room. Som. P. Sharma has a valid comment on their living pattern: 'In a word, they are living not as father and son but as two strangers in the same house.'[120]

The generation gap between Jagan and Mali is also held responsible for their strained relation. After all, how can Jagan tolerate unscrupulous immoral Mali who lives a married life with Grace without marrying her? How can he approve of his eating beef and meat freely? Naturally, Jagan leaves his house in search of peace. He hands over the keys of the house and the shop to his so-called cousin. Next, he instructs him to deliver them to Mali. Of course, there is a generation gap between Jagan and Mali, but its treatment, in M. K. Naik's opinion, looks shabby:

> ...the allied themes of the clash of generations and East-West confrontation are handled too sketchily to yield significant artistic results....Mali's westernism appears to be as skin-deep as Jagan's Gandhism and takes very superficial forms like eating beef and tinned food, drinking and putting on a suit.[121]

This very weak presentation of the generation gap causes the weakness of the novel. Further, if we take a stock of their relationship we find the relation between Jagan and Mali undergoing changes. In the beginning, Mali avoids and ignores Jagan. When Jagan becomes aware of Mali's sinful life with Grace after his return from the U. S. A., it is his turn to keep away from Mali.

When Jagan fails to achieve the possible compromise within the world, he looks at his life afresh. He thinks he is responsible only for his own growth–his own salvation. He realises that now he should not stick to the shop or Mali: 'who are we to get him [Mali] out or to put him in.'[122] Therefore, he decides: 'I am going somewhere, not carrying more than what my shoulder can bear... I am a free man.'[123] 'He leaves the world, therefore, not to take up the uncompromising role of *sanyasi,* but rather the intermediary stages of *Vanaprastha* or retreat to the forest.[124]

Jagan makes his retreat to an abandoned shrine where he can watch 'a goddess come out of a stone.'[125] In this way, 'Jagan disentangles himself from "a set of repetitions performed for sixty years," from emotional subservience as a parent... .'[126] Jagan's action really conforms to the traditional Hindu ethics. 'The theory of ashrama sees life as a pilgrimage through four different stages.'[127] S. Radhakrishnan in *The Hindu View of Life* has explained Manu's theory of renunciation:

> According to Manu, one must enter the third stage when one becomes a grandfather, or one's skin begins to show wrinkles or one's hair turns grey. When one's bodily powers wane, it is time to depart to the forest and prepare oneself for the true life of the spirit. The main objective of this stage is to escape from the bustle of the world into the solitude of the forest to meditate on the higher problems.[128]

Shirley Chew's concept of detachment may be corelated to Manu's theory of Sanyasa:

> Detachment, when it is meaningful, follows after engagement with living. Sometimes the effort is to emerge from a cocoon of routine and sufficiency application and sacrifice.[129]

A true analysis of Jagan's character reveals the degeneration of the young true Gandhian into the hypocrite of the later years. Even old Jagan's renunciation is 'charmingly freckled with an appealing human flaw.'[130] After all how can a hypocrite renounce the world whose heart has been corrupted beyond redemption? 'If old Jagan's Gandhism is only skin-deep (as it unmistakably appears to be) his renunciation cannot be authentic either.'[131] The greatest proof of his false renunciation is his carrying the bank book and the key to the back door of the house.

Whatever may be the quality of Jagan's Sanyasa, the theme of renunciation recurs in Narayan's novels. In Narayan's early novels, Sanyasa is used as the means of escape from the rules of society and the means of expressing one's individuality. Chandran in *The Bachelor of Arts* is always stationed in the world. Consequently, he fails as a *sanyasi* and resumes his role of householder for which he is a fit man. Savitri fails as a *sanyasin* because 'however much she desires her individuality, her emotional attachments in the world are too great to allow it (Sanyasa).' [132] Raju has also been seen in the role of s*anyasi* for his personal gains, but he is found identifying himself with it. In this process, 'his identity is affirmed, but his individuality is annihilated in the will of the people...' [133]

Jagan's quality of Sanyasa is different. He embraces Sanyasa to fulfill some necessary obligation of life. The conversation between Jagan and the Bearded Man playing the role of the guru reflects the true nature of his *Sanyasa*:

> '...God knows I need a retreat. You know, at some stage in one's life one must uproot oneself from the accustomed surroundings and disappear so that others may continue in peace.[134]

However, he fails because he has not been able to desert the world completely.

Unlike Srinivas, Jagan is not an intellectual. He has not gone through ten principal *Upanishads*. *The Gita* is the only source of wisdom for him. 'Yet, he is fully conscious of the traditional goals prescribed for human life by the Hindu religious thinkers and the traditional ordering of life in terms of Ashramas.'[135] Jagan's reliance on traditional wisdom is shared by others in his community, but a conversation between the Bearded Man and Jagan questions Jagan's authenticity as true follower of the *Gita:*

> 'I can help you to get the supplies if you like. As Lord Krishna says in *the Gita,* it is all in one's hand. Make up your mind and you will find the object of your search.'
> The bearded man... butted in to remark, 'Ah, *The Gita* is a treasure, truly a treasure-house of wisdom.'
> 'I never spend a moment without reading it.' '... *The Gita* also says every man must perform his duty in the right spirit and the right measure. Do you think you are doing that?' Jagan's composure was lost. He merely said, 'Oh!' and covered his confusion with a simper.[136]

G. S. Amur genuinely feels, 'Jagan throughout the transaction uses *The Gita* more as a decoy rather than as religious authority accounts for the controlled irony in the passage.'[137]

Jagan lacks consistency of character. G. S. Amur has brilliant comments on the incongruity of Jagan's character:

> The man who preaches conquest of taste is maker of sweets; Jagan simplifies his life by giving up salt, sugar and rice but goes on accumulating wealth...; Jagan's appreciation of the quietness

> of the garden is accompanied by an oppressive sense of fear;... even when he sets out to the forest, instead of carrying the sacrificial fire as the Shastras enjoined, he takes with him his bank book and is not in the least embarrassed when his cousin makes a sarcastic reference to it.[138]

Nevertheless, in spite of these incongruities, 'Jagan is realistic, and more of a whole, distinct character than Srinivas, Nataraj, or even Margayya.'[139] Jagan, from one viewpoint, is a pathetic figure. His wife is already dead. He lives almost a solitary life. His other relatives look down upon him as an outcast. His so-called daughter-in-law, Grace, belongs to an alien culture. His son lives with Grace without marrying her. He is aggrieved because he was not accorded a big farewell while leaving for the forest as he was given during the Quit-India Movement. Uma Parameswaran is sympathetic to Jagan's pitiable condition:

> ...Jagan's plight arouses genuine pity because he is essentially too naive to conceal his feelings and fears successfully. He is too naive to see the obvious difference between Mali's brusque, disconnected or imperious letters and Grace's long, chatty, informative ones; too naive to see why Nataraj can rush Mali's prospectus through the press in a week while his own *Nature Cure and Natural Diet* has languished for years at Nataraj's office.[140]

Still his character looks real because 'the pathetic side of Jagan is... nicely balanced by his comic gratitude at thus being, released from family obligations.'[141]

> Otherwise they would be making constant demands on his time and energy, compelling him to spend his time in family conclaves, sitting on carpets with a lot of kinsmen exchanging banalities ...Thus he had escaped the marriages of his nieces...[142]

Uma Parameswaran establishes brilliant contrast between Jagan and Margayya:

> Margayya's shrewdness evokes the reader's admiration but his miserliness is unequivocally clear. Jagan is not as obsessed with money as Margayya is and is as reluctant as Margayya to spend any of it, but he does not stint when it comes to keeping his two loves, the purity of his sweets and the welfare of his son.[143]

The list of minor characters in the novel is very short if compared to the list of *The Man-Eater of Malgudi.* Mali and Grace are a unique pair. Their uniqueness lies in their westernised outlook to some extent. Mali's views on life and culture do not tally with his conservative father, Jagan. P. S. Sundaram thinks that this clash originates from 'the influence of the West from which Jagan is wholly free and to which Mali seems wholly to succumb.'[144] M. K. Naik has judged these two characters in a broader perspective: 'Mali's Westernism appears to be skin-deep as Jagan's Gandhism.'[145] In fact, Mali may not be out and out an American but he represents the views of 'a whole new generation of scooter-riding, alcohol smuggling boys.'[146] His views on marriage and love are dangerously materialistic and devoid of any emotion. Mali meets Grace in Michigan and soon falls in love with her. They take the decision to marry after they reach India, but they have 'totally different conception of man-woman relationship from ours.'[147] O. P. Sexena in his famous article 'Cupid's Caprice in R. K. Narayan's Novels' comments:

> They are attuned to free sex and consider marriage only a formality without taking into consideration the Hindu outlook, they indulge in it without inhibitions.[148]

Naturally, Jagan is deeply hurt and disgusted. He feels that his 'home is tainted now,'[146] and his own house 'looks like somebody else's home.'[150]

Mali and Grace come to India with a plan of installing a factory to manufacture story-writing machines. Jagan is requested to finance the plan. Jagan does not help owing to his distrust of Mali. Mali and Grace anticipate the death of their plan and decide to part with each other. 'Their union which has been planned on commercial lines and is governed by economic values alone, can no longer stand the falling prospects... The prospect of their marriage fails with the failing of their embryonic enterprise.'[151] O. P. Saxena evaluates them rightly: 'Mali and Grace represent the most commercially mechanised society–a society which has learnt to rely more and more on the use of machines and computers. It is a society of beings who cut through feeling to accept the creed of crude animality.'[152] Really their relationship is based on mercenary considerations because whereas he exploited only his father before going to America, on his return he exploits both his father and his American wife or rather mistress.[153] In Narayan's concept of human values such a relationship is bound to die out.

Cousin is 'an excellent comic creation, the irony of whose parasitical existence is brought out from time to time.'[154] He does not bear any name except 'Cousin' because he claimed cousinhood with many others in the town (totally incompatible, at times), but if challenged he could always overwhelm the sceptic with genealogy.'[155] He is a great lover of sweets and poses himself to be a self-appointed sweet-taster. He visits Jagan's shop every day to taste sweets and to entertain him with local gossip or to flatter him, for flattery was his sole business in life. Moreover, he is perhaps the only link between Jagan and Mali.

We cannot undermine an eccentric like Chinna Dorai, the sculptor turned hair-dye-maker. He quotes *The Gita* and *The Upanishads* off and on. When provoked he sings 'not in a falsetto, but a full-throated voice without inhibition...'[156] First, Jagan views him with suspicion but later on Chinna Dorai's impact on Jagan seems revolutionary: He (Jagan) suddenly realised how narrow his whole existence had been. And at sixty he feels he is on the verge of 'a new *Janma*.'[157]

These characters have been drawn so life-like that we are led to believe Narayan's 'interest in character than in story.'[158]

REFERENCES

The Man-Eater of Malgudi

1. R. K. Narayan, 'Gods, Demons and Modern Times,' *The Literary Criterion,* 10, No. 3 (Winter 1972), pp. 47-48.
2. *R. K. Narayan,* p. 97.
3. M. K. Naik, *The Ironic Vision: A Study of the Fiction of R. K. Narayan* (New Delhi, 1983), p. 65.
4. *Ibid.,* p. 74.
5. K. R. S. Iyengar, *Indian Writings in English* (Delhi, 1983), p. 380.
6. Harish Raizada, *R. K. Narayan: A Critical Study of His Works* (New Delhi, 1969), p. 154.
7. *The Indo-Anglian Novel and the Changing Tradition,* p. 93.
8. *Ibid.*
9. V. Panduranga Rao, 'The Art of R. K. Narayan,' *The Journal of Commonwealth Literature,* 5 (July 1968), p. 37.
10. *Ibid.*
11. Maurice Dolbier, 'The Man-eater,' *New York Herald Tribune,* 9 February 1961, p. 33.
12. Rosanne Archer, 'In Malgudi Again with the Beguiling Narayan,' *New York Herald Tribune,* 12 February 1961, p. 33.

13. L. Wheildon, 'Narayan's "Man-Eater" Best in Wonderful Series,' *Boston Herald,* 12 February 1961, Sec IV, p. 3.
14. Alan Prince-Jones, ' Satire, Heavy and Light,' *Harper's,* 222 (April 1961), pp. 100-101.
15. Ved Mehta, 'Indian Host,' *Saturday Review of Literarture,* 44, 11 March 1961, p. 29.
16. Charles Poore, 'Books of The Times,' *New York Times,* 9 February 1961, p. 29.
17. Charles W. Mann, 'Jr. Review,' *Library Journal,* 86, 1 March 1961, p. 1017.
18. Collier Ford, 'Between Book Ends,' *St Louis Post Dispatch,* Sec C, 10 July 1961, p. 2.
19. Mary McGreogory, 'Mr Narayan Depicts Village Life in India,' Sec C, *Washington star,* 12 February 1961, p. 5.
20. Leon Bell Bagai. 'The Man-Eater of Malgudi' is Whimsical Whodunit,' *Los Angeles Times,* 26 February 1961.
21. Lakshmi Holmstrom, *The Novels of R. K. Narayan* (Calcutta, 1973), p. 70.
22. Nirmal Mukherji, 'Some Aspects of the Literary Development of R. K. Narayan,' *The Banasthali Patrika,* Vol 5, No.13 (July 1969), p. 83.
23. Alfred P. Klauder, 'Mostly Top-Notch,' *Christian Century,* 78 (13 September 1961), p. 182.
24. 'The Art of R. K. Narayan,' p. 37.
25. Shirley Chew, *Readings in Commonwealth Literature* (London, 1973), p. 67.
26. Lakshmi Holmstrom, *The Novels of R. K. Narayan* (Calcutta, 1973), p. 70.
27. *The Critical Response*, p. 121.
28. R. K. Narayan, *The Man-Eater of Malgudi* (Mysore, 1984), p. 7.
29. *The Critical Response,* p. 121.
30. *R. K. Narayan: A Critical Appreciation*, p. 135.
31. *Ibid.*, p. 136.
32. Shirley Chew, *Readings in Commonwealth Literature* (London, 1973), p. 71.
33. *Ibid.*
34. *The Man-Eater of Malgudi*, p. 66.
35. *The Man-Eater of Malgudi*, p. 67.
36. P. S. Sundaram, 'Malgudi: The World of R. K. Narayan' Part II, *The Indian P.E.N.*, 43, Nos. 3-4 (March-April 1977), p.2.

37. *The Man-Eater of Malgudi*, p. 71.
38. *The Man-Eater of Malgudi*, p. 92.
39. *The Ironic Vision: A Study of the Fiction of* R. K. *Narayan*, p. 71.
40. *The Man-Eater of Malgudi*, p. 105.
41. *The Ironic Vision: A Study of the Fiction of* R. K. *Narayan*, p. 72.
42. *Ibid.*
43. *The Man-Eater of Malgudi*, p. 207.
44. *The Man-Eater of Malgudi*, p. 74.
45. *The Man-Eater of Malgudi*, p. 158.
46. *Ibid.*
47. *The Man-Eater of Malgudi*, p. 208.
48. B. Parvathi, *Studies in Indian Fiction in English* (Gulbarga, 1987), p. 119.
49. *Ibid.*
50. *The Man-Eater of Malgudi*, p. 94.
51. *The Man-Eater of Malgudi*, p. 94.
52. *The Man-Eater of Malgudi*, p. 93.
53. *The Man-Eater of Malgudi*, p. 182.
54. *Critical Essays on Indian Writings in English*, p. 216.
55. *Indian Writing in English*, pp. 70-71.
56. *The Ironic Vision: A Study of the Fiction of* R. K. *Narayan*, pp. 70-71.
57. *Ibid.*, p. 71.
58. *Perspectives on* R. K. *Narayan*, p. 9.
59. *The Man-Eater of Malgudi*, p. 13.
60. R. K. *Narayan: A Critical Appreciation*, p. 137.
61. *Indian Writings in English*, p. 382.
62. *Ibid*, p. 383.
63. P S. Sundaram in *Explorations in Modern Indo-English Fiction* ed. R.K. Dhawan (New Delhi, 1982), p. 150.
64. *The Indo-Anglian Novel and the Changing Tradition*, p. 93.
65. H.M. Williams in *Perspectives on* R. K. *Narayan*, p. 10.
66. *The Ironic Vision: A Study of the Fiction of* R. K. *Narayan*, p. 67.
67. *Ibid.*

68. *The Man-Eater of Malgudi*, p. 15.
69. *The Indo-Anglian Novel and the Changing Tradition*, p. 93.
70. *Perspectives on* R. K. *Narayan*, p. 9.
71. *The Man-Eater of Malgudi*, p. 38.
72. *The Man-Eater of Malgudi*, p. 242.
73. R. K. *Narayan*, p. 107.
74. *Ibid.*
75. *Ibid.*
76. James Dale in R. K. *Narayan: A Critical Spectrum*, ed. Bhagwat S. Goyal (Meerut, 1983), p. 96.
77. *The Ironic Vision: A Study of the Fiction of* R. K. *Narayan*, p. 77.
78. *Ibid.*, p. 75.
79. *Ibid*, p. 74.
80. *The Man-Eater of Malgudi*, p. 5.
81. *The Ironic Vision: A Study of the Fiction of* R. K. *Narayan*, p. 74.
82. *Studies in Indian Fiction in English*, p. 121.
83. *Ibid.*
84. *The Man-Eater of Malgudi*, pp. 122-23.
85. *The Man-Eater of Malgudi*, p. 126.
86. M. K. Naik, *The Ironic Vision: A Study of the Fiction of* R. K. *Narayan* (New Delhi, 1983), p. 75.

The Vendor of Sweets

87. Bruce F. Macdonald, *Perspectives on* R. K. *Narayan* ed. Atma Ram (Ghaziabad, 1981), p. 151.
88. Atma Ram (ed.), *Perspectives on* R. K. *Narayan* (Ghaziabad, 1981), p. 160.
89. Lakshmi Holmstrom, *The Novels of* R. K. *Narayan* (Calcutta, 1973), p. 74.
90. B. S. Goyal (ed.), R. K. *Narayan:* A *Critical Spectrum* (Meerut, 1983), p. 102.
91. H.M. Williams, *Indo–Anglian Literature (1800-1970): A Critical Survey* (Bombay, 1967), p. 62.
92. R. K. Dhawan (ed), *Explorations in Modern Indo-English Fiction* (New Delhi, 1982), pp. 126-127.
93. *Ibid.*, p.132.

94. Warren French, *Kansas City Star,* 16 April 1967, Sec D, p. 6.
95. John Gale, *New Republic*, 156, 13 May 1967, pp. 30-31.
96. Ronald White, *New York Times Book Review*, 14 May 1967, p. 46.
97. Mary H. Freeman, *Savannah News,* 28 May 1967, p. 8.
98. Lois Hartley, *Boston Heralds,* 28 July 1967, Sec. C, p. 17.
99. Anthony West, 'Books,' *New Yorker,* 43 (14 October 1967), pp. 122-123.
100. Lakshmi Holmstrom, *The Novels of R. K. Narayan* (Calcutta, 1973), p. 74.
101. John Gale, *New Republic*, 156, 13 May 1967, p. 31.
102. Ved Mehta, *John is Easy to Please* (Harmondsworth, 1974), p. 153.
103. R. K. Narayan, *The Vendor of Sweets,* (Mysore, 1981), p. 15.
104. *Ibid.*
105. *Ironic Vision: A Study of the Fiction of R. K. Narayan,* p. 80.
106. *Ibid.*, p. 81.
107. *The Vendor of Sweets*, p. 47.
108. *The Vendor of Sweets*, p. 183.
109. *The Vendor of Sweets*, p. 138.
110. *The Vendor of Sweets*, p. 16.
111. *The Vendor of Sweets*, p. 109.
112. *The Vendor of Sweets*, p. 19.
113. *The Vendor of Sweets*, p. 20.
114. *The Vendor of Sweets*, p. 117.
115. Som P. Sharma in *Perspectives on R. K. Narayan*, p.162
116. Uma Parameswarn, *A Study of Representative Indo-English Novelists,* (New Delhi, 1976), p. 82.
117. *The Vendor of Sweets*, p. 23.
118. *The Vendor of Sweets*, p. 29.
119. *Perspectives on R. K. Narayan*, p.1.
120. *Ibid.*
121. *The Ironic Vision: A Study of the Fiction of R. K. Narayan*, p. 82.
122. *The Vendor of Sweets*, p. 190.
123. *The Vendor of Sweets*, pp. 190-91.
124. *The Novels of R. K. Narayan*, p.74.

125. *The Vendor of Sweets*, p. 191.
126. *Readings in Commonwealth Literature*, p. 58.
127. *Ibid.*
128. S. Radhakrishnan, *The Hindu View of life*, (London, 1960), p. 64.
129. *Readings in Commonwealth Literature*, p. 59.
130. *The Journal of Commonwealth Literature*, 5 (July 1968), p. 121.
131. *The Ironic vision:* A *Study of the Fiction of* R. K. *Narayan*, p. 82.
132. *The Novels of* R. K. *Narayan*, p. 73.
133. *Ibid.*
134. *The Vendor of Sweets*, p. 126.
135. G. S. Amur in *Explorations in Modern Indo-English Fiction*, ed R. K. Dhawan, (New Delhi, 1982), p. 126.
136. *The Vendor of Sweets*, pp. 105-06.
137. *Explorations in Modern Indo-English Fiction*, p. 126.
138. *Ibid.*, p. 130.
139. Uma Parameswaran, *A Study of Representative Indo-English Novelists* (New Delhi, 1976), p. 62.
140. *Ibid.*, p. 82.
141. R. K. *Narayan* (New Delhi, 1983), p. 149.
142. *The Vendor of Sweets*, p. 148.
143. *A Study of Representative Indo-English Novelists*, p. 82.
144. R. K. *Narayan*, p. 111.
145. *The Ironic Vision: A Study of the Fiction of* R. K. *Narayan*, p. 82.
146. A. N. Kaul, *Considerations (New* Delhi, 1977), p. 60
147. R. K. Narayan, 'English in India.' *The Times of India*, 2 December 1964.
148. *Glimpses of Indo-English Fiction.* vol. III, (New Delhi, 85), p. 55
149. *The Vendor of Sweets*, p. 143.
150. *Ibid.*, p. 138.
151. O.P. Saxena, *Glimpses of Indo-English Fiction*, vol. III. (New Delhi, 1985), p. 56.
152. *Ibid.*
153. *Considerations*, p. 60.

154. *The Ironic Vision: A Study of the Fiction of* R. K. *Narayan*, p. 83

155. *The Vendor of Sweets,* p. 13.

156. *The Vendor of Sweets*, p. 111.

157. *The Vendor of Sweets*, p. 182.

158. R. K. *Narayan*, p. 109.

7

NOVELS OF TRANSFORMATION: THE PAINTER OF SIGNS AND A TIGER FOR MALGUDI

> If you want something you never had, do
> something you've never done.
>
> —Annonymous

THE PAINTER OF SIGNS

The Painter of Signs was first published in 1976. Like Narayan's other novels, this novel has also received the attention of several eminent critics and scholars. William Walsh finds the novel 'both slim and packed.'[1] And yet he notices that 'by the end of it a character has been evolved, a predicament analysed, a world constructed: a point of view defined.'[2] In M. K. Naik's opinion, the novel is thematically 'a light weight'[3] from the viewpoint of its narrative outline. He also adds that '*The Vendor of Sweets* at least had made some attempt to raise ethical issues. *The Painter of Signs* makes no such attempt and only carries vestiges of some of the motifs presented successfully in the earlier novels.'[4] S. P. Bharadwaj considers it to be 'the outcome of R. K. Narayan's mature, creative years,'[5] though he finds a sense of continuity in this novel:

> Narayan here again, as ever before, is seen at his best as a smiling spectator of all that is absurd and incongruous in human nature, social environment, tradition and the material advancement of the modern days.[6]

Bhardwaj also gives credit to the novel because it 'highlights the change in human outlook with regard to some of the cherished ideals, established institutions and accepted values.... The ideals of family obedience and reverence to elders in the family are gradually dropped for the sake of keeping one's own individuality intact.'[7] O. P. Mathur too finds elements of modernity in this novel because it portrays 'the process of modernization of Malgudi which has now reached a state where it can be compared with New York.'[8] P. S. Sundaram corroborates the ideas of S. P. Bhardwaj and O. P. Mathur: 'How Malgudi has changed beyond recognition?'[9] He goes on to illustrate his point:

> There is a hydroelectric project somewhere in the Mempi Hills, jeeps and lorries make traffic difficult on Market Road, and hippie-like youths with side burns recall by their appearence Stevenson and Faradey. More than all this there is a young lady entirely uninhibited in matters of sex...[10]

E. J. Kalinnikov points out that 'legends from the Mahabharata'[11] have been exploited in this novel. M. K. Naik also confirms 'the use of an ancient Hindu legend'[12] in the modern context in the novel. To elucidate the point he says that the Santhanu-Ganga parallel has been employed consciously in the novel[13]. Bhagwat S. Goyal likes the novel because Narayan 'explores the theme of man's quest for identity through its protagonist, Raman who is a painter of signs.'[14]

The Painter of Signs is a story of Raman, the young painter of signboards in Malgudi. He is proud of his painting and colour combination. Once he gets an order for a signboard from the Family Planning Officer. His work is appreciated by Daisy, in charge of the Family Planning Mission. Daisy lectures to the villagers about Family Planning, but her lecture does not bear much fruit because it is neutralised by a temple priest. The bullock cart driver views Raman and Daisy as a newly-wedded couple. Raman enjoys this misunderstanding because he is in love with Daisy. Besides, the ride in the cart provides him the much-awaited proximity. Raman tries to express his love to Daisy when she is expected to lie in the cart but Daisy deserts the cart in advance sensing his intention. Moreover, Daisy feels hurt at his indecent behaviour. Raman grows normal in a week or so when he is assured that he is not to be put behind bars because of his mischief. Suddenly Daisy appears on the scene. She has a brief talk with him and their courtship begins. They decide to marry. Raman's aunt leaves the house to note this unwelcome decision, but Daisy just in the nick of the time changes her mind about marrying him. She does so because of her commitment to the Family Planning Mission. Raman once again starts his job as a painter of signs.

The main character of the novel is Raman. He paints signs for others. His job does not earn him only bread but 'it has aesthetic, philosophical and social implications, which make him a kind of intellectual generalist looking for his moorings in the society.'[15] He is seen engaged in polemics with a lawyer who desires his name to be written in slanted letters. Raman explains to him his philosophy of calligraphy to the lawyer: 'The letters on a lawyer's board must always stand up proudly, and not lie supine. Head erect.'[16] He also elucidates the point that slanted and supine letters would indicate the lawyer's cowardice. At times, Raman is sad to note that people do not appreciate the art:

> 'I took it up because I loved calligraphy; loved letters, their shape and stance and shade. But no one cares for it, no one notices these values.'[17]

He joined the profession because of his inherent aesthetic sense, but today people seem to be ignorant of this sense. He gets some amount of satisfaction from Daisy's appreciation of his art:

> It (signboard painting) was an important link in society, among various types of people and their activities. But for signboards, people would wallow in isolation, no one would know what another was doing or what was happening.[18]

Thus, Raman is all the time aware not only of aesthetic meaning but also of the social meaning of his profession. Raman claims that his signboard signifies respectability and nobility of purposes, but how many of those whose signboards he writes can be graced with these labels

Raman is a self-styled rationalist. He wishes to establish the Age of Reason in the World:

> 'I want a rational explanation for everything,' he cried, 'otherwise my mind refuses to accept any statement. I am a rationalist and I don't do anything unless I see some logic in it.'[19]

Therefore, he tries to get rid of the irrational attraction he has for Daisy. However, it sounds surprising that a man proclaiming the dictum of 'Be Scientific, please, scientific,'[20] falls the prey to an unwomanly woman. M. K. Naik also shares this view: 'an ironical study of the discomfiture of a self-declared rationalist caught in the coils of love, but as the novel progresses, Raman's rationalism fades out into sheer "Daisy-ism" and the narrative slides into the familiar grooves of the love-story of a weak and infatuated youth and his strong-willed lass.'[21] Raman appears to be fickle-minded. On one occasion, he is lost with the girl's thought and the next moment he indulges in 'self-criticism': [22]

> The girl at the river–was she a girl or lady or woman or just a female? ... The glimpse of the thigh below the hem of her tucked-up sari had monopolized his attention, and then the quick and desperate effort to get away from the resulting sequence of thoughts, imagery, and wishful speculations: Why did I run away from the steps? Just my principle and disciplining my mind against sex–obsessive sex.[23]

Raman's entire experience with Daisy proves to be something of an unreal, though enchanting dream, but he is back in the solid world of reality.

Though Raman is a rationalist, on several occasions he appears to represent Narayan's own philosophy of neutrality or non-commitment. This is why when the lawyer mentions dirt on the board he feels panicky at the sudden threat of a problem. 'He wanted to remain non-committal as long as possible and for a moment wished he could hop on his cycle and run away.'[24] Is it the way a staunch rationalist should behave? On a closer analysis, we find him an escapist. He is easily cowed down by any crisis and prefers to seek the easiest way out.

He is a typical symbol of the bourgeois hypocrisy. He claims to hate money and sex: 'Money and sex, he reflected, obsessive thoughts, too much everywhere–literature, magazines, drama, or cinema deal with nothing but sex all the time.'[25] Nonetheless, he is all the time obsessed with them. He is also aware of the various corruptions prevalent in the society but finds himself unable to take any action against it:

> What about the American milk powder meant for the orphans of India and sold on the black market? What about the government hospital surgeon who flourished his knife like an assassin and made money and acquired the much-coveted building sites beyond the railway crossing! And that wholesale grain-merchant who cornered all the rationed articles and ran the co-operative stores meant for the poor? Raman would expose them

> to the world if someone paid him and provided him with a spacious wall, but ironically enough, he wrote signboards for most of them.[26]

Raman shows his irritation at the illiteracy in society. When the bangle-seller disapproved of Raman's signboard

> … the world was peopled by persons who expected 'cash' to be written in green. The fault is in the educational system and the political leadership. People who ought to mould the taste of the public and help their minds to grow were busy otherwise.[27]

'Raman's relationship with Daisy of the Family Planning Centre... passes through four phases.'[28] In the first phase he is attracted to her and tries to resist the temptation. The second phase places him in the company of Daisy on a tour of the nearby village for a Family Planning Survey. On their downward journey, Raman tries to make a pass at Daisy that she rejects. The third phase witnesses Daisy's developing her relation with Raman to the extent of courting, dating and pre-marital sex. She also promises to marry, though Raman's aunt cannot swallow the idea of their marriage. In utter frustration, she leaves the house for Kasi. In the last stage, Daisy backs out. She advances logic that her commitment to the mission does not provide room for married life. In fact, love relationship between Raman and Daisy forms the main crux of the novel. R. K. Narayan tries to sum up the relationship:

> Of course, the story is set in Malgudi, but it is pretty changed Malgudi... My hero, who goes to paint a sign for the centre falls passionately in love with the young woman in-charge. But her one passion is birth control.[29]

Of course, the story is set in Malgudi, but neither Daisy belongs originally to Malgudi nor all the incidents are confined to its limits. Raman and Daisy spend a considerable period in the neighbouring villages. They are a modern pair of lovers. O. P. Saxena confirms their modern outlook:

> They are the veritable products of their time and contemporary thinking. The complexities, uncertainties, mixed-motivations and obscure lines of modern life shape the nature of the love-relationship between Raman and Daisy.[30]

Raman, the self-declared 'rationalist' [31] and lover of 'logic,'[32] behaves most illogically on several occasions. He runs after Daisy. He imagines her talking to him in the most seductive manner while he lies 'tossing in bed that night.'[33] He tries to restrict his fancy for the girl but fails even to follow Gandhian principles of looking down while talking. Thus, 'an edifice of self-discipline laboriously raised in a life-time seemed to be crumbling down.'[34] He realizes that he suffers from 'love-sickness.'[35] Raman's relationship with Daisy in the beginning has been evaluated well by O. P. Saxena:

> The purely physical attraction of Raman toward Daisy remains only one-sided for quite a long time. He finds Daisy hopelessly cold and encouraging. She, quite unemotionally maintains sobriety and distance of an executive. He is amazed how Daisy is so immune from sex, though she is all the time busy in explaining to men and women the anatomy of sex and all its sexual apparatus. She is a riddle to him. She looks so dispassionately while he … continues to pursue.[36]

During the trip to the neighbouring village with Daisy, he follows her 'as a sort of trailer'[37] rather than a fellow-companion. While coming back they are put in a very romantic situation. Raman grows mischievous in the bullock cart and drags her to satisfy his queries on birth control devices. He misconceives that such a talk may develop an understanding between them. Daisy does not feel inclined towards him in spite of the talk related to sex. By chance, they spend the night in a solitary place as one bullock gets hurt. Raman makes some advances to Daisy on the assumption that 'women liked an aggressive lover'.[38] He also argues within himself that it is unworthy of a man to let slip a 'god-given moment meant for action.'[39] The god-given moment does not bear fruit as Daisy, sensing his intention, leaves the cart before hand. He feels humiliated. He enjoys the cart man's presumption that they are husband and wife. Daisy instantly corrects the cartman. 'Make no mistake. We are not married.'[40] Raman just to tease her shares the cartman's view. Daisy feels irritated and shocked and warns him:

> ... Taking advantage! You will learn your lesson like others who have learnt their lessons. I'll see that you go to jail for this.[41]

Consequently, they fall apart.

Although Daisy is sore at Raman's indecent behaviour, she slowly softens towards Raman. One fine evening she visits his house in an unusually gay mood. They get lost in a confidential chat. That develops in physical union because love to her is quite 'mechanical'[42]: '... his hand seemed to move by itself and find hers, which felt cold and soft. She did not reject his touch. . .'[43] Raman also wins over her by persuasion: 'I like you, I feel lost without you.'[44] No doubt, she offers herself willingly to Raman but she has a mission in life. Therefore, even after she promises to marry, she does not stick to it. O. P. Saxena gives an explanation for her betrayal: 'when the enchanting experience of sexual enjoyment tires her out, she declines to marry.'[45] Moreover, her commitment to her job is stronger. Even marriage does not mean total submission to her:

> Daisy had laid down two conditions before accepting his proposal. One, that they should have no children, and two, if by mischance one was born she would give the child away and keep herself free to pursue her social work. Raman was not to object or modify this in any manner.[46]

> Their relationship is based on youthful passion and natural attraction between a man and a woman. However, it is also governed by the exigencies and urgencies of commerce and profession, as also by new values regarding married life... Daisy is an independent woman and cannot pawn her independence for any promise or comfort of a family life. ... It is Daisy's commitment to her work which terminates their relationship.[47]

The story of Raman runs parallel to the story of king Santhanu in *The Mahabharata.* Raman promises to behave like 'the ancient King Santhanu.'[48] When Daisy lays down the condition on which she will marry him, 'Raman like Santhanu is so much infatuated with love that he is prepared to accept marriage on any condition. Daisy, like Ganga, is a woman whose past is shrouded in a mystery. Ganga's real identity is revealed to Santhanu only at the end. Furthermore, it is possible to see a connection between Daisy's passion for social work and the altruism shown by the divine Ganga ....'[49] However, there is a vital difference between these two stories: 'In the Santhanu-Ganga story, the laying down of the conditions is both the starting point of the eventful narrative to follow and the pivot of the entire action; in Narayan's novel, the stipulation of the conditions comes virtually towards the end of the story....'[50] Naik observes meaning in the use of the Santhanu-Ganga story: 'The whole point in employing this kind of a strategy of juxtaposing antiquity and contemporaneity is to demonstrate how the basic imperatives of the human condition remains the same, in spite of difference in time, place, milieu, even the plane of experience.'[51]

Raman confirms to the regular pattern of Narayan's main character: 'from average to the extraordinary and back again to a more poignant stage of average.'[52] Here we disagree with William Walsh's view that 'Raman undoubtedly seems to develop from within.' [53] He suffers throughout the tragedy of Hamlet–to be or not to be. He is always busy with Daisy's thought and still declares that 'the man-woman relationship was not inevitable and that there were other more important things to do in life than marrying.'[54] He submits to Daisy during loving moments: 'You command, I'm ever your slave.'[55] Besides, his emotional outburst can also be noticed even after her betrayal: 'I'll love no one except you.'[56]

Raman's one striking quality is that he 'conducts his business with the world on the basis of a double dialogue, one with his interlocutor and another, inner one with himself.'[57] For instance, when he bargains with the lawyer, he talks explicitly about materials, concessions and costs but the same time thinks; 'here is the fellow, with nothing settled but talks of style…'[58] William Walsh comments that 'his inward speech is sharper and plainer than his more civil and accommodating utterance.'[59] Daisy, if compared to Raman, 'is not divided.'[60] She is 'all of a piece throughout.'[61]

Daisy, a representative of woman's liberation movement, dislikes the joint family system. She ignores family honour and flees to Madras where she is educated by a missionary organisation. She is a woman of strong conviction and indomitable will. 'But with all this strength within her, there pulsates the soft heart of a female under the ribs'.[62] Of course, she has her 'moments of weakening' but she is all the time aware of her mission which is of supreme importance to her. S. Krishnan sums up Narayan's view about Daisy's whole personality:

> This girl in my new novel is quite different. Not only she is not dependent on men, she actually had no use for them as an integral part of her life… She is a very strong character. All the same, when you read the novel you will find she is very feminine also. There is a conflict. That is the whole point.[63]

She refuses to play the role of a homemaker and discards the idea of housekeeping: 'I don't like all this obsession with a house and the keeping of it.'[64] M. K. Naik comments on her unconventional outlook: 'Daisy's refusal to fill the role of the traditional Hindu housewife, her passion for social work, and her changing moods... raise expectations of an absorbing study of the New Hindu Woman of the post-Independence period.'[65] However, 'Narayan's New Hindu Woman remains as unconvincing as the traditional Hindu wife in *The Dark Room.*'[66]

We can cite several occasions when 'she enjoys the rapture of the flesh:'[67]

> (Once) very gently, he (Raman) withdrew his hand and edged away. But she suddenly turned over on her side and with her eyes still closed, threw her arms around his neck and drew him nearer and lay unmindful as his fingers fumbled with her clothes.[68]

Here it would not be out of place to mention Narayan's fitting remark: 'when a couple, even if they are characters in my own novel, want privacy, I leave the room.'[69] Thus, it is obvious that she wants to satisfy her physical passion but rejects the idea of marriage: '... Married life is not for me. I have thought it over. It frightens me. I am not cut out for the life you imagine.'[70] When asked during an interview by S. Krishnan how he (Narayan) came to give such an unorthodox cast of mind to Daisy, so different from Savitri of *The Dark Room,* Narayan explains: '... In *The Dark Room* I was concerned with showing the utter dependence of woman on man in our society. I suppose I have moved along with the times.'[71]

'There is the usual quota of eccentrics.'[72] For example, the young lawyer likes the letters on his name board to be slanted to the left according to astrologer's direction. Gupta, the businessman, 'started a new business under a new name each year in order to confound the sales tax, income tax, and all the governmental tax-devisers.'[73] The second-hand bookseller starts dancing over the patterns and designs that book-worms create on the book covers and insides. He has a theory about the entire thing. The owner of Bhandari Stores has 'a waxed moustache so finely... pointed that if stepped too close it might puncture your eyes.'[74] The Town Hall professor is capable of delivering sermons on any issue. The Police Inspector hates monkeys. Raman's neighbour, an accountant, is 'a replica of the Common Man created by the cartoonist Laxman.'[75] Finally, there is an old man, the village temple priest capable of telling your past and future. These characters may be interesting but they are not the organic part of the novel because they 'seem to have no thematic connection direct or indirect ... to their counterparts in *The Man-Eater of Malgudi* possess.'[76]

A TIGER FOR MALGUDI

A Tiger for Malgudi was first published in 1983. This novel came out after a gap of seven years. Naturally, some committed readers of R. K. Narayan have inferred that perhaps R. K. Narayan was at the dead end of his creative career. However, the publication of this novel proves that R. K. Narayan has still much of creative genius left in him. Unlike other novels, this novel has not received the attention of several critics because of its recent arrival. However, it has received the attention of R. M. Verma in his essay entitled 'A Thematic study of A Tiger for Malgudi' published in his book *Some Aspects of Indo-English Fiction.* He places it at the highest pedestal as he finds this novel 'Narayan's masterpiece.'[77] He also goes on to add that 'for the wide reading public of Narayan both at home and abroad it is simply a beautiful novel.'[78]

Unlike other earlier novels, Narayan adds a long 'Introduction' to the novel. This introduction traces the genesis of the novel in very clear terms:

> During the Kumbh Mela Festival, which recurs every twelve years at the confluence of the three rivers Ganga, Yamuna and Saraswati in Allahabad, a vast crowd gathers for a holy bath in the rivers. Amidst that ocean of humanity also arrives a hermit with a companion, a tiger. He does not hold the animal on a leash since he claims they were brothers in previous lives. The tiger freely moves about without hurting or scaring anyone. Such a combination seemed incredible when I read reports of it and saw the photographs. But as I got used to the idea, I began to speculate on its possibilities for a novel.[79]

Later on, he also encounters a picture of a young tiger pleading, 'I'd love to get into a good book.'[80] He promptly answered back, 'surely you will get into my book …'[81] One more reason behind writing this novel is that Narayan appears bored with human beings as the subject of the novel:

> Humans have monopolized the attention of fiction writers. Man in his smugness never imagines for a moment that other creatures may also possess ego, values, outlook and the ability to

> communicate, though they may be incapable of audible speech... I wished to examine what the result would be if I made a tiger the central character in a novel.[82]

Narayan also rationalizes the choice of a tiger as a subject matter of the novel 'so that the chief character may not be trampled upon or lost sight of in hole.'[83]

This novel has been marked out from his earlier novels for various reasons. First, the story of the novel seems to move parallel to the best of *The Panchatantra* or the famous Buddhist work *Jatakas*. Also, in this novel Narayan tries to perfect the theme of renunciation and create a real *sanyasi*. Raju in *The Guide* enacts as an imposter Sadhu, though towards the end, he is found to be achieving some qualities of a genuine saint. However, Swami in *A Tiger for Malgudi* remains genuine throughout the novel. He attains his spiritual height after long years of hard and patient sadhana. The renunciation of this Swami has been caused by 'an inner compulsion' [84] very much in the style of Siddhartha. The Swami sees the whole globe as one and its problems non-fragmentarily. He explains this point to his wife who has come to him to plead for his homecoming:

> My past does not exist for me, nor a future. I live for the moment ... I have erased from my mind my name and identity... It would be unthinkable to slide back. You must live your own life and leave me to live mine and end it my own way.[85]

This novel witnesses a clear departure from Narayan's other novels in relation to the depiction of man-woman relationship. The wife of the Captain has not been painted as a traditional submissive woman of *The Dark Room* or *The English Teacher* nor as an independent liberated woman of *The Painter of Signs*. Narayan portrays here a nagging wife, though she is somewhere rooted to the soil. That is why she commits suicide as she comes to know about her husband's death, Further, Narayan deals with the theme of communal disharmony for the first time in this very novel. He discusses some of the well-known causes of communal riots:

> If you are ready to hate and want to destroy each other, you may find a hundred reasons–a diversion of canal water in your field... rumours of molestation of some woman, even the right to worship in a temple, anything may spark off a fight if you are inclined to nurture hatred. [86]

Narayan also wants to establish that all religions preach love but they practise hatred. This leads to riots between the Hindus and the Christians, the Muslims and the Hindus and the Sikhs and the Hindus. Narayan perhaps shares Bertrand Russel's view that religion has done more harm than good. Finally, in this very novel, Narayan first endeavours to propagate the national policy on language–the three-language formula consisting of the regional language, the national language and English:

> He [Captain] delivered his message in at least three languages, as he explained: ... 'in Hindi since it is our national language and given to us by Mahatma Gandhi himself; also in English because as our beloved respected leader Nehru put it, it opens a window on the world. In Tamil, because it is, ah, our Mother Tongue, in which our greatest poets like Kamban and Valluvar composed'.[87]

Nonetheless, here Narayan goes a long way in resolving a major national issue–a choice for a national language. He advocates Hindi as the National language because it is 'given to us by Mahatma Gandhi himself.' [88] Really, in a vast, multi-lingual, multi-cultural country like India, a national link language is urgently needed. R. M. Verma endorses the view that '*A Tiger for Malgudi* sums up much of what modern India is about.'[89] Narayan weaves his story around the Hindu philosophy of Karma, rebirth and transmigration of soul, and other teachings as enunciated in the *Bhgawad Gita.* Besides, he also exposes the rampant corruption in the society in a loud voice. He goes tough with the law enforcing agencies: 'What our country needs most is a tiger for every village and town to keep people disciplined.'[90] Narayan is also not blind to the way government servants attend to public grievances. He makes mockery of bureaucrats who instead of giving relief to the villagers from tiger take to dillydallying tactics:

> The Collector observed them for a moment and said, 'Have you brought your petition in writing'? They looked terrified, having no notion of the world of letters. The Collector felt compassionate and said, 'I can't take action unless there is a written petition. Then I'll fix a date for inspection and take action'.[91]

The other example of the slow functioning of the government department is that the assistant headmaster seeks permission to buy a pin. In fact, 'Narayan is at the peak of his creative originality in *A Tiger for Malgudi,* which will be widely read and long remembered as a political allegory and social satire, for it possibly has not only the merits of George Orwell's *Animal Farm,* but also something more for those who are prepared to look for deeper meanings in this novel.'[92]

A Tiger for Malgudi narrates the story of an aged tiger, Raja lying in the zoo and ruminating on his past. It is not only the story of a tiger from infancy to the old age but also the story of people inhabiting the modern Malgudi with circus and film shooting. Raja's cubhood and youth are spent in the forest enjoying his life and ruling over other animals. His later life passes on in captivity as a circus star. It attains freedom when he breaks loose from a film shooting camp and wanders into the town. The terror-stricken public attempts to shoot him but a master appears on the scene, protects him and adopts him as a friend and finally transforms his inner self completely.

The protagonist of the novel is Raja, a tiger, because the whole novel revolves round him. As the novel opens, the tiger makes us aware of many of his human qualities with only one difference that he cannot make use of human language:

> ...I possess a soul within this forbidding exterior. I can think, analyse, judge, remember and do everything that you do, perhaps with a greater subtlety and sense. I lack only the faculty of speech.[93]

Still he tries to narrate his whole story. Nevertheless, he apprehends that his fierce look may not allow people to listen to him. He himself muses on his terrible look:

> I don't know why God has chosen to give us this fierce make-up, the same God who has created the parrot, the peacock, and the deer, which inspire poets and painters.[94]

During his cubhood he was constantly 'chased, knocked down and hurt by bigger animals and menaced by lesser ones.'[95] As a cub he learns the art of catching miserable creatures such as rabbits, fox, cubs and squirrels for his survival. In due course, he also considers himself a mighty one and attacks weaker creatures fatally. Slowly almost all creatures tremble at his very thought. Some animals instantly announce, 'Here comes our Lord and Master. Keep his path clear.'[96] Overall, there is a general understanding about his undisputed, unquestioned superiority among his jungle community. Surprisingly, Raja is afraid of porcupines and monkeys because they are capable of hopping, climbing, or flying even a short distance. Except these two species of animals, all other creatures maintain a respectable distance from him.

Thus, Raja is blissfully ignorant of the dangers of the world. Suddenly he comes across a tigress with whom he fiercely fights, but contrary to his expectation he gets defeated. He collapses on the ground bleeding from every pore, though he has the satisfaction of leaving the tigress also badly wounded. Instantly a revelation dawns on him that there is no reason to be at enmity with the tigress. This revelation ties them in a bond of friendship that, in due course, turns into a love-relationship. This leads to his fathering a litter of four cubs whom both of them love and guard in their impregnable fortress.

One fine morning the tigress moves into the human habitation in search of prey and thus, loses her life as well as the lives of her four cubs who instinctively follow their mother to death. Then Raja comes to his senses about his strength as compared to the human beings: 'A human being may look small, without prominent teeth or claws, but he is endowed with some strange power, which can manoeuvre a tiger or an elephant as if they were toys.'[97] In course of the frantic search of his wife and children, he stays in and around villages for days together surviving on village cattle. Many times, he has nearly escaped from death but once, unfortunately, he yields to temptation. He is made a captive. The only good luck is that he is not shot dead by the hunter but is taken to the custody of the Captain – the proprieter of the Grand Malgudi Circus. He is trained to perform in the circus and in due course on a film set. Initially, he shirks from acting as a circus star. The Captain tames and trains him for his circus by inflicting the severest sufferings on him. The tiger ultimately learns his lessons to the satisfaction of the Captain and totally submits to his dictates. He develops a compromising attitude to his life and starts loving his changed lifestyle:

> Life was not so bad after all. Captain was not such a monster after all. I began to respect him for his capabilities. I began to admire him–a sort of worshipful attitude was developing in me.[98]

Within a very short period, he turns an established member of that circus because of presenting varieties of difficult and daring shows. Once at a circus show Raja is put near a goat drinking milk from a pot. He tries his best but cannot suppress his hunger. He makes an attempt at the life of the goat leaving it badly hurt. He is punished for it. Finally, he is taken to be good.

One filmmaker wants Raja with him. He also wants a snap of the situation in which Raja is seen fighting with a great wrestler. The tiger reacts over the thought of being used by different persons for different gains. He is simply tired of circus-existence and naturally, every pore of his being hankers for freedom from this life of slavery. His long monologue reflects his concern for the Captain's well-being as well as a thirst for his own freedom:

> Go away before any harm befalls you, my good man. After all, you have fed me and protected me.
>
> I shall honour you for it. But please go away and leave me alone... I won't do any of the meaningless turns... I like this air and freedom. I'm not going to give it up now .[99]

The captain unmindful of his inner cry tries to get the tiger on his legs. In addition, to bring perfection in his show he gives him a very severe blow. The tiger screams loudly in reaction:

> 'Oh, Captian, don't be foolhardy, your life is in danger, go away, leave me before any calamity befalls you.'[100]

However, when the Captain refuses to take the hint, he is killed. The tiger is surprised to know 'that such a family creature, no better than a membrane, stretched over some thin framework, with so little stuff inside, should have held him in fear so long.'[101]

Having killed the Captain, he walks off the place and takes shelter in a school building. He remains there for some time and is locked in the headmaster's room along with the headmaster. Other teachers in order to shoot him first contact the S. P. and then D. F. O. Meanwhile a master turned Swami appears on the scene and creates awareness among people not to consider the tiger a beast. Alphonse who thinks himself to be the bravest and the fittest tries to shoot the tiger without injuring the headmaster. Members of Save Tiger Project also arrive at the scene. They take more interest in saving the tiger than the headmaster, but no one succeeds either in shooting him dead or in capturing him alive.

Swami takes him out of the room and brings him under his spell to such an extent that the tiger meekly follows him to the forest being convinced by the Swami's words, 'I am your friend ...'[102] The tiger gets a great relief at the idea of living his 'familiar life, back to the jungle, to the bed of long grass'.[103] He also goes on to add:

> How grand it'd be to back in the world of bamboo shade and monkeys and jackals! Even the supercilious leopard and the owl I would not mind; compared to human company, they were pleasant...[104]

They stay near a rock. Here Raja is initiated into spiritualism. Though 'God' is unheard of by the tiger, Swami explains him this term: 'You may not understand the word. But let it sink in your mind and ring on your ears, and then tell me later how you feel.'[105] His master further illustrates: 'Remember also He is within everyone of us and we derive our strength from Him.'[106] Before being initiated by the Swami, the tiger measures everything including God in his own terms:

> God must be an enormous tiger, spanning the earth and the sky, with a tail capable of encircling the globe, claws that could hook on the clouds, and teeth that could grind the mountain, and possessing, of course, immeasurable strength to match.[107]

The master corrects his misconception in simple terms by saying that everyone creates and sees him in his own form but he is also something more: 'In *Bhagavad Gita* He reveals himself in a mighty terrifying form which pervades the whole universe in every form of life and action'.[108] In the gracious presence of the Swami, Raja's whole attitude to life changes. He takes to vegetarianism and repents over his past days: 'How I wished I had learnt the art of living on sugarcane and rice, like the elephant and the hippo of the circus...'[109]

Raja is also taught to live in the present and relieve his mind of facts and information because an obsession for these details is the root cause for suffering. He grows meditative and becomes ecstatic whenever he is in close proximity of his meditating master:

> At such moments, I felt lighter at heart and my physical self also became secondary. My sight became clearer; if I lifted my gaze to the horizon, the shining on the land filled me with joy...[110]

Thus, they live in utter isolation but still in utter bliss. Their days pass smoothly until a day when suddenly swami has a revelation of achieving a near *samadhi* stage. Thereupon he decides to disconnect even the last bondage of friendship with Raja:

> No relationship, human or other, or association of any kind could last forever. Separation is the law of life right from the mother's womb.[111]

Before taking leave of Raja, Swami hands him over to the care of a zoo master with the instruction to keep him well as 'he is only a tiger in appearance... He is a sensitive soul who understands life and its problems exactly as we do.'[112] With these words the master hopes to meet him again in the next life, for dying is the only way to prove reincarnation.

The story of Raja undergoes a complete circle. It starts from his cubhood and moves on the old age through the adventures and misadventures of his youth. It does not end with his old, invalid self but paves way for his rebirth. Credit goes to Narayan for describing Raja with human touch and at times establishing superiority of animals over human beings: 'Tigers attack only when they feel hungry, unlike human beings who slaughter one another without purpose or hunger…'[113] R. M. Verma infers:

> 'He must have spent long hours in a zoo to study and watch the life of a tiger, his natural proneness to indolence and the behaviour pattern of other animals...'[114]

The novel has two more important characters who shape and influence Raja's course of life. They are–the Captain and the master turned swami. The captain shapes Raja's exterior while the master transforms his interior. The tiger lives in the company of the Captain because of his helplessness and, therefore, does not love and adore him though he appreciates some of his rare qualities as a circusmanager. However, his togetherness with the master is his own choice because his living with the master is not bondage. It provides an opportunity for his over-all growth. There is a bond of love-relationship between them which later turns into guru-disciple relationship.

The master was once a great champion of the freedom movement. He was also put behind the bars for tearing down the British flag and writing down 'Quit India' on the wall. He has also worked for the Foreign Insurance. Soon he is tired of his routine job and decides to desert this world. He himself confesses:

> I was a man of the world... One day it seemed all wrong, a senseless repetition of activities… I abruptly… fled away from wife,

> children, home, possessions... and left very much in the manner of Siddhartha...[115]

The master turns into a Swami and is now much wiser. His wisdom tames the ferocious tiger like a cat and transforms his pattern of life. His words of wisdom are replete with eternal truth:

> My past does not exist for me, nor a future. I live for the moment, and that awareness is enough for me.[116]
>
> God resides within all of us.[117]
>
> A great power has determined the number of breaths for each individual, we can neither stop them nor prolong ...[118]

In fact, in the master we meet a real ascetic who not only preaches Upanishadic truth but also lives it to attain *Samadhi*. However, the real beauty of this Swami does not lie in his own attainment to godhood but in an attempt to help others to achieve it.

REFERENCES

The Painter of Signs

1. William Walsh, *R. K. Narayan: A Critical Appreciation* (New Delhi, 1983), p. 153.
2. *Ibid.*
3. M. K. Naik, *The Ironic Vision: A Study of the Fiction of* R. K. *Narayan* (New Delhi, 1983), p. 87.
4. *Ibid.*
5. Atma Ram (ed.), *Perspectives on* R. K. *Narayan* (Ghaziabad, 1981), p. 168.
6. *Ibid.*
7. *Ibid.*, p. 174.
8. *Ibid.*, p. 33.
9. P. S. Sundaram, *Explorations in Modern Indo-English Fiction* (New Delhi, 1982), p. 152
10. P. S. Sundaram, 'Malgudi: The World of R. K. Narayan,' Part II, *The Indian P.E.N.*, ed. Sofia Wadia, Vol. 43, No, 3-4 (March-April 1977) p. 3.
11. *Perspectives on* R. K. *Narayan*, p. 24.
12. *The Ironic Vision: A Study of the Fiction of* R. K. *Narayan*, p. 87.
13. *Ibid.*, p. 88.

14. Bhagwat S. Goyal, R. K. *Narayan: A Critical Spectrum* (Meerut, 1983), p. 161.
15. R K. *Narayan: A Critical Spectrum*, p. 162.
16. *The Painter of Signs* (Mysore, 1986), p. 5.
17. *Ibid.*, p. 30.
18. *Ibid.*, p. 32.
19. *Ibid.*, p. 5.
20. *Ibid.*, p. 7.
21. *The Ironic Vision: A Study of the Fiction of* R. K. *Narayan*, p. 89.
22. *The Painter of Signs*, p. 14.
23. *Ibid.*, p. 16.
24. *Ibid.*, p. 10.
25. *Ibid.*, p. 14.
26. *Ibid.*, p. 13.
27. *Ibid.*, p. 25.
28. *The Ironic Vision: A Study of the Fiction of* R. K. *Narayan*, p. 86.
29. S. Krishnan, 'A Day with R. K. Narayan,' *Span* (April 1975), p. 40.
30. O. P. Saxena, *Glimpses of Indo-English Fiction*, Vol.III (New Delhi, 1985), p. 57.
31. *The Painter of Signs*, p. 5.
32. *Ibid.*
33. *Ibid.*, p. 44.
34. *Ibid.*, p. 45.
35. *Ibid.*, p. 46.
36. *Glimpses of Indo-English Fiction*, p. 58.
37. *The Painter of Signs*, p. 63.
38. *Ibid.*, p. 92.
39. *Ibid.*, p. 93.
40. *Ibid.*, p. 99.
41. *Ibid.*, p. 101.
42. *Ibid.*, p. 125.
43. *Ibid.*, p. 126.

44. *Ibid.*, p. 125.

45. *Glimpses of Indo- English Fiction*, p. 61.

46. *The Painter of Signs*, p. 156.

47. O. P. Saxena, 'Cupid's Caprice in R K Narayan's Novels,' *Glimpses of Indo-English Fiction*, p. 62.

48. *The Painter of Signs*, p. 159.

49. *The Ironic Vision: A Study of the Fiction of R. K. Narayan*, pp. 87-88.

50. *Ibid.*, p. 88.

51. *Ibid.*

52. Rajeev Taranath, *Critical Essays on Indian Writings in English*, eds. M. K. Naik, S. K. Desai and G. S. Amur (Dharwar, 1972), p. 296.

53. *R. K. Narayan: A Critical Appreciation*, p. 154.

54. *The Painter of Signs*, p. 45.

55. *Ibid.*, p. 144.

56. *Ibid.*, p. 182.

57. *R. K. Narayan: A Critical Appreciation*, p. 156.

58. *The Painter of Signs*, p. 4.

59. William Walsh, *R. K. Narayan* (New Delhi, 1983), p. 157.

60. *Ibid.*

61. *Ibid.*

62. S. P. Bhardwaj, 'The Painter of Signs – An Analysis,' *Perspectives on R. K. Narayan*, p. 174.

63. 'A Day with R. K. Narayan,' *Span*, p. 42.

64. *The Painter of Signs*, p. 167.

65. *The Ironic Vision: A Study of the Fiction of R. K. Narayan*, pp. 89-90.

66. *Ibid.*, p. 90.

67. *Glimpses of Indo- English Fiction*, p. 62.

68. *The Painter of Signs*, p. 175.

69. R. K. Narayan, 'Editorial Letters,' 4, *The Times of India* (16 November 1980), p. 10.

70. *The Painter of Signs*, pp. 178-179.

71. 'A Day with R. K. Narayan,' *Span*, p. 42.

72. *The Ironic Vision: A Study of the Fiction of* R. K. *Narayan*, p. 90.
73. *The Painter of Signs*, p. 15.
74. *Ibid.*, p. 24.
75. *Ibid.*, p. 159.
76. *The Ironic Vision: A Study of the Fiction of* R. K. *Narayan*, p. 91.

A Tiger for Malgudi

77. R. M. Verma, *Some Aspects of Indo-English Fiction* (New Delhi, 1995), p. 1.
78. *Ibid.*
79. R. K. Narayan, *A Tiger for Malgudi* (Mysore, 1983), p. 7.
80. *Ibid.*
81. *Ibid.*
82. *Ibid.*, pp. 7-8.
83. *Ibid.*, p. 8.
84. *Ibid.* p. 168.
85. *Ibid.*, p. 171.
86. *Ibid.*, p. 165.
87. *Ibid.*, p. 66.
88. *Ibid.*
89. *Some Aspects of Indo-English Fiction,* p. 11.
90. *A Tiger for Malgudi*, p. 155.
91. *Ibid.*, p. 30.
92. *Some Aspects of Indo-English Fiction*, p. 13.
93. *A Tiger for Malgudi*, p. 12.
94. *Ibid.*
95. *Ibid.*, p. 13.
96. *Ibid.*, p. 14.
97. *Ibid.*, p. 28.
98. *Ibid.*, p. 52.
99. *Ibid.*, p. 113.
100. *Ibid.*, p. 114.
101. *Ibid.*, pp. 114-115.

102. *Ibid.*, p. 144.

103. *Ibid.*, p. 146.

104. *Ibid.*

105. *Ibid.*, p. 157.

106. *Ibid.*, p. 158

107. *Ibid.*

108. *Ibid.*

109. *Ibid.*, p. 159.

110. *Ibid.*, p. 165.

111. *Ibid.*, p. 174

112. *Ibid.*, p. 175.

113. *Ibid.*, p. 117.

114. *Some Aspects of Indo-English Fiction*, p. 5.

115. *A Tiger for Malgudi*, p. 161.

116. *Ibid.*, p. 171.

117. *Ibid.*, p. 164.

118. *Ibid.*, p. 142.

8

ORDINARY HERO IN AN EXTRAORDINARY WAY: TALKATIVE MAN, THE STORY OF NAGARAJ, AND GRANDMOTHER'S TALE

People do not decide to become extraordinary.
They decide to accomplish extraordinary things. .
—Edmund Hillary

TALKATIVE MAN

Talkative Man was first published in 1985. Previously the novel was serialised for almost a year in *Frontline.* Later on, it was given the shape of a book. In the postscript, Narayan labels it novel no.14 but in fact, it is the 13th novel. This appears to be the novelist's miscalculation. It may also be a hint towards the fact that his one novel might have gone unpublished. Narayan also claims it to be the shortest one consisting of one hundred sixteen typewritten sheets whereas the minimum requirement for fiction in those days was seventy thousand words. He himself accounts for its being a short novel because it 'came to a halt like a motor car runs out of petrol.'[1] The novel has its genesis in one incident in which Narayan tries to get a man out of Malgudi hurriedly when 'he was planning to seduce and abduct a young innocent school girl.'[2] known to the novelist.

Surprisingly even after a lapse of decades, we do not find many articles on this novel. P. S. Sundaram writes a very short article running into one page and a half in his recent book *R. K. Narayan as a*

Novelist (1988). We know certain facts about the novel from an interview Susan Ram had with R. K. Narayan for *The Telegraph* (11 May 1986). P. S. Sundaram is very critical of the novel: 'Narayan had been reduced to repeating himself in a voice less vibrant than it was. *Talkative Man* has little to recommend it except that it is by R. K. Narayan and recalls some of the scenes and persons of Malgudi.'[3] Here, perhaps, P. S. Sundraram is not aware of the changing inter-personal relationship under the impact of the Western wind. Thus, the novel opens a new vista of relationship, which is based not on certain religious and social commitment but also on one's fancy and fulfilment of the immediate need. Rann, the protagonist, represents the changed aspect of life. Contrary to P.S. Sundaram's criticism, Nandani Saha (2007:102) hails Narayan as a great story teller and appreciates his admiration for storytelling:

> The importance Narayan allots to the storyteller is evident when he designates him as the "source of enchantment" of a village community that is otherwise "isolated from the mainstream of modern life".[4]

The novel tells a story of a widely travelled man called Dr. Rann. In course of his travelling, Talkative Man assures Station Master that he would get rid of Dr. Rann who keeps on staying in the waiting room. Rann is shifted to Talkative Man's house. He tries to seduce Girija, the librarian's granddaughter. Talkative Man prevents the catastrophe by sending a wire to Commandant Sarasa, Rann's wife who has been abondoned by Rann. Sarasa catches hold of her husband and restores the marital peace. Later Rann again elopes with a nurse deserting his wife.

Rann is the central character of the novel because the whole story moves around him. Talkative Man is only the narrator, though he adds to the plot by playing certain important roles in the novel. Rann belongs to Maniyor, a southernmost village and he has tailored his name to sound foreign. He encounters Talkative Man in the reading room and is introduced by the librarian. Rann seeks help from T. M. (an abbreviated form for Talkative Man) but provides him with his wrong whereabouts and mission. He discloses that he belongs to America and is working on a U.N. project and writing a book. He lies to the Station Master and intends staying at the station for a long time. The

Station Master reads Rann's intention and with the help of T. M. gets him displaced. T. M., in spite of his frantic search, does not arrange a house for Rann. Naturally, Rann starts living in T. M.'s house. T. M. develops interest in the stranger and he informs the news-editor about this American. The editor needs Rann's photograph. T. M. creates a situation in which he has been photographed without his knowledge.

Once a woman with the picture of a stranger approaches him. Treating him as a journalist, she asks T. M. about the whereabouts of Rann. She discloses her identity as Rann's wife. T. M. does not disclose Rann's whereabouts but makes him aware that a woman with his photograph is in search of him. Rann gets panicky because of this new disclosure. He comes closer and closer to T. M. and is advised to keep inside because someone is seriously after him. Once the woman visits T. M.'s house in Rann's absence. She is hosted breakfast and she divulges her entire past and present. She is serving the homeguard at Delhi in the capacity of an officer. She went in for love-marriage with Rann even at the cost of her parents' displeasure.

Rann instead of living happily with his wife makes advances towards the librarian's granddaughter. T.M. senses the gravity of the situation and informs his wife of his whereabouts. Rann plans to elope with Girija to the Peak House after his lecture on futureology in a Silver Jubilee celebration comes to an end. Rann's wife arrives at an appropriate hour and receives an envelope and invitation card from the Station Master who receives them from T. M. . On the celebration day, some confusion arises and people start fleeing away. In that very confusion, Rann is led to a car that is already occupied by Sarasa, his wife. Girija's life is spared and T. M. receives appreciation from the librarian. However, Rann and his wife could only live together for nearly six months and one fine morning he flees away with a nurse leaving Sarasa behind to her own fate.

Rann's character has been exposed to us because of the presence of T. M. in the novel. T. M. is a good link, for connecting people. He is a man who goes through the city like a breeze everywhere, who knows many people.

The story of the novel records the impact of the Western ethos on Indians. Some succumb to the effect but others do not leave their roots. Rann succumbs to the Western wind but his wife is rooted in our culture and values. Thus, the novel presents two contrary philosophies of life. A. Hariprasanna (1998:159) attempts to draw a very good parallelism between Savitri and commandant Sarasa.[5] She feels that in *Talkative Man*, Narayan appears to have started where he left off several years ago in *The Dark Room*. Both novels deal with the theme of the suffering wife. In fact, Malgudi has changed, under the impact of modernity, remarkably, since Narayan had written his earlier novel, *The Dark Room*. Naturally, we may witness the attitudinal changes too in Narayan's characters. However, Hariprasanna does not find any change in the woman's condition. Both Savitri and Sarasa suffer because of the immortality of their husbands and both are humiliated by their husbands. However, both are different in their capabilities and perception. Savitri of yesterday does not earn money and so she is compelled to remain dependent on her husband. Just the opposite, Sarasa is financially independent and thus has greater freedom to choose the course of her life. Nevertheless, Sarasa, seems to be more traditional in her values because of her mental make-up and also her love for children. Naturally, she is ready to relinquish everything if only she can retain her husband. Here I agree with Cynthia Vanden Driesen (1993) who finds Sarasa representing a somewhat liberated woman.[6] To elaboarate, Sarasa is not a very weak and dutiful wife fleeing from a callous philandering husband, rather the full-blooded male is afraid of his dominating wife, who will not tolerate his roving eye. Sarasa is pictured as follows:

> A six-foot woman (as it seemed at first sight) dark-complexioned, cropped head and in jeans and a T-shirt with bulging breasts, the first of her kind in the Malgudi area ...[7]

Even her card, which she leaves with the Talkative Man reads "Commandant Sarasa, Home Guards Auxiliary, Delhi"[8] Like any other professional wife, the calls of her profession supersede her love for her husband. Later she explains her situation in a confessional manner: 'I could not give him enough time ... being mostly out on official duties.'[9]

THE WORLD OF NAGARAJ

With high ambition but with little potential, the protagonist of *The World of Nagaraj* is a typical Narayan character. The very first sentence of the novel says: 'Nagaraj fancied himself a man with a mission.'[10] He wants to write the biography of sage, Narada, but he hardly knows anything about him. He knows neither Sanskrit nor any sources of information about the sage. He simply talks about him to people hoping to find someone who can enlighten him. No one understands Nagaraj's obsession. He lives in a world that is unsympathetic to his great ambition. His brother Gopu, who is concerned with practical things in village like gobar gas, insecticide, etc., considers Nagaraj a dreaming idiot. In the house, his wife and his mother are always quarrelling and he did not like to arbitrate between them all the time. Other relatives and outsiders act like intruders, as he wants to concentrate on his subject. In addition to the people in his world, there are his own reflections and memories that distract him away from his subject.

Nagaraj belongs to a rich family of the Kabir Street. His father had money in the bank, a big house in the Kabir Street and vast rice fields in the village. After the death of his father, his property is divided between him and his brother. To his share comes the vast house and he gets a thousand rupees every month from his bank deposits. With no financial worries, he feels supreme contentment sitting on a pyol in the veranda, brooding and watching the activities of the neighbours.

Early in the novel, Nagaraj has developed a strategy of becoming inaccessible to others by wearing an ochre robe. He gets the colour from a *sanyasi* who informs him that when he wears the ochre robe, his mind should only be on God, not on money or the family. He must observe silence, become deaf to other people's voices. In the ochre robe, he feels transformed. His wife has to conduct herself as if he has ceased to exist. It is like experiencing temporary death a little each day so that he can slip into the final state effortlessly. Therefore, whenever he wants to concentrate, he wears ochre robe.

The novel describes the daily routine of Nagaraj and his effort to achieve equanimity. He likes to be out of his house as far as possible so that he does not have to listen to the criticism of his mother and Sita, his wife. Early morning, after coffee, he steps out and strolls along to wake up his friend, Jayaraj, the photographer, who sleeps on a bench in front of his shop at the archway. Jayaraj glances through one-sheet morning pages, ambling along the road to watch stalls and people. He sits on the pyol brooding until his wife gets the water ready for a bath. After bathing and eating, Nagaraj dresses himself in a snow-white dhoti with thread on the edge, a blue shirt and a white upper cloth and goes out. His first shop is at Kanni's stall at the Market corner. Kanni is an old chum of his primary school days. Now middle aged, he sits on a low stool inside his shop and sells cigarettes, soda and betel leaves and tobacco for chewing. After a little gossip, with a betel leaf in his mouth, he moves on to his next shop, Coomar's Boeing Saree Centre. Nagaraj has struck a lasting friendship with Coomar at the Boardless College House when the former is a student of Albert Mission College. Years later, with a little help from Nagaraj, Coomar starts selling saris on a bicyle. In due course of time, Coomar opens a big shop at the corner of the Grove Street and Nagaraj does some bookkeeping for him. After lunch, he occasionally goes to the Town Hall Library and talks to the old librarian about Narada. At times he simply sits on a pyol in the veranda watching people and birds and planning his book about the life of Sage Narada.

The quiet and comforting words of Nagaraj spread on the arrival of his brother's son, Tim, who leaves his own home in the village and comes to live with Nagaraj. When Gopu, Tim's father, comes to take him to the village, Tim refuses to go with him. Nagaraj unobtrusively observes Tim's movements. Tim always gets ready early in the morning. After his coffee, he borrows Sambu's scooter and goes out only to come very late in the night. Tim starts visiting Kismet Club in the New Extension. His late arrival worries Nagaraj but he does not have the courage to seek explanation from his nephew. He finds out from the Principal of Albert Mission School that Tim has been dropped out of the school. Tim's parents want to "tether him … to domestic life,"[11] so get him married to Saroja who sings with a harmonium in a nasal voice.

Now that Tim and Saroja begin to live in his house, Nagaraj finds his peace terribly disturbed. There is incessant chatter and giggling coming from their talk. After Tim leaves for the Kismet, Saroja starts reading aloud from a film magazine, and then she suddenly bursts out singing to the accompaniment of the harmonium.

To get help on his biography of Narada, Nagaraj goes to Karu Pandit who lives in a lane off Ellaman Street. With the help of the Talkative Man, the Pundit agrees to give Nagaraj lessons in the *deva bhasa,* Sanskrit. He even accepts an advance of one hundred rupees. The lessons are to start from some auspicious day that the Pundit finds from the almanac. Meanwhile Nagaraj has to go to the pundit daily to know when he will start the lessons. He has to cut short his stay at the

Silk Centre and leave at two-thirty instead of two after rushing through his ledger work. On the way, he stops at the Boardless for coffee. He walks a couple of miles everyday to Ellaman Lane, but the auspicious moment remains elusive. Everyday the Pundit spends time airing his views on the state of affairs, in general, ignoring the purpose of Nagaraj's visit. The Pundit proves to be very slippery. He tells Nagaraj that one needs 'an auspicious moment or day must be sought in the almanac only at an auspicious moment to begin with'.[12]

Nagaraj faces another predicament. He learns from the talkative man. that Saroja may start singing in Kismet. He feels stunned at the news–a daughter-in-law of the family to sing to a set of drunkards! What would his brother say? In addition, even the neighbours are sometimes impractical. His life is getting more and more complex, but he seeks freedom and peace of mind to write his book. He has to depend on others for that. After a visit to the river in search of peace, he goes to Bari, the stationer, to buy a notebook to write his book. There he comes to know that Bari hails from Aligarh where in his temple people worship god Narada. Bari reads from *Narad Puran*, and translates verses into broken Tamil, Pidgin English and sometimes in his own language. Nagaraj decides to write in English to reach a wider reading public. However, he canot write more than a few words because Bari's reading and comprehension are puzzling. Nowhere can Nagaraj find a mention of Narada. He does not know how to reduce the notes to a cogent, relevant narrative.

Taking a cue from Nagaraj, Saroja also starts getting up early. After Nagaraj finishes his bath, she occupies the bath shed and beats her washing on the granite slab. After washing, she starts humming a film tune before the mirror and then comes to the harmonium. Nagaraj finds that his pen does not move in that noise. At nine, he is filled with a sense of frustration and sits on a pyol, meditating until eleven after which he dresses up and goes out. As usual, he passes by Jayaraj, and then Kanni for betel leaves and goes to Coomar's Sari Centre.

He thinks of moving to the temple to write but Sita suggests that he should work at home wearing his ochre robe (which keeps people away) and cotton wool (which keeps out all sound). His experience of buying cotton wool is hilarious. He goes to Dr. Velu of Velu Medical Hall on the Market Road to get some cotton. He has to give an explanation for why he needs cotton wool. As Nagaraj feels hissing noise in the ear, the doctor suggests several tests to be done at Natwar's polyclinic and laboratory. Nagaraj flees from Dr. Velu and on the way stops at Ganesh Store to buy some cotton. He is able to get only wicks for the oil lamps for gods. He seeks a handful of twisted cotton wicks. As he reaches home, his wife snatches the cotton wicks, saying that she has promised to the gods in the temple to light a hundred wicks. When Nagaraj tells her that he needs a few wicks to plug his ears, she looks horrified at the idea, holds the packet away from him, and says:

> What an evil notion! To misuse god's lamp-wicks! I never thought you would stoop so low. It's a sin to misuse god's wicks.[13]

He has to make sense of his notes about cosmology and cataclysm, without a trace of creation. He is irritated that the old texts start from the beginning of the time and come to the point very slowly. Dressed in his ochre robe but without cotton wool in the ears, he begins to write but cannot concentrate because of the harmonium. Next day he begins without the ochre robe, and is again disturbed. He gets up angrily to stop the harmonium. Saroja happily greets him. Seeing that he is without the ochre robe she knows that she can talk to him at that moment. She tells him that she is trying a new tune and that she wants him to listen to her song and give his opinion. Tapping the keys of the harmonium she sings the song that says, "At midnight I am thinking of you, at dawn I think of you…."[14] He feels shy listening to the song with double meaning from a daughter-in-law of the family. The fury that drives him from his writing room has evaporated. While the girl is still singing, he slips away pretending to have heard a knock on the street door. He realizes that it is going to be impossible to tell the girl to stop. Sita does not want to come to his rescue by telling Saroja to practise music later.

The crisis comes when Tim and Saroja both begin to work in the Kismet Club and live in an outhouse. Gopu comes and creates a scene before the club. The sentry of the club does not allow him to enter the hall. Gopu sits cross-legged in the middle of the entrance. The strongman of the club cannot remove him, but when Gopu comes to know that his son has refused to meet him, he goes to the bus stand to catch a bus to his village.

After the death of his mother, and the departure of Tim, Saroja and Gopu, the house is normal and quiet. He is free from worries about Tim's movements. He can pray in peace and write in peace, sitting in a chair and at a table. He plans to get up at five in the morning and begin writing once again at seven.

At this moment, he hears a van stop before his house. Out of the van come Tim and Saroja with loads of luggage including a folding chair and a large harmonium with bellows to be operated by a foot pedal leaving both hands free from the player to produce the maximum noise. "Got at as good price for my old instrument and I was able to get this and the chair," she explains to Sita. They again occupy the room with the table and the chair. Tim does not explain anything but Saroja tells Sita that Tim has a fight with the Secretary of the club, and that they would not go back to the club any more. Nagaraj dreads that the harmonium will start blaring in the morning and there is no hope of writing any more. Sita can as well take the notebook back to the old room, where at least the ants may relish his notes on Narada. He tells his wife not to be surprised if he wears the ochre robe when he is at home. It will force him not to speak out and upset the children, driving them out again. He will also acquire a lot of cotton wool and pack it all in his ears "so that even a thunderclap may sound like a whisper."[15]

Nandini Saha (2007:102) thinks the story may be divided into three sections.[16] The first section consists of Chapter one to ten and discusses Nagaraj and his life in Kabir Street. Chapter eleven and twelve focus on self-reflexive debate and make up the second section. Saha finds this section unimportant as these two chapters can be easily deleted without affecting the novel's evolution. The third section comprises Chapters Thirteen and Fifteen where the narrative focus shifts back to Nagaraj and his life with his family in Kabir Street. In the last section the narrative records further complications and within these three chapters all problems are solved and normalcy returns to Nagaraj's household. Unlike *Talkative Man*, the end of the novel is not sudden and abrupt. In fact, here the end comes very smoothly as Nagaraj decides not to write a "magnum opus."

In this novel , Nagaraj is painted as very weak and incapable of being a responsible person. His "ochre robe" does not symbolize his strong passion for spiritualism but his suppressed desire to run away from the harsh realities of life and also his inabilities to face the challenges of daily life. That is why, he is called by his father a dreamy fellow. Even Saha considers his retreat into the puja room an 'excuse to escape the hassles of regular life.'[17] Further, he is not strong enough to ask for an explanation from his own nephew when he gets back home from a party in a drunken stage. Nagaraj has to rehearse his "tone of authority and firmness"[18] but he fails to scold his own nephew in spite of his unacceptable behaviour.

A. Hariprasanna (1998:130-31) explains why Narada has been taken as a great renouncer of the world and how he fits into the theme of renunciation quite well[19]. Narada, though a renouncer, moves with ease among gods and demons. He is able to travel any distance according to his sweet will and is welcome in all the different worlds above and below. Sometimes he creates strife by passing some gossip from one quarter to another but always to benefit the world in the end. Therefore, Narada is a true *sanyasi* who moves only for the sake of others and for the benefit of humanity in general. In fact, renunciation has been considered very religiously in the Indian consciousness. Narayan is great in the sense that he takes up this subject of renunciation and suggests that strict adherence to the traditional *asramadharma* is not necessary to renounce the world. He also affirms that this appears to be a negative concept but in fact it is a very positive one that sustains and nourishes both–life and society.

Saha (2007:101-12) has written a long paper to theorize that this novel can be taken as an icon of a Post-Modern Malgudi:

> Times are changing as is evident from the new methods of agriculture, the gobar gas plant, the new bar and restaurant in the town called the Kismet where there is a dress code and Gopu is not allowed inside because of his typical villager's dress. Similarly, in the novel the infiltration of postmodern self-reflexive metafictional elements that commingle with the portrayal of Malgudi produces a new kind of Malgudi novel.[20]

GRANDMOTHER'S TALE

Grandmother's Tale, Narayan's latest work published in 1992 is a "borderline between fact and fiction" (Explanation of *Grandmother's Tale*, p. 0)[21] It is the story of his great-grandmother as narrated by his grandmother and transcreated by the author. It is being treated here because Narayan has given his biography a fictional form. He himself says that 'this is mainly a story-writer's version of hearsay biography of a great- grandmother.'[22] The great grandmother Bala, probably lived in the later period of the East India Company (i.e. the first half of 19th century). Bala marries at the early age of seven to Viswa, a boy of ten. One day Viswa just leaves bidding her goodbye and joins a group of pilgrims going to Pandaripur. Years go by but there is no trace of him. Bala, now a young woman, finds life extremely difficult with the entire *agraharam* gossiping about her husband's tale. She leaves home determined to find him. She undertakes an arduous journey to Poona. She succeeds in locating Viswa and persuading him to return to the South–to their long, happy life in Kumbakonam, where five children were born to them. Bala's death and eventually Viswa's death due to poisoning by his third wife's mother form rest of the narrative. The little girl, Bala is informed of her marriage only a week before the wedding. First, she protests, but it is of no use. On the day of marriage, she realises that she has seen the bridegroom often in the adjoining street. After the weeklong celebration, the bridegroom, Vishwanath, goes back to his school run under a Banyan tree. His friends rag him but his teacher rescues him by saying that marriage is not a bad thing to go in for. She meets her husband only on special occasions. These meetings lack privacy and anyhow she is able to talk only a few words. In the very first meeting, she touches the black patch under his ear. The husband when asked says that the black patch is a lucky sign according to his mother. Gradually they discover an interest in each other's company. As frequent meetings are almost impossible, Viswa finds a way. He manages to reach the backyard of the in-law's house through a dirty lane and is able to watch his wife doing household jobs. After a brief conversation, she goes inside the house. These meetings continue for sometime until one day Viswa informs the girl that he is going away but he asks her to keep it a secret. When asked about the place he replies that he wants to join a group of pilgrims singing a bhajan about Pandaripur and will come later. This is the last time the girl meets him for a long time to come. As days passes by, she secretly starts worrying about him until her mother realises that there is something wrong. When she comes to know about his departure, she informs her husband about it. He goes to the boy's house to ask his whereabouts but he is informed that the boy is living with his in-laws. After a frantic search, they come to know that he is seen with a group crossing the river. Everyone nurses a secret fear that Vishwa is drowned in the river and offerings are promised in the temple for his coming back alive. As the girl matures, people ask about her husband and she gives evasive replies about his whereabouts. Soon she is tired of all this and mostly keeps herself indoors except for a visit to the temple on Tuesday and Friday evenings. She prays for some news about her husband.

In the temple also, women start talking that most probably her husband is no more but she refuses to live like a widow. One day the priest comes to her mother and instructs her not to send her daughter to the temple. Infuriated at this, she tells the priest that her husband is alive and she will not rest until she comes back with him some day to shame them all. Then she runs towards Viswa's house leaving her mother behind. Her mother-in-law asks her to live with them but Bala says that she will live with them when she comes back with her husband. She puts a pinch of vermilion on her brow, prostrates at her mother-in-law's feet who asks her to wait for her father-in-law. Bala leaves the place with some clothes, money, a few gold ornaments and a knife to end her life if she is unable to protect her honour. With only one word Pandaripur in her mind, she takes the right track, joins travellers, and reaches Poona after a year. By this time, she has exhausted all her money and gold jewellery. The language people speak in Poona is alien to her. Somehow, she lands in a rest house. Making the rest house a central place, she starts looking at passers-by hoping to find Viswa. She can remember his face and the black patch under his left ear. Once an elderly woman asks about her in Marathi, she points to her thali (a sign of a married woman) and starts weeping, muttering something in Tamil. They sympathise with her; someone recognises her language and guesses that she is a Madrasi. A person takes her to a Tamilian who has been living in Poona for many years and leaves her at his door. There she finds a man riding on a horse and is dressed like a Marathi. As she wonders about his identity, she continues to sit there praying to her God for help. The servant of the house tries to whisk her away but when she refuses to leave that place, the master of the house summons her. He speaks to her in Marathi and tries to send her away by offering her money. She refuses to leave the place. At this moment, the mistress of the house comes to her rescue. She asks talking in Tamil about her story. Concealing the real purpose behind her stay, she concocts a story and tells her that she is separated from a pilgrim's group.

Surma, the mistress of the house, gives Bala food, shelter, and talks about her garden, her father and her husband. Bala gradually collects information about them. The woman reports that her husband whom she always addresses as Bhatji is a renowned gem and diamond dealer. Long ago, he came to her father's shop in a ragged condition and kept standing in front of the shop for the whole day. Her father who was busy did not notice him but she, who was eighteen at that time, felt pity for him and persuaded her father to talk to that boy. The boy wanted to work and he had come to Poona from a south Indian village. He had visited other parts of the country and had learnt Marathi while in Bombay. The old man was impressed by his adventurous story and gave him a job in his shop and a room to live in. Soon he became the old man's trusted person and got training in the gem business. However, when she disclosed her intention to marry the boy, her father was furious and threatened them with dire consequences. They eloped to Nasik and married secretly in the temple of Trimalaka. Eventually her father accepted them and after his death, the whole property and business came to them. Surma constantly expressed her admiration and love for Vishwanath.

One day Surma goes to the temple leaving the house in Bala's charge. Bala is waiting for this moment. Shutting the front door, she goes upstairs and comes to Viswa's room. When Viswa asks her to go out she says that she has already recognised him and his whiskers, which he had grown on Surma's advice. Therefore, he is not able to hide his face. She said that she had already seen the black patch that was supposed to bring luck. She also says that she has waited for long and shows him the *thali* tied in front of God to her neck. Finally, Viswa is overwhelmed and asks her to be patient and not to upset Surma. Bala is ready to wait but not for a long time. They live separately in the same house and once again, when Surma is away she asks Viswa to return to their own village. At first, he refuses to leave the place and his trade but finally agrees. Bala makes her plan very meticulously.

Viswa assures her that he would tell the truth to Surma and she is not required to live as a domestic servant but as his wife. Bala refuses to stay there. She gives a time limit to return but not without him. He keeps on pleading that he cannot live without Surma but she is adamant. Unconscious of all these developments, Surma is worried to see her husband disturbed. Bala then asks Surma to visit Vitholba temple for a change with Bhatji and herself. They plan a three to four months tour to the South. After a month, they reach Banglore where they camp for three days. On the fourth day, Bala enters the water and threatens to drown herself unless Viswa sends Surma back. Surma now comes to know everything and is ready to live together but Bala refuses to take her to the village. With great tact, she sends Surma back with her entourage. Viswa is pained to leave Surma but there is no way out.

They return to their village where Bala's house has been occupied by someone else who informs her that the old lady has gone to live in Benaras after her husband's death because their only daughter had run away from home a long time back. Viswa's house is not even traceable. He returns after almost 30 years. So they move to Kumbakonam. In Kumbakonam, Viswa settles as a gem dealer and Bala lives satisfactorily as a housewife, giving birth to three daughters and a son. They spend the next twenty years happily in great prosperity. His daughters are married now and the son has become a doctor.

Changes are coming in Viswa's life. His son is posted at Kolar in Mysore. Viswa, now nearing seventy, finds it tedious to continue the gem business. Bala, who, too, has grown old, engages a woman having a twelve-year daughter with her to cook. Gradually, Bala leaves the household to the woman and her daughter. As Bala'a health is declining, a vaid (a doctor expert in traditional medicine) is called for her treatment. His son also arrives a month later but inspite of his best effort she does not survive. After the obsequies are over, Viswanath is persuaded by his married daughter to go with his son. The house is locked up, leaving two rooms for the cook (woman) and her daughter, who work now as caretakers.

Viswa is now with his son's family, consisting of his wife, a son and a daughter. His son's bunglow is spacious and Viswa is looked after well. He sometimes remembers Surma and Bala. His son is a busy person but hands over his salary to his father. After counting the amount (i.e. Rupees. 400), he gives it to his daughter-in-law saying that he has enough money of his own. In due course, the salary is given directly to his daughter-in-law. Now Viswa is restless, as he hopes that again his son will give his salary to him. After a few months when his daughter-in-law gives him the salary bag, he is angry that his son has no time to hand over the salary. He remarks that now his son is a big man. Ignoring the bag, he bolts the door from inside. He feels that his son has no time for him. To teach them a lesson, he leaves the house informing his daughter-in-law that he is going away. He returns to Kumbakonam. The cook woman and his daughter welcome him and one day his daughter (R K Narayan's grandmother) gets the information that his father (Viswa) has married the cook woman's daughter. It is the culmination of a rage against his son. This drastic step proves fatal. The cook is now his mother-in-law. She has an eye on his collection of rare stones. When the old man realises his mistake, he wants to return to Kolar, to his son, but the shrewd woman keeps a strict vigil on him and one day poisons him to death, after taking his signature on the documents. His son, Swaminathan, comes from Kolar and takes charge of his assets. The neighbours mention to him the woman's schemes to grab his wealth. The son disposes of the house and returns to Kolar.

Grandmother's Tale brings out the character of Bala as a Hindu wife whose social identity is determined by marriage. With no moods or vagaries of her own, she tunes herself to the moods and vagaries of her husband. She draws upon her inner resources and her character develops according to her circumstances–happy or unhappy. This *Tale* delineates Bala growing up from an innocent little girl–sitting in the lap of her father at the time of her marriage to a firm, determined, aggressive young woman and finally to a quiet, docile, orthodox Hindu wife.

It would not be out of place here to remind ourselves of what is beguilingly called "unnecessary lesson" which Narayan as a child has to learn. In fact, this is a part of the socialising process that every Indian has to undergo in the past. Now, of course, there are women's magazines and televisions besides mothers' or grandmothers' lessons. A child born as a female becomes a woman and a child born as a male comes to expect from a woman too much by undergoing this socialising process. Narayan refers to this unnecessary lesson in a very clear term:

> The most unnecessary lesson however, is my memory as I realise it now, was a Sanskrit lyric, not in praise of God, but defining the perfect woman–it is said that the perfect woman must work like a slave, advise like a *Mantri* (Minister), look like Goddess Lakshmi, be patient like Mother Earth and courtesan–like in the bed chamber–this I had to recite on certain days of the week.[23]

According to this perfect woman (i.e. a wife, because there is no other role envisaged here for a woman) should be hardworking, intelligent, beautiful, patient (i.e. one who can endure suffering like mother earth) and sexually provocative.

A serious reading of the novel marks it as a biography that borders between fact and fiction though one does know how much of it is fact and how much is fiction. However, from different sources, it appears true that it is a tale of Narayan's great grandmother. A. Hariprasanna (2007:161-63) tries to draw a parallelism between Bala and Vishwa on the one hand and Savitri-Satyaban on the other hand besides discovering some similarities and differences between *Talkative Man* and *The Grandmother's Tale*.[24]

The protagonist of Talkative Man, Sarasa, comes to Malgudi in search of her husband. She finds her husband after a long search but she fails to capture him and live with him for the remaining period of her life. In case of *Grandmother's Tale*, Bala also searches for her missing husband for a very long time, but she succeeds in convincing him to be with her and spend the rest of her life peacefully and harmoniously in Kumbakonam. In *Talkative Man*, Sarasa has been painted as an educated modern woman but Bala of *The Grandmother's Tale* is a traditional homemaker but committed to the institution of marriage.

The story of *Grandmother's Tale* moves parallel to the story of Savitri-Satyaban legend of the *Mahabharata*. As Savitri pursues Yama, Bala follows her husband and finally wins him back from the clutch of his another wife, Surma. The novel is replete with this myth. The narrator of the story says:

> What else could a poor woman like her do to recover her husband? Only a woman can understand it. To a woman, her husband is everything. She cannot lose him. Remember in what condition Bala had left home and what trials she must have gone through to reach Poona and how much misery she faced before she could reach him. Everything is justified, all means are justified in her case. Did not Savitri conquer herself, and trap him into promising her a boon? ... Yama had to yield back Satyavan's life. You should not imagine a greater woman than Savitri for austerity and purity of mind.[25]

Thus, myths and legends of the Vedic times have been followed by the stories of *The Upanishads* and the Jatakas which merge into history blurring the frontiers between history and fiction.[26]

REFERENCES

Talkative Man

1. *Talkative Man*, p. 120.
2. *Ibid.*
3. P.S. Sundaram, *R .K. Narayan as a Novelist* (Delhi, 1981), p.114.
4. Nandani Saha, The world of Nagaraj: A Postmoden Malgudi?, *The Journal of Commonwealth Literature*, 42(2), 101-112, 2007.
5. A. Hariprasanna.*The World of Malgudi: A Study of R. K. Narayan's Novels.* (Delhi, 1998)
6. Driesan, C.V. 'The Novelist Skipped Town …' % A Postscript to the ICASEL Conference – Mysore. Online. Retrieved on 10 April 2008 from *http://wwwmcc.murfoch.edu.au/Reading*Room/listserv/SPAN/34/ Driesen.html
7. *Talkative Man,* p. 39.
8. *Talkative Man,* p. 98.
9. *Talkative Man,* p. 117.

The World of Nagaraj

10. *The World of Nagaraj*, p. 1
11. *Ibid.* p. 86.
12. *Ibid.* p. 115.
13. *Ibid.*, p 140.
14. *Ibid.*, p 142.
15. *Ibid.*, p 185.
16. Nandani Saha, The world of Nagaraj: A Postmoden Malgudi? p. 102.
17. *Ibid.*, p.104.
18. *The World of Nagaraj*, p. 66.
19. A. Hariprasanna. *The World of Malgudi: A Study of R. K. Narayan's Novels.* p. 131.
20. *Ibid.*, p.111.

Grandmother's Tale

21. Explanation of *Grandmother's Tale*, p. 0.
22. *Grandmother's Tale*, p. 8.

23. *Ibid.*, p. 5.
24. A. Hariprasanna. *The World of Malgudi: A Study of* R. K. *Narayan's Novels.* pp. 161-63.
25. *Grandmother's Tale*, pp. 65-66.
26. A. Hariprasanna. *The World of Malgudi: A Study of* R. K. *Narayan's Novels.* p. 163.

9

CONCLUSION

> I think and think for months and years. Ninety-nine times, the conclusion is false. The hundredth time I am right.
>
> —Albert Einstein

R. K. Narayan is great in many respects. He has been perhaps the most prolific Indo-Anglian novelist. He began his literary career with his novel *Swami and Friends* (1935) and ended with his last novel entitled *Grandmother's Tale.* He has fifteen novels and over half a dozen volumes of short stories besides several essays and travelogues to his credit. His literary merit and growing reputations in India and aboard have brought him many laurels. He earned the Sahitya Academy Award (1961), Padma Bhushan (1964), the Royal Society of literature Christopher Benson Award (1964), an honorary doctorate degree from the University of Leeds in 1973, the same degree from Delhi University in 1974, the Benson Medal of the Royal Society of Literature in 1980, honorary membership of the American Academy and Institute of Arts and Letters in 1981, and the lifetime achievement award for a South Asian writer and Padma Vibhushan in 2000. His greatness lies in the fact that the India Mr. Narayan deals with is of ages and sages. It breaks the bounds of cultural experience. He is unique also because he follows no trend but humanity. He unrolls a vast panorama of his country people with men and women who, despite their strengths and weaknesses, have souls. Naturally, a full-length study of his characters, especially principal characters, is warranted to understand the social ethos of Malgudi. His principal characters are of a wide range. His characters constitute a school kid, collegiate, lecturer, officer, printer, financial expert, freedom fighter, guide, publisher, painter of signs, journalist, tiger acting and interacting like human beings, enchantingly leisurely Nagaraj, and a young woman searching frantically for her lost husband. If these characters are classified into three categories–gods, demons and human beings–we discover that not a single principal character is godly. Even the portrait of Gandhi, who is not the principal character, is weak. Gandhi, who has been raised to the position of the Father of the Nation and who is full of divine qualities does not enlarge our awareness in the sense of 'painting a picture larger than life.'[1] Vasu of *The Man-Eater of Malgudi* is really demonic–full of evil qualities and endowed with a giant's strength. Moreover, we know that power corrupts and absolute power corrupts absolutely. Vasu brings untold sufferings to his neighbourhood, and, in this process, he also kills himself. However, Vasu in spite of being the title figure of the novel *The Man-Eater of Malgudi* is not the principal character because the novel is not so much the story of Vasu as that of Nataraj. Moreover, in the perpetual fight between good and evil, Vasu, the evil incarnation, loses the battle in favour of Nataraj. Almost all his main characters are neither saints nor devils. They are ordinary, very ordinary human beings. 'There is nothing very sensational or heroic about them. A little more brightness would have made them too conspicuous for Malgudi.'[2]

The only animal character in the novel, *A Tiger for Malgudi,* a tiger, is Raja. He has been described in the way a human being is normally described. In addition, he behaves as a human being and possesses ego, a philosophy of life and values normally associated with human beings.

Like George Eliot, Narayan creates real men and women. He does not want to meddle with glamorous illusions of life tinged with fanciful imagination. None of his principal characters is a high dignitary. There are 'no maharjas wearing turbans worked with gold and diamonds, no maharanis representing oriental splendour–not even a Nawab Bahadur going for shikar in Mempi Hills of Malgudi.'[3]

Narayan's characters are ordinary in a special sense also. Their ordinariness is the permanent quality but their extra-ordinariness is purely temporal and it withers away soon. This theory is applicable to almost all the principal characters. Taranath discovers a recurring pattern with most of the main characters in Narayan's novels: 'from average to the extraordinary and back again to a more poignant state of averge.'[4] Chandran (*The Bachelor of Arts*), once a forlorn and dejected youth, ready to commit suicide, turns into a Sadhu renouncing the world and finally comes back to the world and lives his life without any memory of the old wounds. Chandran appears an extraordinary fellow while choosing sanyasa but on a deeper analysis, we come to know that his taking to sanyasa is in preference to suicide. That is why a man who is bent upon embracing sanyasa settles down in his life like an ordinary man. Savitri, the principal character in *The Dark Room* is ill-treated by her husband but swallows the insult. Nevertheless, an awareness of her husband's involvement with some other lady compels her to take recourse to the dark room and at some later stage when she gets fed up with the tyranny of her husband, she leaves the house again. Krishna *(The English Teacher),* who is highly concerned about the safe arrival of his baby, grows mature enough to pronounce the Upanishadic truth: 'We come together only to go apart again...a profound unmitigated loneliness is the only truth of life.' [5] This character is unlike other normal characters because in his case we find a movement from ordinariness to extraordinariness. His extraordinariness at the end is reflected in his wanting to revive the old Indian tradition of education. Sriram in *Waiting for the Mahatma* has nothing to do with politics but under the influence of the revolutionary Jagdish, takes to terrorism. He is jailed but he comes out subdued and ready to marry Bharati as the novel ends. So he returns to the same point from where he starts. His political career is only a showmanship. Mr. Sampath begins as a 'printer, becomes a producer-actor, finds disaster overtaking his film company, and emptiness, his relation with Shanti, the actress, ends as a forlorn person whose real job is only to be a printer'.[6] In fact, Sampath gets sick of Shanti soon after running off to the jungle with her and returns to his family, normal once again. Margayya begins as a petty moneylender, having his office under a tree in front of a co-operative bank. He grows prosperous under the influence of Dr. Pal and Madan Lal but he is scandalized by Dr. Pal as a heartless villain. Therefore, his business collapses and at the end, he remains his old original self. Raju (in *The Guide)* also has a superb phase but he is reduced to a prisoner. He begins as a Railway guide, moves on to become Rosie's guide but suddenly finds himself behind the bars. Even his sanyasa is a fake one because he embraces it to earn his livelihood. Nataraj (in *The Man-Eater of*

Malgudi), in the beginning, is found to be printing coloured labels for K.J. and towards the end of the novel again, he is seen busy with the same job. Raman (in *The Painter of Signs),* in the course of painting signboards, comes across Daisy, develops an intimate relationship, and proposes to her but gets disappointment. Moreover, at the end again he is seen painting the board once again. Raja, the protagonist of the novel *A Tiger for Malgudi,* has moments of ecstatic experience but towards the end and in the beginning of the novel he is enjoying the bliss of freedom.

E. M. Forster classifies characters into two categories–flat and round. Nevertheless, this classification does not work out well here because normally Narayan's characters belong to the intermediate shade between flat and round. For instance, Sriram, the hero of *Waiting for the Mahatma,* shares the features of flat as well as round characters. As far as his flatness is concerned, he continues to be the same. The only perceptible difference is his winning over Bharati. Otherwise 'he remains the same: a romantic body, irresponsible, headstrong and bashful.'[7] Even his active contact with Mahatma Gandhi hardly makes any difference because his dominant passion of his life is his love for Bharati. Sampath is flat because he begins and ends as a printer. Nevertheless, he has a greater degree of roundness also. This rotundity lies in that he has a vast experience of life including the job of producer-actor. Krishna *(The English Teacher),* a caring father and husband, grows sad because of his wife's death. Suddenly he finds a ray of hope in his three-year old daughter whose upbringing becomes a sacred duty for him. And with the passage of time he has a realisation of 'the moments of rare immutable joy-moments for which one feels grateful to life and death.'[8] Margayya also appears to be a flat character because he begins and ends his career in the same way explaining some financial aspects. Nevertheless, beneath the surface, he is a round character who undergoes many vicissitudes in life cheerfully because he believes that the world is a stage and one man in his lifetime plays several roles. Thus, Margayya changes a lot. Readers find a transition in his life–from Margayya, the moneylender to Margayya, the philosopher.

We may also draw a distinction between the earlier characters and the later characters of Narayan. Narayan's earlier characters appear to be the different phases of the same person. For instance, the principal characters of *Swami and Friends, The Bachelor of Arts and The English Teacher* refer to the three phases of life, i.e., childhood, youth and householder. However, the later characters are types in themselves and stretch themselves to the world. Naturally, Sampath, Margyya, Raju, Nataraj, Jagan, Raman and Dr. Rann have been involved in a chaos of human relationships and activities.

Generally, Narayan's main characters appear to be tragic ones. Chandran is tragic because he 'wakes to men's preoccupations with themselves, the loneliness of the individual and the callousness of time and is shocked. It is the shock of innocence waking to experience.'[9] Savitri's tragedy lies in her slavery and her extra concern for home and children. This is why, she is not free even to confine herself to the dark room or the temple. Margayya is a tragic figure because both his loves–money and son–disappoint him. All his money is wasted and his son gets spoilt because he takes to drinking, gambling and begins to associate himself with loose women. Raju's tragedy lies in the fact that his acting is taken as his being. Nataraj is a tragic person because he cannot bear to think of his enemy: 'I could never be a successful enemy to anyone. Any enmity worried me day and night. It bothered me like a toothache.'[10] He suffers also because he cannot say 'No' to anyone–whether a tea stall man needs his help to cure a sick elephant, or a monosyllabic poet wishes to get an epic printed in a dreadful hurry. Jagan's life is miserable because of his maladjustment with his son, Mali who is a modern, Westernized youngman believing in the acquisition of immense wealth and having pre–marital sex. Raman is a tragic character because the girl of his choice is a woman's lib enthusiast.

Further, a common thread to bind all principal characters is their belonging to a common class, i.e. middle class. In addition, Narayan writes about them because he knows them best. We may have some instances of upper class people such as Soma Sundram, Deputy Superintendent of Police and Principal Browne, but they are minor characters. Moreover, nearly all main characters are Hindus. It is so not because of Narayan's preference of Hindu religion to other religions. It is so because he is aware of the life in a Hindu family more intimately. Still, his novels do have people from different religions. We have instances of Christians like Mr. Brown and Mr. Ebenzer. One cannot ignore Gaffur, a Muslim playing important role in *The Guide*. However, characters from other religions have been granted minor status. What is more significant here is that Narayan does not describe his people in terms of caste because caste is not a major consideration for him.

As Hindu religion has its origin in very ancient times, characters are also bound by tradition and naturally, they believe in many ancient rituals and superstitions. In fact, they have started taking note of the wind of change, but Narayan accepts them as they are and does not take them to task for their being and commitment. For instance, Chandran is disallowed to marry Malthi because their horoscopes do not tally. Nevertheless, characters' attitudes do change in Narayan's later novels. Raju dares to live with someone else's wife under the same roof and Mali is courageous to live with Grace without marrying her, defying the age-old social convention. In fact, Narayan is aware of the impact of the Western civilization but he is also aware of the roots that lie too deep for the winds of change to disturb them. Further, it is his awareness of the roots that does not allow any character to go his own way for long.

As far as Narayan's control over his characters is concerned, it is implicit. Therefore, he does not allow a great many impossible things such as Sriram's elopement with Bharati or Raju's settling down with Rosie in life. Such actions on the part of characters may also go against their temperament and consequently, make them unconvincing. Of course, his characters are free in motivation. For example, Chandran's taking to Sanyasa grows out from his 'strong urge to be away from the environment which reminds him every moment of the girl he had loved and lost,'[11] though his characters are not always free to act out of their natures. 'Their freedom has several checks–the checks of caste, religion, economy, social prestige, family structure and the pressure of social relationships'.[12]

Narayan seems to agree with Radhakrishnan that 'The worst sinner has a future as the greatest saint has had a past. No one is as good or as bad as he imagines.'[13] Therefore, in his scheme of life, characters are not doomed. Each one of his characters–wicked or virtuous – is drawn with extraordinary tenderness. Consequently, characters emerge as interesting, amusing and convincing figures and make the earth colourful and worth living. Narayan's characters sound good because of their positive outlook towards life. That is why we find Chandran, Sampath, Margayya and Sarasa declaring that all battles are worth fighting. They have always a hope for the future. Even a sinner like Raju finds an ideal worth aspiring for in his death.

Renunciation is simply inseparable from the Indian psyche and so it is very much expected to recur with relation to some of Narayan's characters. A desire to use the theme of renunciation dawned upon Narayan because of several reasons. First, Narayan appears to have a great respect for religion and spiritualism. Next, renunciation is a part of social reality in the Indian society also. We share with A. Hariprasanna, who finds Narayan taking a very comprehensive view of this theme and does not feel that renunciation suggests only running away from home and family:

> The most important thing for the man or woman of genuine renunciation is the achievement of non-attachment, freedom from delusions of all kinds, transcendence of the ego, and serenity of mind...[14]

To elaborate, we may consider the characters of Raju and Jagan. Raju initially plays the role of a holy man to please gullible villagers but slowly gets transformed into a real saintly person and tries to elevate the pitiable condition of villagers. In this case, he gets rid of lots of illusions and also gets a chance to develop a serenity of mind. Jagan is a wealthy and satisfied person but at a certain stage, prefers to renounce all the worldly comfort and withdraws into a grove and becomes a saint in search of self-realization.

To sum up, Narayan's characters have variety. Narayan himself takes pride in the wide range of characters: 'All morning I wandered. At every turn, I found a character fit to go into a story.'[15] Writing about her characters George Eliot said:

> There are few prophets in the world; few sublimely beautiful; few heroes. I can't afford to give all my love and reverence to such varieties; I want a great deal of those feelings for my everyday fellowmen, especially for the few in the foreground of the great multitude whose faces I know ... And I would not ... be the clever novelist who could create a world so much better than this, in which we get up in the morning to do our daily work, that would be likely to turn a harder, colder eye on the dusty streets and the common green fields, on the real breathing men and women. [16]

Like George Eliot, Narayan succeeds in creating 'the real breathing men and women'. In addition, these breathing men and women have been created in line with the social and moral ethos of Malgudi. So, Narayan's characters and place (i.e. Malgudi) are inseparable.

REFERENCES

1. P. S. Sundaram, *R. K. Narayan* (New Delhi, 1973), p. 88.
2. N. Mukherji, *The World of Malgudi,* An unpublished doctoral dissertation, Louisiana State Univ., 1960, p. 107.
3. *Ibid.,* p. 42.
4. M. K. Naik, S. K. Desai and G. S. Amur (eds). *Critical Essays on Indian Writings in English* (Dharwar, 1972), p. 296.
5. R. K. Narayan, *The English Teacher* (Mysore, 1970), p. 203.
6. *Critical Essays on Indian Writings in English* (Dharwar, 1972), p. 296.
7. Nirmal Mukherji, *The World of Malgudi,* p. 64.
8. *The English Teacher*, p. 214.
9. P. S. Sundaram, *R. K. Narayan as a Novelist (Delhi, 1988)*, p. 30.
10. R. K. Narayan, *The Man-Eater of Malgudi* (New York, 1961), p. 98.
11. *The World of Malgudi,* p. 121.
12. *Ibid.,* p. 162.
13. S. Radhakrishnan, *The Hindu View of Life* (London, 1927), p. 71.
14. A. Hariprasanna, *The World of Malgudi: A Study of R.K.Narayan's Novels.* (New Delhi, 1998), p. 198.
15. Susan Ram, '50 years of Story Telling,' *The Telegraph,* 11 May, 1986, p. 7.
16. George Eliot, *Scenes of Clerical Life* (Boston, 1907), p. 62.

BIBLIOGRAPHY

PRIMARY SOURCE

Novels

Narayan, R. K. (1971), *Swami and Friends*. Mysore: Indian Thought Publications, (First Pub.1935).

——(1982), *The Bachelor of Arts*. Mysore: Indian Thought Publications, (First Pub. 1937).

——(1986), *The Dark Room*. Mysore: Indian Thought Publications, (First Pub. 1938).

——(1970), *The English Teacher*. Mysore: Indian Thought Publications, (First Pub. 1945).

——(1983), *Mr. Sampath*. Mysore: Indian Thought Publications, (First Pub. 1949).

——(1984), *The Financial Expert*. Mysore: Indian Thought Publications, (First Pub. 1952).

——(1971), *Waiting for the Mahatama*. Mysore: Indian Thought Publications, (First Pub. 1955).

——(1983), *The Guide*. Mysore: Indian Thought Publications, (First Pub. 1958).

——(1984), *The Man-Eater of Malgudi*. Mysore: Indian Thought Publications, (First pub. 1961).

——(1981), *The Vendor of Sweets*. Mysore: Indian Thought Publications, (First pub. 1967).

——(1986), *The Painter of Signs*. Mysore: Indian thought Publications, (First Pub. 1977).

——(1983), *A Tiger for Malgudi*. Mysore: Indian Thought Publications, (First Pub. 1983).

——(1986), *Talkative Man*. Mysore: Indian Thought Publications, (First Pub. 1985).

——(1993), *The World of Nagaraj*. Mysore: Indian Thought Publications, (First Pub. 1990).

——(1997), *Grandmother's Tale*. Mysore: Indian Thought Publications, (First Pub. 1992).

Short Stories

Narayan, R. K. (1945), *Cyclone & Other Stories*. Mysore: Indian Thought Publications.

——(1943), *Malgudi Days*. Mysore: Indian Thought Publications.

——(1947), *An Astrologer's Day and Other Stories*. London: Eyre and Spottswide.

——(1950), *Dodu and Other Stroies*. Mysore: Indian Thought Publications.

——(1979), *Lawley Road and Other Stories*. Delhi: Orient Paperback, (First Pub. 1956)

——(1970), *A Horse and Two Goats*. Mysore: Indian Thought Publications,.

——(1974), *The Reluctant Guru: Short Tories and Anecdotes*. Delhi: Hind Pocket books..

——(1981), *Old and New*. Mysore: Indian Thought Publications.

——(1985), *Under the Banyan Tree and Other Stories*. London: Heinemann.

——(1992), *Malgudi Landscapes: The Best of R.K. Narayan*. Ed. S. Krishnan, New Delhi: Penguin (India).

——(1993), *Salt and Sawdust: Stories and Table Talk*. New Delhi: Penguin Books.

Others

Narayan, R. K. (1956), *Next Sunday*: Delhi: Orient Paperback.

——(1971), *My Dateless Diary* (travel in America). Delhi: Orient Paperback, (First Pub., 1960).

——(1973), *Gods, Demons and Others*. Mysore: Indian Thought Publications, (First Pub. 1965).

——(1975), *My Days*: A Memoir. Mysore: Indian Thought Publications.

SECONDARY SOURCE

Books

Agnihotri, G. N. (1984), *Indian Life and Problems in the Novels of Mulk Raj Ananad, Raja Rao and R. K. Narayan.* Meerut: Shalabh Book House.

Bhatnagar, M.K., ed. (2002), *New Insights into R.K.Narayan.* New Delhi: Atlantic Publishers and Distributors.

Cecil, David (1972), *Early Victorian Novelists.* Ludhiana: Kalyani Publishers.

Chew, Shirley (1973), "A Proper Detachment: The Novels of R.K. Narayan." *Readings in Commonwealth Literature.* London: Oxford University Press.

Coomaraswamy, Anand K. (1956), *The Transformation of Nature in Art.* New York: Dover Publications.

——(1909), *Essays in Indian Naturalism.* Madras: G. A. Natesh and Co.

Das, Kamala (1970), *The Golden Treasury of Indo- Anglian Poetry 1828-1965*, Ed. V. K. Gokak. New Delhi: Sahitya Academy.

Dhawan, R. K. (ed.) (1982), *Explorations in Modern Indo-English Fiction.* New Delhi: Bahri Publications Pvt. Ltd.

Goyal, B. S. (1983), *R. K. Narayan: A Critical Spectrum.* Meerut: Shalabh Book House.

Hariprasanna, A. (1998), *The World of Malgudi: A Study of R.K.Narayan's Novels.* New Delhi: Prestige Publishers.

Holmstrom, Lakshmi (1973), *The Novels of R. K. Narayan.* Calcutta: Writer's Workshop.

Ibsen, H. (1966), *Three Plays.* New York: Dell Publishing Co. Inc.

Iyengar, K. R. S. (1984), *Indian Writings in English.* New Delhi: Sterling Publishers Pvt. Ltd.

Mehta, Ved. (1974), *John is Easy to Please.* Hardmondsworth: Penguin Books.

Mukherji, Nirmal. "The World of Malgudi: A Study of the Novels of R. K. Narayan." An unpublished Ph.D. dissertation, Louisiana State University, 1960.

Mukherjee, Meenakshi (1971), *The Twice Born Fiction.* New Delhi: Arnold Heinemann.

Naik, M. K. (1979), *Aspects of Indian Writing in English.* Delhi: Macmillan

Naik, M. K. (1988), *The Ironic Vision: A Study of the Fiction of R. K. Narayan.* New Delhi: Sterling Publishers Pvt. Ltd.

Naipaul, V. S. (1968), *An Area of Darkness*. Hardmondsworth: Penguin Books.

Naipaul, V. S. (1997), *India: A Wounded Civilazation*. New York: Penguin.

Narasimhaiah, C. D. (1969), *The Swan and the Eagle*. Simla: Indian Institute of Advanced Studies.

——(1970), Indian Literature of the Past Fifty Years 1917-1967. Banglore: University Press.

Parameswaran, Uma (1976), "Native Genius—R. K. Narayan." *A Study of Representative Indo-English Novelists*. New Delhi: Vikash Publishing House Pvt. Ltd.

Parvathi, B. (1987), "Man and Eater: R. K. Narayan's The Man-Eater of Malgudi." *Studies in Indian Fiction in English*. Ed. G. S. Balrama Gupta. Gulbarga: Journal of Indian Writings in English Publications.

Philip, David Scott (1986), "R. K. Narayan: The Reinvented Traditionalist." *Perceiving India through the Works of Nirad C. Choudhary, R. K. Narayan and Ved Mehta*. New Delhi: Sterling Publications Pvt. Ltd.

Radhakrishnan, S. (1973), *The Hindu View of Life*. London: George Allen and Unwin Ltd.

Raghavacharyulu, D. V. K. (1980), "The Sense of Life in R. K. Narayan and Naipaul." *The Critical Response*. New Delhi: The Macmillan Company of India Ltd.

Raizada, Harish (1969), *R. K. Narayan: A Critical Study of His Works*. New Delhi: Young Asia Publications.

Ram, Atma (1981), *Perspectives on R. K. Narayan*. Ghaziabad: Vimal Prakashan.

Ram, Susan and N. Ram (1996), *R. K. Narayan: The Early years 1906-1945*. New Delhi: Viking.

Ramteke, S. R. (1998), *R.K. Narayan and His Social Perspective*. New Delhi: Atlantic Publisher.

Rao, A. V. Krishna (1972), "R. K. Narayan: The Novel of Affirmation." *The Indo-Anglian Novel and the Changing Tradition*. Mysore: Rao and Raghvan.

Sankaran, Chitra (1993), *The Myth Connection: The Use of Hindu Mythology in Some Novels of Raja Rao and R. K. Narayan*. New Delhi: Allied Publishers.

Saxena, O. P. (1985), "Cupid's Caprice in R. K. Narayan's Novels." *Glimpses of Indo-English Fiction*. Vol III. New Delhi: Jainsons Publications.

Sharma, K. K., ed. (1977), *Indo-English Literature: A Collection of Critical Essays on Indian Creative Writers in English*. Ghaziabad: Vimal Prakashan.

Sidhu, N. S. (1992), *A Critical Study of the Novels of R. K. Narayan*. New Delhi: Bahri Publications.

Singh, Bhupal (1934), *A Survey of Anglo-Indian Fiction*. London: Oxford University Press.

Singh, Promod Kumar (1999), *The Novels of R. K. Narayan: A Critical Evaluation*. New Delhi: Atlantic Publishers.

Singh, R. S. (1971), *The Guide: Some Aspects*. Delhi: Doaba House.

Srinath, C.N. (2005), *R. K. Narayan: An Anthology of Criticism*. Delhi: Pencraft International.

Sundaram, P. S. (1973), *R. K. Narayan*. New Delhi: Arnold Heinemann.

Sundaram, P. S. (1988), *R. K. Narayan as a Novelist*. Delhi: B. R. Publishing Corporation.

Taranath, Rajeev (1972), "The Average as the Positive—A Note on R.K. Narayan." *Critical Essays on Indian Writings in English*. Eds. M. K. Naik, S. K. Desai and G. S. Amur. Dharwar: Karnataka University.

Varma, R. M. (1985), "A Thematic Study of *A Tiger for Malgudi*." *Some Aspects of Indo-English Fiction*. New Delhi: Jainsons Publications.

Walsh, William (1983), *R. K. Narayan: A Critical Appreciation*. New Delhi: Allied Publishers Pvt. Ltd.

Williams, H. M. (1976), *Indo-Anglian Literature (1800-1970): A Survey*. Bombay: Orient Longman.

Journal Articles/Interviews

Ahluwalia, Harsharan Singh ((1982), "The Guide on Stage: Its Production and Reception." *Indian Journal of English Studies* 22(1982-83): 87-97. Also published in *Punjab Journal of English Studies* 1: 70-81.

——(1984), "Narayan's Sense of Audience." *ARIEL: A Review of International English Literature* 15 (January): 59-65.

——(1989), "Rosie and Daisy: Two Liberated Women in the Fiction of R. K. Narayan." *Voice from India: Critical Essays on Literature*. Eds. Jasbir Jain & Francine E. Krishna. Jaipur: Printwell Publishers. pp. 59-65.

Archer, Rosanne (1961), "In Malgudi Again with the Beguiling Narayan." *New York Herald Tribune* 19 Feb.

Bagai, Leon Bell (1961), "*Man-Eater of Malgudi* is Whimsical Whodunnit." *Los Angeles Times* 26 Feb.

Barr, Donald (1957), "Three Minds in Trouble." *New York Times Book Review* 12 May 4.

Beals, Palmer Margaret (1957), "Light Side of India." *Chatonooga Times* (Tenn) 13 Oct. 20.

Case, Edward M. (1954), "Critic Says New Novels Show Indian Truly Great Writer." *Buffalo Evening News* Sec II, 13 Nov.: 10.

Desai, Anita (1985), "Timeless Tales." *India Today* 20 (16 Nov.): 152-53.

Deshpande, Shashi (2007), "R. K. Narayan: A Personal View." *The Journal of Commonwealth Literature* 42: 65-71.

Dolbier, Maurice (1961), "The Man-Eater." *New York Herald Tribune* 9 Feb.: 33.

Freeman, Mary H. (1967), "Review of *The Vendor of Sweets*." *Savannah News* 28 May 8.

Freemantle, Anne (1957), "Absurd and Credible Events." *Commonweal* 66 (2 Aug.) : 452.

French, Warren (1967), "Add Malgudi to Places as Real as Yoknopatawpha." *Kansas City Star* 16 April: Sec D: 6.

Ford, Collier (1961), "Between Book Ends." *St. Louis Post Dispatch*, 10 July: Sec C: 2.

Gale, John (1967), "Out of India." Review of The *Vendor of Sweets*. *New Republic* 156 (13 May): 30.

Getleen, Frank (1953), "The Little Life of Everyman." *Commonweal* 58 (8 May): 126.

Gilluray, Arthur Mac (1958), "Review." *Best Sellers* 18 (1 April).

Godden, Rumer (1953), "Under a Banyan Tree Sat One with a Knowledge of the Human Heart." *New York Herald Tribune Book Review* 19 Apr.: 3.

Habich, William (1958), "A Comic Novel from India." *Lousville Courier Journal* Sec 4 (20 July): Sec 3. 88.

——(1958), "Hero of Indin Novel 'Reluctant' Holy Man." *Los Angeles Times* 10 August.

Hartley, Lois (1967), *Boston Herald*, 28 July Sec C: 17.

Haverstick, John (1957), "Sly Rascal." *Saturday Review of Literature* 40 (11 May): 20.

Hitrac, Joseph (1954), "Hindu Huckleberry." *Saturday Review of Literature* 37 (6 Nov.): 27.

Hoover, Robert (1958), "Humor and Substance in a Novel." *Columbia Dispatch* 6 April: 12.

Inge, Welford (1957), "They Share Some Fears." *Oklahoman* (Oklahoma City, Okla) 20 Oct.: 27.

Jones, Alan Prince (1961), "Satire, Heavy and Light." *Harper's*, 222 (April).

Jones, Edgar L. (1958), "Delightful Humbug." *Baltimore Sun*, Sec A (16 March).

Kantak, V.Y. (1970), "The Achievement of R. K. Narayan." Narasimhaiah, C.D. (ed) *Indian Literature of the Past Fifty Years*. Banglore: Univesity Press, 133-146.

Kaul, A. N. (1972), "R. K. Narayan and the East –West Theme," *Indian Literature*. Simla: Indian Institute of Advanced Studies.

Klauder, Alfred P. (1961), "Mostly Top- Notch." *Christian Century* 78 (13 Sept.): 1082.

Krishnan, S. (1975), "A Day with R. K. Narayan." *Span* April:40.

Mann, Charles W. (1961), "Jr. Review." *Library Journal* 86 (1 March): 1017.

McGregory, Mary (1961), "Mr. Narayan Depicts Village Life in India." *Washington Star* (12 Feb.): Sec. C: 5 .

Mehta, Ved (1961), "Indian Host." *Saturday Review of Literature* 44 (11 March).

Mish, John L. (1958), "Review."*Library Journal* 83 (5 April): 1230.

Muehl, John Frederick (1953), "Indian Operator." *Saturday Review of Literature* 36 (18 April): 22-23.

Mukherji, Nirmal ((1969), "Some Aspects of the Literary Development of R. K. Narayan." *The Banasthali Patrika* 5.13: 76-87.

Narayan, R. K. (1983), In an Interview Given to S. Krishna, Quoted by Hilda Pontes in *R. K. Narayan*, Ed. Nissim Ezekiel. New Delhi: Concept Publishers.

Narasimhaiah, C. D. (1961), "R. K. Narayan's 'The Guide.' *The Literary Criterion 4.4* (Summer): 63-92.

Narayan, R. K. (1972), "Gods, Demons and Modern Times." *The Literary Criterion* 10. 3 (Winter).

Narayan, R. K. (1980), "Editorial Letters." *The Times of India* 16 Nov. 'Replies to the Questionnaire.' *Kakatiya Journal of English* 1.3 (1978)

Parton, Margaret (1953), "A Novel from India, Shimmering Between Laughter and Tears." *New York Herald Tribune Book Review* 29 Nov.: 53.

"Publications Received." Review of *The English Teacher. Social Libraries* 44 (Dec. 1953): 417.

Parton, Margaret (1958), "Rare Fine Tale from India." *New York Herald Tribune Book Review*, 16 March: 5.

Parton, Margaret (1958), "The Reluctant Swami." *Time* 24 March: 116.

Poore, Charles (1961), "Books of the Times." *New York Times* 9 Feb.: 29.

Ram, Susan (1986), "50 Years of Story Telling." *The Telegraph* 11 May: 7.

Rao, Ranga (2007), "R. K. Narayan: An Indian Perspective." *The Journal of Commonwealth Literature* 36: 117-21.

Rao, V. Panduranga (1971), "Tea with R. K. Narayan." *The Journal of Commonwealth Literature* (June): 79-80.

——(1968), "The Art of R. K. Narayan." *The Journal of Commonwealth Literature* 5 (July): 29-40.

Rau, Santha Rama (1958), "Man with Answers." *Saturday Review of Literature* 14 (3 May): 21.

"Review." *Booklist*, 53, 15 July 1957: 579.

Srinath, C. N. (1981), "R. K. Narayan's Comic Vision: Possibilities and Limitations." *World Literature Today* 55.3: 416-19.

Sundaram, P. S. (1977), "Malgudi: The World of R. K. Narayan." *The Indian P.E.N.* 'Part II. 43. 3-4 (March-April)" 1-8..

Saha, Nandani (2007), "The World of Nagaraj: A Postmodern Malgudi?" *The Journal of Commonwealth Literature*, 42: 101-112.

Tharoor, Shashi (1994), "Revisiting R. K. Narayan." *Indian Review of Books* 16 Oct.-15 Dec.: 21-23.

Thwaite, Anthony (1976), "The Painter of Signs." *Times Literary Supplement* 7.6 (20 June): 3.

Trivedi, Harish (2007), "R. K. Narayan at 100" *The Journal of Commonwealth Literature* 42: 1-5.

Updike, John (1975), "R. K. Narayan: A Writer Immersed in his Material." *Span* (April).

Uttam, Krishna (1980), "Interview with R. K. Narayan." *The Deccan Herald* 29 June: 6.

Venkatachari, K. (1969), "R. K. Narayan's Novels: Acceptance of Life." *Osmania Journal of English Studies* 7.1: 51-65.

West, Anthony (1953), "Happy and Happy Go Lucky." *New Yorker* 29 (25 April): 129-30.

——(1953), "'Tis Love,'Tis Love." Review of *The English Teacher. New Yorker* 29 (31 Oct.): 126-27.

——(1958), "Books." Review of *The Guide. New Yorker* 34 (19 April): 145.

——(1967), 'Review of *Vendor of Sweets*." *New Yorker* 43 (14 Oct.): 222-23.

Weston, Christine (1957), "Odd, Entertaining Doings in a Small Town in India." *New York Herald Tribune Book Review* (2 June): 6.

Wheildon, L. (1961), "Narayan's 'Man-Eater' Best in Wonderful Series." *Boston Herald* Sec IV (12 Feb.): 3.

White, Ronald (1967), *New York Times-Book Review* 14 May: 46.

Willis, Carol (1958), "Glimpses of Life in India Proves Odd, Fascinating." *Buffalo Evening News*, Sec 11 (12 April): 10.

Online Articles

Datta, Nandan (2008), "The Life of R. K. Narayan." 04 Oct.<http://calitreview.com/21/print>.

Driesan, C.V. (2008), "The Novelist Skipped Town …' % A Postscript to the ICASEL Conference–Mysore." 10 Apr.<http://www.mcc. murfoch.edu.au /ReadingRoom/listserv/SPAN/34/Driesen.html>.

Lahiri, Jhumpa (2006), "Narayan Days." *Boston Review* July-August. 02 Oct. 2008 <http://bostonreview.net/BR31.4/lahiri.html>.

Mason, Wyatt (2008), "The Master of Malgudi." 30 Sept. <http://www.newyorker.com /archive/2006/12/18/061218crbo_books?currentPge = all>.

Mishra, Pankaj (2008), "The Great Narayan." 30 September <http://www.nybooks.com/articles/14016>.

Naipaul, V. S. (2008), "The Master of Small things." 09 September <http://www.time.com/time/printout/0,8816,128162,00.html>

Narsimhan, C.V. (2001), "Remebering R. K Narayan." Frontline 18.11 (26 May-8 June) 04 October. 2008 <http://www.hindunet.com/fine/f11811/18111330.htm>.

Ram, N. (2008), "I am Giving you a lot of Trouble." 10 October. <http://www. rediff.com/news/2001/may/15 spec.htm>

Ram, N. (2008), "Reluctant Centenarian." 04 Oct.<http://www.hindu.com/mag/2006/10/08/stories/2006100800050100.htm>.

Ram, Susan and Ram, Narasimhan (2008), 'R.K. Narayan: India's Greatest writer, Illuminating the Human Condition through Small-town Life,' 4 Oct. <http://www.guardian.co.uk/news/2001/may/14/guardi ano bituaries.books/print>.

Sarkar, Anoop (2008), "R.K. Narayan: A Profile." 20 Oct.<http://tamilnation.org/hundredtamils/rknarayan.htm>.

Tharoor, Shsshi (2008), "Comedies of Sufferings." 2 Oct. <http://www.hinduonet.com/2001/07/08/stories/13080675.htm>.

INDEX

J

K

L

M